VANESSA-ANN'S

COZY Crocheted AFGHANS

VANESSA-ANN'S
COZY
Crocheted
AFGHANS

OXMOOR
HOUSE.

For The Vanessa-Ann Collection
Owners: Jo Packham and Terrece Beesley
Designers: Carrie Allen, Terrece Beesley, Marlene Lund,
    Jo Packham, Jerri Smith
Staff: Kathi Allred, Gloria Zirkel Baur, Sandra Durbin Chapman,
    Holly Fuller, Susan Jorgensen, Margaret Shields Marti, Barbara
    Milburn, Lisa Miles, Pamela Randall, Lynda Sessions Sorenson,
    Florence Stacey, Nancy Whitley

Photographer: Ryne Hazen

Book Design: The Baker Design Group

*The Vanessa-Ann Collection appreciates the trust and cooperation of the
individuals and businesses listed below for allowing us to photograph on
their premises and to enjoy their treasures:*
    The Black Goose, Midvale, UT
    Penelope Hammons, Layton, UT
    Home-Spun at The Rock Loft, Fruit Heights, UT
    Kaylene Interiors, Ogden, UT
    Nick Kotok, Ogden, UT
    The Lion House, Salt Lake City, UT
    Anita Louise, The Bearlace Cottage, Park City, UT
    Madsen Furniture, Salt Lake City, UT
    Panache, Ogden, UT
    Susan Pendleton, Ogden, UT
    RC Willey, Salt Lake City and Syracuse, UT
    Trends and Traditions, Ogden, UT
    Wicker and Willow, Salt Lake City, UT

Library of Congress Catalog Number: 92-080723
ISBN: 0-8487-1095-0
Manufactured in the United States of America

First Printing

Editor-in-Chief: Nancy J. Fitzpatrick
Senior Editor, Editorial Services: Olivia Wells
Director of Manufacturing: Jerry Higdon
Art Director: James Boone

Vanessa-Ann's Cozy Crocheted Afghans
from the *Crochet Treasury* series

Editor: Margaret Allen Northen
Editorial Assistant: Shannon Leigh Sexton
Copy Chief: Mary Jean Haddin
Assistant Copy Editor: Susan Smith Cheatham
Production Manager: Rick Litton
Associate Production Manager: Theresa L. Beste
Production Assistant: Pam Beasley Bullock
Crochet Stitch Illustrations: Barbara Ball

*We dedicate this book
to Carrie and Marlene:
For your creativity and inspiration,
for your dedication and
perserverance: You've
done it again!
J and T*

CONTENTS

INTRODUCTION

Prepare to wrap yourself in a warm and wonderful afghan. In the hands of The Vanessa-Ann Collection, the time-honored craft of crochet takes on the unexpected. We look to nature for the patterns and the colors we use, but it is the innovation of today's yarns and the influence of contemporary styles that make each afghan in this book outstanding.

Every afghan in this collection is unique. If your interest is in an intricate textural pattern, turn to Vintage Aran and create a masterpiece of cables in the Irish fisherman tradition. Or, if you wish to craft a lacy feminine throw, try your hand at Fancy Filigree or Picots & Pearls. If you love to cross-stitch, choose Snowmen or Bunnies 'n Carrots to embellish a crocheted throw with a playful design. The variety of projects goes on and on—each one a cozy afghan just waiting to be crocheted by you.

PINK DOGWOODS

*Bring a bit of spring inside with
pink dogwood blossoms cross-stitched
on an afghan-stitch throw.*

Pictured on cover and preceding pages.

FINISHED SIZE

Approximately 50″ x 57″, not including edging.

MATERIALS

Worsted-weight acrylic (110-yd. ball): 33 eggshell.
Size H (14″-long) afghan hook, or size to obtain gauge.
Size G crochet hook.
Paternayan Persian wool (8-yd. skein): see color key.

GAUGE

4 sts and 4 rows = 1″ in afghan st.

DIRECTIONS

Note: See page 141 for afghan st instructions.

Afghan: With eggshell, ch 198, work 227 rows afghan st. Sl st in ea vertical bar across. Do not fasten off last lp.

Border: With size G crochet hook, ch 1, * (sc, ch 1, sc) in corner st, sc in ea st to next corner, rep from * around, sl st in first sc. Fasten off.

Edging: **Row 1:** With size G crochet hook and eggshell, ch 29, dc in 7th ch from hook, (ch 1, sk 1 ch, dc in next ch) twice, ch 3, sk next 2 ch, sc in next ch, ch 3, sk next 2 ch, dc in ea of next 5 ch, ch 3, sk next 2 ch, sc in next ch, ch 3, sk next 2 ch, dc in next ch, ch 1, sk 1 ch, dc in last ch, turn.

Row 2: Ch 4 for first dc and ch 1, dc in next dc, ch 1, dc in next sc, ch 3, sc in next dc, ch 5, sk 3 dc, sc in next dc, ch 5, sc in next dc, ch 3, (dc in next dc, ch 1) twice, sk 1 ch, (dc, ch 1, tr) in next ch, turn.

Row 3: Ch 5 for first tr and ch 1, dc in tr, (ch 1, dc in next dc) twice, ch 3, sc in next dc, ch 3, 5 dc in next ch-5 lp, ch 3, sc in next ch-5 lp, ch 3, dc in next sc, (ch 1, dc in next dc) twice, ch 1, sk 1 ch, dc in next ch, turn.

Row 4: Ch 4 for first dc and ch 1, (dc in next dc, ch 1) 3 times, dc in next sc, ch 3, sc in next dc, ch 5, sk 3 dc, sc in next dc, ch 5, sc in next dc, ch 3, (dc in next dc, ch 1) twice, sk 1 ch, (dc, ch 1, tr) in next ch, turn.

Row 5: Ch 5 for first tr and ch 1, dc in tr, (ch 1, dc in next dc) twice, ch 3, sc in next dc, ch 3, 5 dc in next ch-5 lp, ch 3, sc in next ch-5 lp, ch 3, dc in next sc, (ch 1, dc in next dc) 4 times, ch 1, sk 1 ch, dc in next ch, turn.

Row 6: Ch 4 for first dc and ch 1, (dc in next dc, ch 1) 5 times, dc in next sc, ch 3, sc in next dc, ch 5, sk 3 dc, sc in next dc, ch 5, sc in next dc, ch 3, (dc in next dc, ch 1) twice, sk 1 ch, (dc, ch 1, tr) in next ch, turn.

Row 7: Ch 5 for first tr and ch 1, dc in tr, (ch 1, dc in next dc) twice, ch 3, sc in next dc, ch 3, 5 dc in next ch-5 lp, ch 3, sc in next ch-5 lp, ch 3, dc in next sc, (ch 1, dc in next dc) 6 times, ch 1, sk 1 ch, dc in next ch, turn.

Row 8: Ch 4 for first dc and ch 1, (dc in next dc, ch 1) 5 times, dc in next dc, ch 3, (sc in next dc, ch 5) twice, sk 3 dc, sc in next dc, ch 3, dc in next sc, (ch 1, dc in next dc) 3 times, turn.

Row 9: Sl st in ch-1 sp, sl st in next dc, ch 4 for first dc and ch 1, (dc in next dc, ch 1) twice, dc in next sc, ch 3, sc in next ch-5 lp, ch 3, 5 dc in next ch-5 lp, ch 3, sc in next dc, ch 3, (dc in next dc, ch 1) 5 times, sk 1 ch, dc in next ch, turn.

Row 10: Ch 4 for first dc and ch 1, (dc in next dc, ch 1) 3 times, dc in next dc, ch 3, (sc in next dc, ch 5) twice, sk 3 dc, sc in next dc, ch 3, dc in next sc, (ch 1, dc in next dc) 3 times, turn.

Row 11: Sl st in ch-1 sp, sl st in next dc, ch 4 for first dc and ch 1, (dc in next dc, ch 1) twice, dc in next sc, ch 3, sc in next ch-5 lp, ch 3, 5 dc in next ch-5 lp, ch 3, sc in next dc, ch 3, (dc in next dc, ch 1) 3 times, sk 1 ch, dc in next ch, turn.

Row 12: Ch 4 for first dc and ch 1, dc in next dc, ch 1, dc in next dc, ch 3, (sc in next dc, ch 5) twice, sk 3 dc, sc in next dc, ch 3, dc in next sc, (ch 1, dc in next dc) 3 times, turn.

Row 13: Sl st in ch-1 sp, sl st in next dc, ch 4 for first dc and ch 1, (dc in next dc, ch 1) twice, dc in next sc, ch 3, sc in next ch-5 lp, ch 3, 5 dc in next ch-5 lp, ch 3, sc in next dc, ch 3, dc in next dc, ch 1, sk 1 ch, dc in next ch, turn.

Row 14: Ch 4 for first dc and ch 1, dc in next dc, ch 1, dc in next sc, ch 3, sc in next dc, ch 5, sk 3 dc, sc in next dc, ch 5, sc in next dc, ch 3, (dc in next dc, ch 1) twice, sk 1 ch, (dc, ch 1, tr) in next ch, turn.

Rep rows 3-14 as est until 40 points have been made, ending after row 12. Fasten off.

Assembly: With right sides facing, whipstitch edging to afghan, easing fullness around corners. Arrange edging so that there are 10 points across each long edge, 8 points across each short edge, and 1 point centered on each corner.

Match and whipstitch ends of edging together.

Cross-stitch: Referring to photo for positioning, use 2 strands of wool to cross-stitch design according to chart. Repeat design as necessary to work 3 diagonal rows of flowers across afghan.

Color Key

Paternayan Persian Wool
(used for sample)

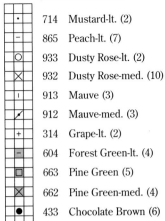

·	714	Mustard-lt. (2)
−	865	Peach-lt. (7)
O	933	Dusty Rose-lt. (2)
X	932	Dusty Rose-med. (10)
I	913	Mauve (3)
/	912	Mauve-med. (3)
+	314	Grape-lt. (2)
▦	604	Forest Green-lt. (4)
▢	663	Pine Green (5)
⊠	662	Pine Green-med. (4)
●	433	Chocolate Brown (6)

Note: The number of 8-yd. skeins required for each color is indicated in parentheses.

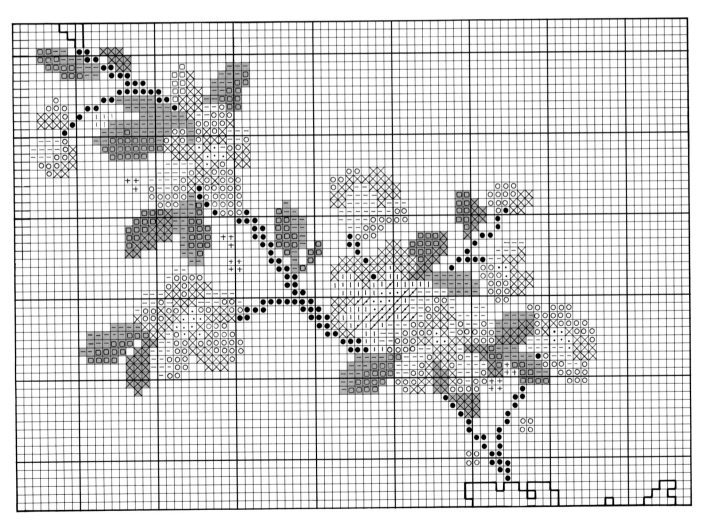

Cross-stitch Chart

9

SWEET DREAMS

The shades of a pastel rainbow are yours
when you vary the color of one of the
two strands of yarn.

FINISHED SIZE
Approximately 45″ x 67″.

MATERIALS
Worsted-weight acrylic (230-yd. skein): 3 each pink, peach, yellow, green, blue.
Size K crochet hook, or size to obtain gauge.

GAUGE
5 dc = 2″.

DIRECTIONS
Note: Use 2 strands of yarn held tog as 1.

Afghan: **Row 1:** With 2 strands of pink, ch 120, hdc in 3rd ch from hook and ea ch across, turn = 119 sts.

Row 2: Ch 3, dc in first st, * sk next 2 sts, sc in next st, sk next 2 sts, (dc, ch 3, sc, ch 3, dc) in next st, rep from * across to last 3 sts, sk 2 sts, sc in last st, turn.

Row 3: (Ch 3, hdc in next ch-3 lp) across, dc in first ch of beg ch-3 on prev row, turn.

Row 4: Ch 4, sc in next lp, (ch 3, sc in next lp) across, ch 2, hdc in top of beg ch-3 on prev row, turn.

Row 5: Ch 3 for first dc, 3 dc in ea lp across, dc in 2nd ch of beg ch-4 on prev row, turn.

Row 6: Ch 3 for first dc, * sk next dc, dc in next st, keeping last lp of ea st on hook, work 3 dc around post of dc just made, yo and through all lps on hook (post-cl made), ch 1, sk next dc, dc in ea of next 3 dc, rep from * across, dc in top of tch, turn.

Row 7: Ch 3 for first dc, * sk next dc, dc in next st, post-cl around dc just made, sk next dc, (dc, ch 1, dc) in next post-cl (V-st made), rep from * 19 times more, dc in top of tch, turn.

Row 8: Ch 3 for first dc, * dc in ch-1 of next V-st, post-cl around dc just made, V-st in next post-cl, rep from * 19 times more, dc in top of tch, turn.

Row 9: Ch 3 for first dc, * dc in first dc of next V-st, ch 1, dc in last dc of same V-st, ch 1, dc in next post-cl, ch 1, rep from * across, dc in top of tch, turn = 62 dc.

Row 10: Ch 2 for first hdc, (dc in next ch-1 sp, hdc in next dc) across, turn = 121 sts.

Row 11: Ch 2 for first sc and ch 1, working in bk lps only, (sk next dc, sc in next hdc, ch 1) across, sc in last st, turn.

Row 12: Fasten off 1 strand of pink. Join 1 strand of peach and work with 1 strand ea of pink and peach. Ch 1, working in ft lps only, sc in next ch, (ch 1, sk next sc, sc in next ch) 60 times, sc in last st, turn.

Row 13: Ch 3 for first dc, (dc in next sc, dc in next ch) across, turn = 121 sts.

Row 14: Ch 3, dc in first st, * sk next 2 sts, sc in next st, sk next 2 sts, (dc, ch 3, sc, ch 3, dc) in next st, rep from * across to last 6 sts, sk 2 sts, sc in next st, sk 2 sts, (dc, ch 3, sc) in last st, turn.

Rows 15-20: Rep rows 3-8.

Row 21: Rep row 8 once more.

Row 22: Rep row 9.

Row 23: Fasten off pink. Join a 2nd strand of peach and rep row 10.

Rows 24-30: Rep rows 14-20.

Row 31: Rep row 9.

Row 32: Fasten off 1 strand of peach. Join 1 strand of yellow and rep row 10.

Rows 33-39: Rep rows 14-20.

Row 40: Rep row 9.

Row 41: Fasten off peach. Join a 2nd strand of yellow and rep row 10.

Rows 42-48: Rep rows 14-20.

Row 49: Rep row 9.

Row 50: Fasten off 1 strand of yellow. Join 1 strand of green and rep row 10.

Rows 51-57: Rep rows 14-20.

Row 58: Rep row 9.

Row 59: Fasten off yellow. Join a 2nd strand of green and rep row 10.

Rows 60-66: Rep rows 14-20.

Row 67: Rep row 9.

Row 68: Fasten off 1 strand of green. Join 1 strand of blue and rep row 10.

Rows 69-75: Rep rows 14-20.

Row 76: Rep row 9.

Row 77: Fasten off green. Join a 2nd strand of blue and rep row 10.

Rows 78-84: Rep rows 14-20.

Rows 85 and 86: Rep rows 9 and 10.

Row 87: Ch 1, sc in ea st across. Fasten off.

Edging: With right side facing and afghan turned to work across pink short edge, join 2 strands of pink with sl st in corner, ch 1, sc in ea st across. Fasten off.

Tassel (make 4): *Note:* See page 141 for tassel diagrams. For each tassel, wind each color of yarn 16 times around a 21″ piece of cardboard. Use pink to wrap 2 tassels and blue to wrap 2 tassels. Attach pink-wrapped tassels to corners at pink end of afghan and blue-wrapped tassels to corners at blue end of afghan.

RICKRACK REVIVAL

Add a touch of old-fashioned warmth to your life with the muted colors and plush fringe of this piece.

FINISHED SIZE

Approximately 43″ x 60″, not including fringe.

MATERIALS

Worsted-weight acrylic (165-yd. skein): 4 rose ombre.

Worsted-weight acrylic (280-yd. skein): 2 each brown, rose; 4 light rose.

Size K crochet hook, or size to obtain gauge.

GAUGE

3 sts = 1″.

DIRECTIONS

Afghan: **Row 1:** With rose ombre, ch 110, sc in 2nd ch from hook and ea ch across, turn = 109 sts (including beg ch-1).

Row 2: Ch 1, sk next st, * hdc in next st, dc in next st, 3 tr in next st, dc in next st, hdc in next st, sc in next st, rep from * 17 times more, turn. Fasten off.

Row 3: Join brown, ch 1, sc in ea of next 3 sts, * 3 sc in next st, sc in ea of next 2 sts, pull up a lp in ea of next 3 sts, yo and pull through all lps (sc dec over 3 sts made), sc in ea of next 2 sts, rep from * across, end with sc dec over last st and tch, turn. Fasten off.

Row 4: Join rose, rep row 3. Fasten off.

Row 5: Join light rose, ch 4 for first tr, tr in next st, * dc in next st, hdc in next st, sc in next st, hdc in next st, dc in next st, keeping last lp of ea st on hook, tr in ea of next 3 sts, yo and pull through all lps on hook (tr dec over 3 sts made), rep from * across, end with tr dec over last st and tch, turn. Fasten off.

Row 6: Join rose ombre, ch 1, sc in ea st across, turn = 109 sts.

Row 7: Ch 1, hdc and dc in next st, * sk 2 sts, (sc, hdc, dc) in next st, rep from * across, turn = 109 sts.

Row 8: Ch 1, sk next st, * (sc, hdc, dc) in next st, sk 2 sts, rep from * across, sc in last st, turn = 109 sts.

Row 9: Ch 1, sc in ea st across, turn. Fasten off.

Row 10: With light rose, rep row 2.

Row 11: With rose, rep row 3.

Row 12: With brown, rep row 3.

Row 13: With rose ombre, rep row 5.

Rows 14-17: With light rose, rep rows 6-9 = 109 sts after row 17.

Rep rows 2-17 as est 7 times, ending after row 13. Fasten off.

Edging: **Rnd 1:** With right side facing and afghan turned to work across long edge, join rose ombre in first st of row 1 (corner st), ch 1, * work 1 or 2 sc in side of ea row across to corner, sc in corner **, sc in ea st to next corner, sc in corner, rep from * to **, rep row 2 across short edge to beg corner, sl st in first sc.

Rnd 2: Ch 1, sc in ea st across to next corner, sc in corner, rep row 2 across short edge to next corner, sc in corner, sc in ea st to next corner, sc in corner, sl st in first sc. Fasten off.

Fringe: Knot 1 (10″) strand of rose ombre yarn in each stitch across short edges of afghan.

FLOWER GARDEN

*Join an openwork edging to squares
embellished with cross-stitched flowers
for an unusual coverlet.*

FINISHED SIZE
Approximately 32″ x 40″, not including edging.

MATERIALS
Worsted-weight acrylic (110-yd. ball): 11 willow, 6 blue.
Size H (10″-long) afghan hook, or size to obtain gauge.
Size E crochet hook.
DMC or Anchor embroidery floss (8-yd. skein): see color key on page 16.

GAUGE
5 sts and 4 rows = 1″ in afghan st.
Square = 8″.

DIRECTIONS
Note: See page 141 for afghan st instructions.

Square (make 10 ea willow, blue): Ch 40, work 32 rows afghan st. Sl st in ea vertical bar across. Fasten off.

Assembly: Afghan is 4 squares wide and 5 squares long. Whipstitch squares together in a checkerboard pattern.

Edging: **Rnd 1:** With size E crochet hook, right side facing, and afghan turned to work across short edge, join willow with sc in corner, * sc in ea st to next corner, (sc, ch 1, sc) in corner, rep from * around, sc in beg corner, ch 1, sl st in first sc.

Rnd 2: Ch 4 for first sc and ch 3, * 3 dc in same corner, (sk 4 sts, sc in next st, ch 3, 3 dc in same st) across short edge to corner, sc in corner sp, ch 3, 3 dc in same corner, (sk 3 sts, sc in next st, ch 3, 3 dc in same st) across to corner, sc in corner sp, ch 3, rep from * around, end with sl st in base of beg ch-4.

Rnd 3: Sl st in ea of next 3 ch, sc in same sp, (ch 7, sc in next ch-3 sp) around, end with ch 4, dtr in first sc.

Rnd 4: Sc in same lp, (ch 7, sc in next lp) around, end with ch 4, dtr in first sc.

Note: To work cl, keeping last lp of ea st on hook, work sts as specified in pat, yo and pull through all lps on hook.

Rnd 5: * Ch 7, (3-tr cl, ch 3, 3-tr cl, ch 3, 3-tr cl) in next lp for corner, (ch 7, sc in next lp) twice, [ch 7, 3-tr cl in ea of next 3 lps, (ch 7, sc in next lp) 5 times] 3 times, ch 7, 3-tr cl in ea of next 3 lps, (ch 7, sc in next lp) twice, rep from * around, except work directions bet [ ] 4 times across ea long edge, end with ch 4, tr in base of beg ch-7.

Rnd 6: Sc in same lp, ch 7, sc in next lp, ch 7, 3-tr cl in next ch-3 sp, ch 3, 3-tr cl in next ch-3 sp, (ch 7, sc in next lp) 3 times, * ch 4, tr in sc just made, sc in top of next cl, ch 3, sk 1 cl, sc in top of next cl, ch 4, tr in sc just made, sc in next lp, (ch 7, sc in next lp) 5 times, rep from * 3 times more, end last rep with (ch 7, sc in next lp) twice, cont around afghan as est and working pat rep as needed, end with ch 4, tr in first sc.

Rnd 7: Sc in same lp, (ch 7, sc in next lp) 6 times, * ch 7, (3-tr cl, ch 5) twice in ch-3 sp, 3-tr cl in same sp, (ch 7, sc in next lp) 5 times, rep from * 3 times more, end last rep with (ch 7, sc in next lp) 7 times, cont around afghan as est and working pat rep as needed, end with ch 4, tr in first sc.

Rnd 8: Sc in same lp, (ch 7, sc in next lp) around, ch 4, tr in first sc.

Rnds 9 and 10: Sc in same lp, (ch 7, sc in next lp) 3 times, * ch 7, (sc, ch 7, sc) in next lp for corner, (ch 7, sc in next lp) across to corner lp, rep from * around, ch 4, tr in first sc.

Rnd 11: Ch 4 for first tr, 2-tr cl in same lp, * ch 1, (3-tr cl, ch 7, sl st in 4th ch from hook to make a picot, ch 3, 3-tr cl) in next lp, rep from * around, end with (3-tr cl, ch-7 picot, ch 3) in beg lp, sl st in top of beg cl. Fasten off.

Cross-stitch: Charts are on page 16. *Note:* For better coverage, separate the 6 strands of floss and put them back together before cross-stitching. Stitch design with all 6 strands of floss. Centering design on square, work single flower design on each willow square and multi-flower design on each blue square. Backstitch around each cross-stitch, using matching thread.

Color Key

Anchor		DMC (used for sample)	
24		776	Pink-med. (36)
75		3733	Dusty Rose-lt. (28)
76		3731	Dusty Rose-med. (5)
875		503	Blue Green-med. (25)
876		502	Blue Green (33)

Note: The number of 8-yd. skeins required for each color is indicated in parentheses.

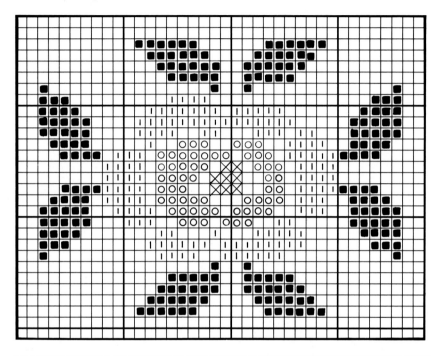

Single Flower Cross-stitch Chart

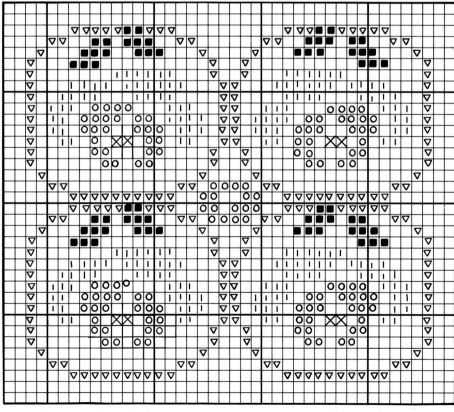

Multi-flower Cross-stitch Chart

PICOTS & PEARLS

*Ribbon flowers and pearls
on shades of mint beckon you to wrap
yourself in this soft throw.*

FINISHED SIZE

Approximately 50″ x 70″.

MATERIALS

Sportweight brushed acrylic (135-yd. skein): 17 mint green.

Sportweight viscose ribbon-type yarn (103-yd. ball): 2 mint green.

Size G crochet hook, or size to obtain gauge.

700 (6-mm) pearlized beads.

20 yards (1″-wide) mint green sheer ribbon.

Mint green sewing thread.

GAUGE

Small panel = 7″ wide.

DIRECTIONS

Small panel (make 3): With acrylic yarn, ch 27.

Row 1: Sc in 2nd ch from hook, (ch 5, sk 4 ch, sc in next ch) 5 times, turn.

Row 2: * Ch 5, (sc, ch 3, sc) in center ch of next ch-5 lp, rep from * 4 times more, ch 2, dc in next sc, turn.

Row 3: Ch 1, sc in first dc, * ch 5, (sc, ch 3, sc) in center ch of next ch-5 lp, rep from * 3 times more, ch 5, sc in 3rd ch of tch, turn.

Rows 4-112: Rep rows 2 and 3 alternately, ending after row 2.

Row 113: (Ch 5, sc in center ch of next ch-5 lp) 5 times. Do not fasten off.

Work around panel in sc as foll: (2 sc in ea sp, sc in ea st) across ea long edge, sc in corner, (3 sc in ea ch-5 lp, sc in ea sc) across ea short edge, end with sl st in first sc. Fasten off.

Large panel (make 2): With acrylic yarn, ch 50.

Row 1: Sc in 2nd ch from hook, ch 2, sk 3 ch, (2 dc, ch 2, 2 dc) in next ch, * ch 5, sc in 4th ch from hook to make a picot, sk 3 ch, sc in next ch, ch 2, sk 3 ch, (2 dc, ch 2, 2 dc) in next ch, rep from * 4 times more, ch 2, sk 3 ch, sc in last ch, turn.

Row 2: Ch 4, tr in ea of next 2 dc, * ch 3, keeping last lp of ea st on hook, tr in ea of next 2 ch, yo and pull through all lps (cl made), ch 3, tr in next dc **, cl over next 2 dc (sk picot bet dc), tr in next dc, rep from * 5 times more, end last rep at **, tr in next dc, tr in sc, turn.

Row 3: Ch 3, work 2 dc in first st, * ch-5 picot, sc in next cl, ch 2 **, (2 dc, ch 2, 2 dc) in next cl, rep from * 5 times more, end last rep at **, sk next tr, 2 dc in next tr, dc in top of tch, turn.

Row 4: Ch 4, tr in base of tch, * ch 3, tr in next dc, cl over next 2 dc (sk picot), tr in next dc, ch 3 **, cl over next 2 ch, rep from * 5 times more, end last rep at **, cl in tch, turn.

Row 5: Ch 1, sc in cl, * ch 2, (2 dc, ch 2, 2 dc) in next cl **, ch-5 picot, sc in next cl, rep from * 5 times more, end last rep at **, ch 2, sc in tch, turn.

Rows 6-68: Rep rows 2-5 for pat, ending after row 4. Do not fasten off.

Work around panel in sc as foll: (2 sc in side of ea dc or tr, sc in top of ea row) across ea long edge, sc in corner, (2 sc in ea ch-sp, sc in ea st) across ea short edge, sl st in first sc. Fasten off.

End panel (make 2): With acrylic yarn, ch 8.

Row 1: Sc in 8th ch from hook, ch 5, turn.

Row 2: Work 3 dc in ch-8 lp, ch 3, turn.

Row 3: Work 3 sc in ch-5 lp, ch 3, dc in same lp, ch 5, turn.

Row 4: Work 3 dc in ch-3 sp, ch 3, 3 dc in next ch-3 sp, ch 3, turn.

Row 5: Work 3 sc in ch-3 sp, ch 3, 3 sc in ch-5 lp, ch 3, dc in same lp, ch 5, turn.

Row 6: Work 3 dc in ch-3 sp, (ch 3, 3 dc in next ch-3 sp) across, ch 3, turn.

Row 7: Work (3 sc in next ch-3 sp, ch 3) across, 3 sc in ch-5 lp, ch 3, dc in same lp, ch 5, turn.

Rows 8-11: Rep rows 6 and 7 twice.

Row 12: Work 3 dc in ch-3 sp, ch 3, [(dc, ch 1, dc, ch 1, dc) in next sp] 5 times, ch 5, turn.

Row 13: Sc in next ch-1 sp, (ch 3, sc in next ch-1 sp) 9 times, ch 3, 3 sc in next ch-3 sp, ch 3, 3 sc in ch-5 lp, ch 3, dc in same lp, ch 5, turn.

Row 14: Work (3 dc in next ch-3 sp, ch 3) twice, [sk next sp, (dc, ch 1, dc, ch 1, dc) in next sp] 5 times, leave last lp unworked, ch 5, turn.

Row 15: Sc in next ch-1 sp, (ch 3, sc in next ch-1 sp) 9 times, (ch 3, 3 sc in next sp) twice, ch 3, 3 sc in ch-5 lp, ch 3, dc in same lp, ch 5, turn.

Row 16: Work (3 dc in next ch-3 sp, ch 3) 3 times, [sk next sp, (dc, ch 1, dc, ch 1, dc) in next sp] 5 times, leave last lp unworked, ch 5, turn.

Row 17: Sc in next ch-1 sp, (ch 3, sc in next ch-1 sp) 9 times, (ch 3, 3 sc in next sp) 3 times, ch 3, 3 sc in ch-5 lp, ch 3, dc in same lp, ch 5, turn.

Row 18: Work (3 dc in next ch-3 sp, ch 3) 4 times, [sk next sp, (dc, ch 1, dc, ch 1, dc) in next sp] 5 times, leave last lp unworked, ch 5, turn.

Row 19: Sc in next ch-1 sp, (ch 3, sc in next ch-1 sp) 9 times, (ch 3, 3 sc in next sp) 4 times, ch 3, 3 sc in ch-5 lp, ch 3, dc in same lp, ch 5, turn.

Row 20: Work (3 dc in next ch-3 sp, ch 3) 5 times, [sk next sp, (dc, ch 1, dc, ch 1, dc) in next sp] 5 times, leave last lp unworked, ch 5, turn.

Row 21: Sc in next ch-1 sp, (ch 5, sc in next ch-1 sp, ch 3, sc in next ch-1 sp) 4 times, ch 5, sc in next ch-1 sp, (ch 3,

3 sc in next sp) 5 times, ch 3, 3 sc in ch-5 lp, ch 3, dc in same lp, ch 5, turn.

Rep rows 12-21 as est 6 times. Fasten off.

Assembly: Hold 1 small panel and 1 large panel with right sides facing and pieces turned to work across 1 long edge, join ribbon yarn in corner of first panel, ch 3, dc in corner of 2nd panel, (sk 1 st on first panel, dc in next st on first panel, sk next st on 2nd panel, dc in next st on 2nd panel) across. Fasten off.

Join rem panels as est, alternating small and large.

Work in same manner to join an end panel to each short edge of afghan, except use tr instead of dc.

Edging: With right side facing and afghan turned to work across long edge, join acrylic yarn with sc in side of last dc on end panel just below unworked lp. * Sc in next sp, (sc, ch 5, sl st in top of sc just made to make a picot, sc) in side of next dc, rep from * 4 times more, 2 sc in next sp, ch-5 picot, 2 sc in side of joining tr, sc in top of tr, ch-5 picot, 3 sc in side of next tr, ch-5 picot, sc in corner of panel, (sc in ea of next 3 sc, ch-5 picot) to st at corner of panel, sc in corner st, 2 sc in side of joining tr, ch-5 picot, sc in top of tr, 2 sc in side of next tr, ch-5 picot, sc in ea of next 2 sts, [(sc, ch-5 picot, sc) in next sp, sc in ea of next 2 sts, ch-5 picot, sc in next st, (2 sc, ch-5 picot) in next sp, sc in ea of next 3 sts, ch-5 picot, 2 sc in next sp **, sc in next st, ch-5 picot, sc in ea of next 2 sts, (sc, ch-5 picot, sc) in next sp] twice, end last rep at **. Fasten off. Rep to work edging across rem long edge.

Finishing: Sew a bead to each picot on large panels. Sew beads to ribbon-yarn joining stitches as desired (see photo).

To make ribbon flowers, cut various lengths of ribbons and gather. Tack to afghan as desired (see photo).

SIMPLY COUNTRY

The distinctive corner rings on this piece are created by interweaving chains covered with half-double crochet stitches.

FINISHED SIZE
Approximately 19″ x 46″, not including edging.

MATERIALS
Sportweight cotton (120-yd. ball): 6 each olive, beige.
Size G crochet hook, or size to obtain gauge.

GAUGE
1 pat rep = 2¾″.
1 row = 1″.

DIRECTIONS
Throw: **Row 1** (right side): With olive, ch 88, sc in 2nd ch from hook, ch 2, sk 1 ch, sc in next ch, * sk 3 ch, work a shell of (3 tr, ch 4, sc) in next ch, ch 2, sk 1 ch, (sc, ch 4, 3 tr) in next ch for shell, sk 3 ch, sc in next ch, ch 2, sk 1 ch, sc in next ch, rep from * across, turn.

Row 2: Ch 4 for first dc and ch 1, dc in ch-2 sp, * ch 1, sk 3 tr, sc in top of ch-4 at point of shell, ch 2, keeping last lp of ea st on hook, work 2 dc in next ch-2 sp, yo and pull through all lps on hook (cl made), ch 2, sc in top of ch-4 at point of shell, ch 1 **, (dc, ch 1, dc) in next ch-2 sp (V-st made), rep from * across, end last rep at **, dc in last sp, ch 1, dc in sc, sk tch, turn. Join beige and ch 1 with both yarns held tog as 1. Do not fasten off olive, carry yarn not in use up side of work.

Row 3: With beige, sc in first st, ch 2, sk next ch and dc, sc in next ch-sp, * (3 tr, ch 4, sc) in next ch-2 sp, ch 2, sk cl, (sc, ch 4, 3 tr) in next ch-2 sp, sc in next sp, ch 2, sk V-st, sc in next ch-1 sp, rep from * across, end with sc in 3rd ch of tch, turn.

Row 4: With beige, rep row 2.

Rows 5 and 6: With olive, rep row 3, then row 2.

Rows 7 and 8: With beige, rep row 3, then row 2.

Rep rows 5-8 as est for pat, changing colors every 2 rows for a total of 98 rows. To end row 98, work last dc to last 2 lps, pick up beige, yo with both yarns tog and pull through rem lps. Fasten off beige, cont working with olive.

Border: Rnd 1: Ch 1, 2 sc in corner, 2 sc in side of ea dc and sc to next corner, 3 sc in corner, sc in next sp, sc in next st, 3 sc in next sp, (sc in ea of next 3 sc, 3 sc in next sp) across to corner, sc in last sc, sc in last sp, 3 sc in corner, 2 sc in side of ea dc and sc to next corner, 3 sc in corner, sc in next sp, sc in dc, sc in sp, sc in top of ch-4 at point of shell, * 2 sc in next sp, sc in cl, 2 sc in next sp, sc in top of ch-4 at point of shell, (sc in next sp, sc in dc) twice, sc in next sp, sc in top of ch-4 at point of shell, rep from * to corner, end with sc in beg corner, sl st in first sc. Fasten off.

Rnd 2: Join beige with sl st in center corner st, ch 4 for first dc and ch 1, dc in same st, * dc in ea st to corner, (dc, ch 1, dc, ch 1, dc) in center corner st, rep from * around, end with (dc, ch 1) in beg corner, sl st in 3rd ch of beg ch-4 = 198 sts across ea long edge and 87 sts across ea short edge (not including corner sts). Fasten off.

Rnd 3: Join olive with sl st in center dc of corner, ch 1, 2 sc in same st, sc in ch-1 sp, * sc in ea dc to corner, sc in ch-1 sp, 3 sc in center dc of corner, sc in ch-1 sp, rep from * around, sc in ch-1 sp of beg corner, sc in same st as beg, sl st in first sc. Fasten off.

Corner rings: **First ring:** With beige, ch 20, join with a sl st to form a ring. Ch 2 for first hdc, 40 hdc in ring, sl st in top of beg ch-2. Fasten off.

2nd ring: Work as for first ring.

3rd ring: With right sides up, lay 2 rings side-by-side. With beige, ch 20, insert ch down through center of first ring and up through center of 2nd ring, join with a sl st in first ch of ch-20 to form a ring. Ch 2 for first hdc, 40 hdc in ring, sl st in top of beg ch-2. Fasten off.

Rep to make 4 grps of 3 rings ea.

Assembly: Tack first ring of 1 group to 5th stitch before center corner stitch. Tack 2nd ring of same group to 5th stitch after same corner stitch. Tack the 3 rings together in 8th stitch from joining with throw on first 2 rings. Repeat to join a group of rings to each corner of throw.

Edging: **Rnd 1:** Join olive with sc in 11th st before first corner ring on short edge of throw, sk 2 sts, 8 tr in next st, sk 5 hdc on ring from joining, * (sc in next st on ring, ch 3, sk 3 sts, 3 dc in next st, ch 3, sk 3 sts) twice, sk 3 sts, sc in next st and in 8th st from joining on center ring at the same time, ch 3, sk 2 sts, 3 dc in next st on center ring, (ch 3, sk 3 sts, 3 dc in next st) 4 times, ch 3, sk 2 sts, sc in next st on center ring and in 9th st from joining on 3rd ring at the same time, (ch 3, sk 3 sts on 3rd ring, 3 dc in next st, ch 3, sk 3 sts, sc in next st) twice, sk 7 sts on edge of throw beyond joining of 3rd ring, 8 tr in next st, sk 2 sts, sc in next st, sk 2 sts, [8 tr in next st, sk 3 sts, sc in next st, sk 3 sts] across to 9 sts before next ring joining, sk 2 sts, 8 tr in next st, sk 5 sts from joining on first ring at next corner, rep from * around, end with sl st in first sc. Fasten off.

Rnd 2: Join beige in same st as last sl st, ch 1, * sc in ea st to corner rings, (sc in ea st, 3 sc in ea ch-3 sp) around corner rings, rep from * around, end with sl st in beg ch-1. Fasten off.

LAVENDER FIELDS

The mile-a-minute technique makes it easy
to fashion these scalloped strips of
lavender and pink.

FINISHED SIZE
Approximately 46″ x 60″.

MATERIALS
Sportweight cotton (137-yd. ball): 9 lavender, 8 pink.

Sportweight vicose ribbon-type yarn (103-yd. ball): 7 white.

Size F crochet hook, or size to obtain gauge.

GAUGE
1 ch-link = 1″.

Strip = 3″ x 60″.

DIRECTIONS
Strip A (make 8): With lavender, (ch 4, tr in 4th ch from hook) 55 times = 55 ch-links.

Rnd 1: Ch 1, working across tr edge of ch-links, sc in first ch-link, * (ch 5, sc in same st as ch-link tr) 55 times, rep from * down opposite side of ch-links to beg, end with sl st in first sc.

Rnd 2: Ch 3 for first dc, 3 dc in same st, * [8 dc in next ch-5 lp, (dc, ch 3, dc) in next ch-5 lp] 27 times, 8 dc in next ch-5 lp **, 8 dc in next sc, rep from * to ** once more, 4 dc in same st as beg, sl st in top of beg ch-3. Fasten off.

Rnd 3: Join white with sc bet last dc and rnd-2 beg ch-3, (ch 5, sk 2 dc, sc bet next 2 dc) twice, [* (ch 5, sk 4 dc, sc bet next 2 dc) twice, ch 3, sc in ch-3 sp, ch 3, sk next dc, sc bet next 2 dc, rep from * 26 times more, (ch 5, sk 4 dc, sc bet next 2 dc) twice], (ch 5, sk 2 dc, sc bet next 2 dc) 4 times, rep bet [ ] once, ch 5, sk 2 dc, sc bet next 2 dc, ch 5, sl st in first sc. Fasten off.

Rnd 4: Join lavender with sc in 3rd ch of 3rd ch-5 lp from end of strip, ch 3, sc in center ch of ea ch-5 lp around, sl st in first sc.

Strip B (make 7): Work as for strip A, using colors as foll:
Rnds 1 and 2: Pink.
Rnd 3: White.
Rnd 4 (joining rnd): Join pink with sc in 3rd ch of 3rd ch-5 lp from end of strip, * (ch 1, sl st in center ch of corresponding lp on strip A, ch 1, sc in center ch of next lp on strip B) across to end of strip, (ch 3, sc in center ch of next lp) 5 times, rep from * once more to join another strip A, end with sl st in first sc. Fasten off.

Rep to join rem strips as est.

Trim: Working down tr edge of base ch-links of first strip, join pink with sl st in first ch-link, [* (ch 4, dc, ch 4, sl st) 3 times in same ch-link, (ch 3, sl st, ch 3, sl st) in ea of next 5 ch-links, ch 3, sl st in next ch-link, rep from * 8 times more, (ch 4, dc, ch 4, sl st) 3 times in last ch-link], sl st in ch-4 edge of same ch-link, working down opposite side of ch-links, rep bet [ ] once more, sl st in beg sl st. Fasten off.

Rep to work pink trim on ea lavender strip and lavender trim on ea pink strip.

Edging: Join white with sc in any lp, (ch 5, sc in next lp) around, end with sl st in first sc. Fasten off.

EVENING OMBRE

*Swirl irridescent ombre yarn
into round motifs for an afghan that
mirrors the violet hues of sunset.*

FINISHED SIZE

Approximately 45″ x 60″.

MATERIALS

Sportweight brushed acrylic (135-yd. skein): 18 green/blue/lavender ombre.

Size E crochet hook, or size to obtain gauge.

GAUGE

Large motif = 7½″.

DIRECTIONS

Large motif (make 48): **First motif:** Ch 12, join with sl st to form a ring.

Rnd 1: Ch 3 for first dc, 31 dc in ring, sl st in top of beg ch-3 = 32 sts.

Rnd 2: Ch 6 for first dc and ch 3, (sk 1 st, dc in next st, ch 3) 15 times, sl st in 3rd ch of beg ch-6 = 16 sps.

Rnd 3: Sl st into next sp, ch 3 for first dc, 3 dc in same sp, ch 1, (4 dc in next sp, ch 1) around, sl st in top of beg ch-3, turn work to wrong side, sl st into ch-1 sp, turn work back to right side.

Rnd 4: Ch 7 for first dc and ch 4, dc in same sp, (dc, ch 4, dc) in ea ch-1 sp around, sl st in 3rd ch of beg ch-7.

Rnd 5: Sl st into next sp, ch 3 for first dc, (2 dc, ch 3, 3 dc) in same sp, (3 dc, ch 3, 3 dc) in ea ch-4 sp around, sl st in top of beg ch-3.

Rnd 6: Sl st into next sp, ch 3 for first dc, (2 dc, ch 1, 3 dc) in same sp, work a shell of (3 dc, ch 1, 3 dc) in ea ch-3 sp around, sl st in top of beg ch-3.

Rnd 7: Sc in sp before sl st, * (ch 5, sk 2 sts, sc in next st) twice, ch 5, sk 1 st, sc in sp bet shells, rep from * around, end with sl st in first sc. Fasten off.

2nd motif: Rep rnds 1-6 as for first motif.

Rnd 7 (joining rnd): Rep rnd 7 of first motif to last 2 shells, ch 5, sk 2 sts, sc in next st, ch 2, sc in corresponding lp on first motif, ch 2, sk 2 sts, sc in next st on 2nd motif, ch 2, sc in next lp on first motif, ch 2, sc in sp bet shells on 2nd motif, (ch 2, sc in next lp on first motif, ch 2, sk 2 sts, sc in next st on 2nd motif) twice, ch 5, sl st in first sc on 2nd motif. Fasten off.

Cont to make and join motifs as est for a throw 6 motifs wide and 8 motifs long.

Small motif (make 35): *Note:* Small motifs are joined in the openings bet rows of large motifs.

Ch 8, join with a sl st to form a ring.

Rnd 1: Ch 3 for first dc, 23 dc in ring, sl st in top of beg ch-3 = 24 sts.

Rnd 2: Ch 6 for first dc and ch 3, (sk 1 st, dc in next st, ch 3) around, sl st in 3rd ch of beg ch-6 = 12 sps.

Rnd 3 (joining rnd): Sl st into next sp, ch 3 for first dc, dc in same sp, * dc in ch-5 lp 2 lps before joining of 2 large motifs, tr in next lp, dtr in joining st, tr in next lp on next large motif, dc in next lp, keeping last lp of ea st on hook, work 2 dc in beg sp on small motif, yo and pull through all lps on hook (cl made), ch 2, sc in next lp on large motif, ch 2, sc in next sp on small motif, ch 2, sc in ea of next 2 lps on large motif, ch 2, sc in next sp on small motif, ch 2, sc in next lp on large motif, ch 2, cl in next sp on small motif, rep from * around, end with sl st in top of beg ch-3. Fasten off.

VICTORIAN FINERY

*Fancy textured yarns and popcorn stitches
come together for an afghan
full of the opulence of the Victorian era.*

FINISHED SIZE

Approximately 37″ x 53″, not including edging.

MATERIALS

Worsted-weight mohair-wool blend (90-yd. skein): 8 dark pink (A), 9 pink (B).

Worsted-weight mohair-wool blend bouclé (90-yd. skein): 10 pink (C).

Size I crochet hook, or size to obtain gauge.

GAUGE

6 dc and 3 rows = 2″.

DIRECTIONS

Flower square (make 10): With B, ch 3, dc in 3rd ch from hook to form a ring.

Rnd 1: (Ch 5, sc in ring) 7 times, ch 5, sc in top of beg dc of ring.

Rnd 2: * (Ch 7, sc in bk lp of next sc) twice, ch 7, sc in same sc for corner, rep from * 3 times more, sl st in base of beg ch-7. Fasten off.

Rnd 3: Join A with sc in center of any corner lp, sc in same lp, * (ch 2, sc in next lp) twice, ch 2, 3 sc in next corner lp, rep from * around, sc in same lp as beg, sl st in first sc.

Rnd 4: Ch 1, working in bk lps only, 2 sc in same st, * sc in next sc, (2 sc in next ch-2 sp) 3 times, sc in next sc, 3 sc in center st of corner, rep from * around, sc in same st as beg, sl st in first sc. Fasten off.

With wrong sides facing and working through bk lps only, whipstitch squares tog to make a row of 10 squares.

Afghan: **Row 1** (wrong side): With B, ch 103, dc in 4th ch from hook and ea ch across = 101 sts (including beg ch-3), turn.

Row 2 (right side): Ch 3 for first dc, dc in next st, work 5 dc in next st, drop last lp from hook, insert hook in first st of grp, pick up dropped lp and pull through (popcorn made), dc in ea of next 5 sts, (popcorn in next st, dc in ea of next 5 sts) 15 times, popcorn in next st, dc in ea of next 2 sts = 17 popcorns, turn.

Row 3: Ch 3 for first dc, dc in ea dc and popcorn across, turn.

Row 4: Ch 3 for first dc, dc in ea of next 2 sts, (popcorn in next st, dc in ea of next 3 sts, popcorn in next st, dc in next st) across, end with dc in ea of last 2 sts = 32 popcorns, turn.

Row 5: Ch 3 for first dc, dc in ea dc and popcorn across = 101 sts, turn.

Row 6: Ch 3 for first dc, (dc in ea of next 3 sts, popcorn in next st, dc in next st, popcorn in next st) 16 times across, dc in ea of next 4 sts, turn.

Row 7: Rep row 5.

Row 8: Ch 3 for first dc, dc in ea of next 4 sts, (popcorn in next st, dc in ea of next 5 sts) across = 16 popcorns, turn.

Row 9: Rep row 5. Fasten off.

Row 10: With wrong sides facing and working in bk lps only, whipstitch row of flower squares to top edge of row 9.

Row 11: With right side facing and piece turned to work across long edge of squares, join B in corner, ch 3 for first dc, working in bk lps only, work 10 dc across ea square (sk sts as necessary) = 101 sts, turn.

Row 12: Ch 3 for first dc, dc in ea dc across, turn.

Row 13: Ch 3 for first dc, dc in next st, (popcorn in next st, dc in ea of next 11 sts) 8 times, popcorn in next st, dc in ea of last 2 sts, turn.

Row 14 and foll even-numbered rows: Ch 3 for first dc, dc in ea dc and popcorn across = 101 sts, turn.

Row 15: Ch 3 for first dc, dc in ea of next 2 dc, (popcorn in next st, dc in ea of next 9 sts, popcorn in next st, dc in next st) 8 times, dc in ea of last 2 sts, turn.

Row 17: Ch 3 for first dc, dc in ea of next 3 sts, (popcorn in next st, dc in ea of next 7 sts, popcorn in next st, dc in ea of next 3 sts) 8 times, dc in last st, turn.

Row 19: Ch 3 for first dc, dc in ea of next 4 sts, (popcorn in next st, dc in ea of next 5 sts) across, turn.

Row 21: Ch 3 for first dc, dc in ea of next 5 sts, (popcorn in next st, dc in ea of next 3 sts, popcorn in next st *, dc in ea of next 7 sts) across, end last rep at *, dc in ea of last 6 sts, turn.

Row 23: Ch 3 for first dc, dc in ea of next 6 sts, (popcorn in next st, dc in next st, popcorn in next st *, dc in ea of next 9 sts) across, end last rep at *, dc in ea of last 7 sts, turn.

Row 25: Ch 3 for first dc, dc in ea of next 7 sts, (popcorn in next st *, dc in ea of next 11 sts) across, end last rep at *, dc in ea of last 8 sts, turn.

Row 27: Rep row 23.

Row 29: Rep row 21.

Row 31: Rep row 19.

Row 33: Rep row 17.

Row 35: Rep row 15.

Row 37: Rep row 13.

Rows 38 and 39: Ch 3 for first dc, dc in ea st across. Fasten off after row 39, do not turn.

Row 40: With right side facing, join A in top of row-39 beg ch-3, ch 3 for first dc, sk next dc, (2 dc bet next 2 dc, sk 2 dc) across, dc in last dc = 101 sts, turn.

Note: Work 2-dc cl as foll: keeping last lp of ea st on hook, work 2 dc in next st, yo and pull through all lps on hook.

Row 41: Ch 3 for first dc, sk 2 dc, * (2-dc cl, ch 3, 2-dc cl) in next sp, sk 4 dc, rep from * 24 times more, end last rep with sk 2 dc, dc in last st, turn.

Row 42: Ch 3 for first dc, * (2-dc cl, ch 3, 2-dc cl) in ea ch-3 sp across, dc in last st. Fasten off, do not turn.

Row 43: With right side facing, join C in top of row-42 beg ch-3, ch 3, * popcorn in next ch-3 sp, ch 3, sc bet next 2 cl, ch 3, rep from * across, end with sc in last dc = 25 popcorns, turn.

Row 44: Ch 6 for first dc and ch 3, (sc in top of next popcorn, ch 4) across, end last rep with ch 3, dc in base of row-43 beg ch-3, turn.

Row 45: Sc in top of same dc, (ch 3, popcorn in next lp, ch 3, sc in next sc) across, end with ch 3, popcorn in last lp, dc in 3rd ch of tch = 26 popcorns, turn.

Row 46: Ch 1, sc in top of same dc, (ch 4, sc in top of next popcorn) across, turn.

Row 47: Ch 1, sc in same sc, (ch 3, popcorn in next lp, ch 3, sc in next sc) across = 25 popcorns. Fasten off, do not turn.

Row 48: With right side facing, join A in row-47 beg ch-3 sp, ch 3 for first dc, 2-dc cl in same sp, * sk popcorn, (2-dc cl, ch 3, 2-dc cl) in next sc, rep from * across, end with 2-dc cl in last ch-3 sp, dc in same sp, turn.

Rows 49-52: Ch 3 for first dc, 2-dc cl in same dc, * (2-dc cl, ch 3, 2-dc cl) in next ch-3 sp, rep from * across, end with (2-dc cl, dc) in last st. Fasten off after row 52, do not turn.

Row 53: With right side facing, join B in top of row-52 beg ch-3, (ch 8, sc, ch 3, dc) in same st, * sc in next ch-3 sp, (dc, ch 3, sc, ch 8, sc, ch 3, dc) in next ch-3 sp (3-petal flower made), rep from * 11 times more, sc in last st, turn.

Row 54: Ch 3 for first dc, dc in same st, * (dc, ch 3, sc, ch 3, dc) in next ch-8 lp, sk last petal of flower, 2 dc in next sc, rep from * 11 times more, (dc, ch 3, sc) in last ch-8 lp, turn. Fasten off.

Row 55: With right side facing, join C in top of first row-54 sc, ch 6 for first dc and ch 3, sc in next lp, [ch 3, popcorn bet next 2 dc, (ch 3, sc in next lp) twice] 12 times, ch 3, dc in last st, turn.

Row 56: Ch 3 for first dc, (2 dc in next sp, 3 dc in next

sp, 2 dc in next sp, dc in next popcorn) 12 times, 2 dc in ea of last 2 sps, turn.

Row 57: Ch 3 for first dc, dc in ea dc across = 101 sts. Fasten off.

Note: Work remainder of afghan across unworked side of foundation ch.

Row 1: With right side facing, join A in same ch as last dc of row 1, ch 3 for first dc, dc in ea st across = 101 sts.

Row 2: Rep row 41.

Rows 3 and 4: Rep row 42. Fasten off.

Rows 5-7: Join C, rep rows 43-45. Fasten off after row 7.

Rows 8 and 9: Join A, rep rows 48 and 49. Fasten off after row 9.

Row 10: Join B, rep row 53 across, end with sc in next ch-3 sp, (dc, ch 3, sc) in sp bet last 2-dc cl and last dc, turn.

Row 11: Ch 4 for first tr, tr in same sc, 2 dc in sc bet 3-petal flowers, rep row 54 across, turn. Fasten off.

Row 12: With right side facing, join C in first sc, ch 6 for first dc and ch 3, sc in next lp, rep row 55 across, end with ch 3, sc in next lp, ch 3, dc in sc at base of ch-8 lp, turn.

Row 13: Ch 3 for first dc, dc in next sp, (dc in next popcorn, 2 dc in next sp, 3 dc in next sp, 2 dc in next sp) 12 times, dc in next popcorn, dc in ea of last 2 sps = 101 sts, turn.

Row 14: Ch 3 for first dc, dc in ea st across. Fasten off.

Edging: **Rnd 1:** With right side facing and afghan turned to work across long edge, join A in corner, ch 2 for first sc and ch 1, sc in same st, * work 147 sc across to corner st, (sc, ch 1, sc) in corner, work 99 sc across to next corner st, (sc, ch 1, sc) in corner, rep from * around, sl st in first ch of beg ch-1.

Rnd 2: Ch 3 for first dc, (dc, ch 3, 2-dc cl) in same st, * [sk 2 sts, (2-dc cl, ch 3, 2-dc cl) in next st] 49 times, sk 1 st, (2-dc cl, ch 3, 2-dc cl) in corner st, [sk 2 sts, (2-dc cl, ch 3, 2-dc cl) in next st] 33 times, sk 2 sts, (2-dc cl, ch 3, 2-dc cl) in corner st, rep from * around, sl st in top of beg ch-3. Fasten off.

Rnd 3: Join C with sc in ch-3 sp before corner sp, * ch 7, (sc, ch 7, sc, ch 9, sc, ch 7, sc) in next ch-3 sp, ch 7, sc in next ch-3 sp, rep from * around, sl st in first sc. Fasten off.

Rnd 4: With right side facing and afghan turned to work across long edge, join A with sc in corner ch-9 lp, (ch 3, sc in next lp) twice, dc in next sc, sc in next lp, [(ch 3, sc in next lp) 4 times, dc in next sc, sc in next lp], * sk next 3 lps, sc in next lp, push sk lps to front of work, dc in next sc, sc in next lp **, (rep bet [ ] twice, rep from * to ** once) 7 times, rep bet [ ] 3 times for corner section, (rep from * to ** once, rep bet [ ] twice, rep from * to ** once, rep bet [ ] once) 3 times, work corner section as est, cont around afghan as est, end with sl st in first sc. Fasten off.

Rnd 5: With right side facing and afghan turned to work across long edge, join C with sc in ch-3 sp before corner sc, (ch 5, sc in next ch-3 sp) 6 times, * ch 11, sk across to next ch-3 sp, sc in ch-3 sp, (ch 5, sc in next ch-3 sp) 7 times **, rep from * 7 times more, (ch 5, sc in next ch-3 sp) 4 times, [rep from * to ** once, ch 11, sk across to next ch-3 sp, sc in ch-3 sp, (ch 5, sc in next ch-3 sp) 3 times] twice, rep from * to ** twice, (ch 5, sc in next ch-3 sp) 4 times, cont around afghan as est, end with sl st in first sc.

Rnd 6: Sl st into next lp, (sc, ch 3, popcorn, ch 3, sc) in corner ch-5 lp, (ch 3, sc in next lp, ch 3, popcorn in next lp) twice, * ch 3, sc in next lp, ch 3, (popcorn, ch 7, popcorn, ch 7, popcorn) in next ch-11 lp, (ch 3, sc in next lp, ch 3, popcorn in next lp) 3 times, rep from * 6 times more, ch 3, sc in next lp, ch 3, (popcorn, ch 7, popcorn, ch 7, popcorn) in next ch-11 lp, (ch 3, sc in next lp, ch 3, popcorn in next lp)

twice, ch 3, sc in next lp, ch 3, (sc, ch 3, popcorn, ch 3, sc) in next lp for corner, cont around afghan as est, end with sl st in first sc.

Rnd 7: Sl st backward into last rnd-6 sc, ch 4, tr in same st, (ch 4, tr bet ch and tr) 3 times (4-ch-link lp made), sc in first sc after corner, [ch 4, tr in same st, ch 4, tr bet ch and tr (2-ch-link lp made), sc in sc after next popcorn] twice, * (make 2-ch-link lp as est, sk next popcorn, sc in next ch-7 lp) twice, (make 2-ch-link lp, sk next popcorn, sc in next sc) 4 times, rep from * to corner, make 4-ch-link lp, sc in first sc after corner, cont around afghan as est, end with sl st in base of beg ch-link. Fasten off.

FLOWERY FANTASY

*Start with a variegated yarn
to quick-crochet the strips for
this charming throw.*

FINISHED SIZE
Approximately 48″ x 54″.

MATERIALS
Fingering-weight cotton-acrylic blend (230-yd. ball): 7 white.

Fingering-weight cotton (150-yd. ball): 8 variegated pastel.

Size E crochet hook, or size to obtain gauge.

GAUGE
1 ch-link = 1″.
Strip = 5½″ x 54″.

DIRECTIONS
Strip A (make 5): With white, (ch 4, tr in 4th ch from hook) 45 times = 45 ch-links.

Rnd 1: Ch 3 for first dc, working across tr edge of ch-links, 7 dc in same ch-link, 5 dc in ea of next 43 ch-links, 15 dc in last ch-link, working down opposite side of ch-links, 5 dc in ea of next 43 ch-links, 7 dc in last ch-link, sl st in top of beg ch-3. Fasten off.

Rnd 2: Join variegated pastel with sl st in same st as last sl st, ch 3 for first dc, working in bk lps only, (2 dc in next dc, dc in next dc) 3 times, 2 dc in next dc, * sk 2 dc, (5 dc in next dc, sk 4 dc) 43 times, sk 2 dc **, (2 dc in next dc, dc in next dc) 7 times, 2 dc in next dc, rep from * to ** once more, (2 dc in next dc, dc in next dc) 3 times, 2 dc in next dc, sl st in top of beg ch-3.

Rnd 3: Ch 3 for first dc, working in bk lps only, 2 dc in

same st, (sk 2 dc, work a shell of 5 dc in next dc) 3 times, (sk 4 dc, 5-dc shell in next dc) 44 times, (sk 2 dc, 5-dc shell in next dc) 6 times, (sk 4 dc, 5-dc shell in next dc) 44 times, (sk 2 dc, 5-dc shell in next dc) twice, sk 2 dc, 2 dc in same st as beg ch-3, sl st in top of beg ch-3 = 100 shells around. Fasten off.

Rnd 4: Join white with sl st in same st as last sl st, * (ch 3, sl st, ch 5, sl st, ch 3, sl st) in same st, ch 3, sc in sp bet shells, ch 3, sl st in center dc of next shell, rep from * around, end with sl st in same st as beg sl st. Fasten off.

Strip B (make 5): Rep rnds 1-3 as for strip A.

Rnd 4 (joining rnd): Join white with sl st in same st as last sl st, * (ch 3, sl st, ch 5, sl st, ch 3, sl st) in same st, ch 3, sc in sp bet shells, ch 3, sl st in center dc of next shell **, rep from * twice more, [ch 3, sl st in same st, ch 2, sl st in corresponding ch-5 lp on strip A, ch 2, (sl st, ch 3, sl st) in same st on strip B, ch 3, sc in sp bet shells on strip B, ch 3, sl st in center dc of next shell on strip B] 45 times, rep from * to ** 5 times, rep bet [ ] 45 times to join another strip A, rep from * to ** twice. Fasten off.

Rep to join rem strips as est.

Trim: Join white with sc in top of rnd-2 beg ch-3, working in ft lps only, (ch 3, sk next dc, sc in next dc) 5 times, * ch 3, sk next dc, sc in sp bet shells, (ch 3, sk next dc, sc in next dc) twice **, rep from * 43 times more, (ch 3, sk next dc, sc in next dc) 9 times, rep from * to ** 44 times, (ch 3, sk next dc, sc in next dc) 4 times, ch 3, sl st in first sc. Fasten off.

Rep to work trim on ea strip.

COTTON CANDY

*With just a few simple stitches,
a yarn as light and fluffy as spun sugar
becomes a child-sized throw.*

FINISHED SIZE

Approximately 47″ square.

MATERIALS

Bulky-weight cotton-acrylic-mohair blend (105-yd. ball): 10 pink with white accents.

Sportweight brushed acrylic (156-yd. ball): 1 white.

Size I crochet hook, or size to obtain gauge.

GAUGE

9 dc and 4 rows = 3″.

DIRECTIONS

Throw: **Row 1:** With pink, ch 103, dc in 4th ch from hook and ea ch across, turn = 101 dc.

Row 2: Ch 3 for first dc, dc in ea st across, turn.

Row 3: Ch 3 for first dc, dc in ea of next 4 sts, * sk 2 sts, 5 dc in next st (shell made), ch 2, sk 4 sts, dc in ea of next 5 sts, rep from * 7 times more, turn.

Row 4: Ch 3 for first dc, dc in ea of next 4 sts, * shell in first st of next shell, ch 2, dc in ea of next 5 dc bet shells, rep from * across, turn.

Rows 5-41: Rep row 4.

Row 42: Ch 3 for first dc, dc in ea dc and ch across, turn = 101 dc.

Row 43: Ch 3 for first dc, dc in ea dc across. Fasten off.

Edging: **Rnd 1:** Join white with sl st in top of first st of row 43, ch 2 for first hdc, 2 hdc in same st, * work 99 hdc across to next corner, 3 hdc in corner, work 100 hdc across to next corner, 3 hdc in corner, rep from * around, sl st in top of beg ch-2. Fasten off.

Rnd 2: Join pink with sl st in first st of any corner, ch 3 for first dc, 4 dc in same st (beg shell made), * ch 2, sk next st, dc in last st of corner grp, dc in ea of next 4 sts, (sk next 2 sts, shell in next st, ch 2, sk 4 sts, dc in ea of next 5 sts) to next corner grp, shell in first st of corner grp, rep from * around, sl st in top of beg ch-3, turn.

Rnd 3: Sl st into next dc, ch 3 for first dc, dc in ea of next 4 dc, (shell in first st of next shell, ch 2, dc in ea of next 5 dc bet shells) around, sl st in top of beg ch-3, turn.

Rnd 4: Ch 2 for first hdc, hdc in same st, 4 hdc in next ch-2 sp, * 2 hdc in ea of first 2 sts of corner shell, 3 hdc in next st for corner, 2 hdc in ea of last 2 sts of same corner shell, 2 hdc in ea of next 5 dc, (4 hdc in next ch-2 sp, 2 hdc in ea st of next shell, 2 hdc in ea of next 5 dc) across to corner shell, rep from * around, sl st in top of beg ch-2, turn. Fasten off.

Rnd 5: Join white with sl st in center st of any corner, ch 3 for first dc, beg shell in same st, * ch 2, sk next 4 sts, dc in next st, sk 2 sts, shell in next st, rep from * around, end with sl st in top of beg ch-3, turn. Fasten off.

Rnd 6: Join pink with sl st in first st of any shell, ch 3 for first dc, beg shell in same st, * ch 2, dc in dc bet shells, shell in first st of next shell, rep from * around, sl st in top of beg ch-3, turn.

Rnd 7: Sl st into next dc, ch 3 for first dc, * shell in first st of next shell, ch 2, dc in dc bet shells, rep from * around, sl st in top of beg ch-3, turn.

Rnd 8: Ch 3 for first dc, * shell in first st of next shell, ch 2, dc in dc bet shells, rep from * around, sl st in top of beg ch-3, turn.

Rnd 9: Sl st into ch-2 sp, * ch 3, sl st in first st of next shell, ch 3, sl st in center st of same shell, ch 3, sl st in last st of same shell, ch 3, sl st in next ch-2 sp, rep from * around, sl st in beg sl st. Fasten off.

TWINING IVY

*For cool evenings on the patio
or to accessorize the garden room, cross-stitch
ivy vines on panels of deep green.*

FINISHED SIZE

Approximately 35″ x 47″, not including edging.

MATERIALS

Worsted-weight acrylic (110-yd. ball): 25 dark green.
Size H (10″-long) afghan hook, or size to obtain gauge.
Paternayan Persian wool (8-yd. skein): see color key.
Size H crochet hook.
Amber beads (color #5110, available from Quilter's Resource, 2211 North Elston, Chicago, IL 60614).
Dark green sewing thread.
Beading needle.

GAUGE

9 sts and 8 rows = 2″ in afghan st.

DIRECTIONS

Note: See page 141 for afghan st instructions.

Panel (make 3): With dark green, ch 52, work 192 rows afghan st. Sl st in ea vertical bar across. Fasten off.

Cross-stitch: Stitch design with 2 strands of wool. With last row of afghan stitch at top, center design on panel and begin cross-stitching 3 rows from top edge. Work 3 repeats of design plus 1 partial design to fill each panel, stopping 3 rows from end of panel.

Assembly: Holding 2 panels with wrong sides facing and working through both pieces, join dark green with sl st in corner, * ch 1, sl st in next st, rep from * to next corner. Fasten off. Rep to join rem panel.

Edging: **Rnd 1:** With size H crochet hook, right side facing, and afghan turned to work across short edge, join dark green with sc in corner, * sc in ea st to next corner, (sc, ch 1, sc) in corner, rep from * around, sc in beg corner, ch 1, sl st in first sc = 154 sts across ea short edge and 190 sts across ea long edge.

Rnd 2: Ch 1, sc in same sp, * (ch 6, sk 5 sts, sc in next st) across to corner, ch 6, sc in corner sp, rep from * around, sl st in first sc.

Rnd 3: Ch 1, sc in same st, (ch 3, 3 dc in next lp, ch 3, sc

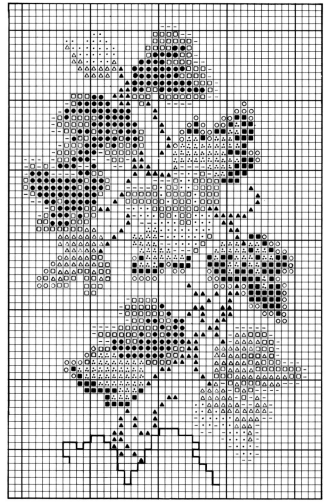

Cross-stitch Chart

Color Key

**Paternayan Persian Wool
(used for sample)**

·	612	Hunter Green (8)
△	611	Hunter Green-dk. (9)
O	604	Forest Green-lt. (6)
∴	603	Forest Green-med. (9)
■	600	Forest Green-dk. (8)
-	644	Khaki-lt. (9)
▲	641	Khaki-dk. (9)
□	652	Olive (18)
●	651	Olive-dk. (9)

Note: The number of 8-yd. skeins required for each color is indicated in parentheses.

in next sc) around, sl st in first sc.

Rnd 4: Ch 1, sc in same st, * ch 8, sk 3-dc grp, (tr, dc, hdc, sc in next ch-3 sp), sc in next sc, rep from * around, sl st in first sc.

Rnd 5: * Sl st into next lp, ch 4, (dc, hdc, sc) in same lp, sc in next tr, ch 8, sk dc-hdc-sc grp, sc in next sc, rep from * around, sl st in base of beg ch-4.

Rnd 6: Sl st in ea of 4 ch, ch 1, (sc in ch-4 sp, ch 6, sc in ch-8 lp, ch 6) around, sl st in first sc.

Rnd 7: Sl st into next lp, ch 3 for first dc, 2 dc in same lp, * ch 3, (sc in next lp, ch 3, 3 dc in next lp, ch 3) to corner lp, (sc, ch 3, 3 dc, ch 3, sc) in corner lp, ch 3, 3 dc in next lp, rep from * around, end with dc in top of beg ch-3, sl st into next sc.

Rnds 8-12: Rep rnds 4-7, ending after rnd 4. Fasten off after rnd 12.

Vine (make 2): Ch 3, dc in 3rd ch from hook, (ch 3, dc bet ch and dc to make a ch-link) 4 times, * ch 6, sc in 5th ch from hook (picot made), ch 8, sc in 5th ch from hook (picot made), ch 7, dc in 4th ch from hook, [ch 7, sc in 5th ch from hook (picot made)] twice, ch 7, dc in 4th ch from hook, (ch 3, dc bet ch and dc to make a ch-link) twice, ch 3, 2 dc bet ch and dc, [ch 7, sc in 5th ch from hook (picot made)] 3 times, ch 7, dc in 4th ch from hook, ch 3, 4 dc bet ch and dc, drop last lp from hook, insert hook in top of ch-3, pick up dropped lp and pull through (popcorn made), ch 3, dc in top of popcorn, (ch 3, dc bet ch and dc) 4 times, rep from * until piece measures 4½ to 5 yards long. Fasten off. (*Note:* It is not necessary to work the picots, ch-links, and popcorns as described. Vary the vine by working the sts as desired.)

Finishing: Referring to photo, arrange a vine along each seam between panels and tack in place. Arrange beads on afghan as desired and stitch in place.

HOMESPUN CLASSIC

*Openwork hexagons accented with
shell stitches make this throw
a classic example of the art of crochet.*

FINISHED SIZE
Approximately 44″ square.

MATERIALS
Sportweight cotton (115-yd. ball): 7 blue, 6 green, 10 brown.
Size E crochet hook, or size to obtain gauge.

GAUGE
Large motif = 9″.

DIRECTIONS
Note: Since large motifs are joined while working rnd 10, work motifs in rows according to placement diagram (on page 38). Begin with motif A in lower left-hand corner of diagram.

Large motif (make 25): **First motif: Rnd 1:** With blue, ch 8, dc in first ch, (ch 4, dc in same st) twice, ch 4, sl st in 4th ch of beg ch-8 = 4 sps around.

Rnd 2: Sl st into next sp, ch 3 for first dc, (2 dc, ch 2, 3 dc) in same sp, * ch 2, (3 dc, ch 2, 3 dc) in next sp, rep from * twice more, ch 2, sl st in top of beg ch-3. Fasten off.

Rnd 3: Join green with sl st in ch-2 sp after prev sl st, working in bk lps only, ch 1, sc in ea dc and ch around, sl st in first sc = 40 sts. Fasten off.

Note: For rnds 4 and 6, carry color not in use around by working over it with the next grp of sts. To change colors, bring up new color as last yo of st in prev color.

Rnd 4: Join blue with sl st in last rnd-3 sc, working in bk lps only, ch 1, sc in next st, ch 2, sc in next st, * sc in next st, join brown and work (sc, 5 dc, sc) in next st (shell made), with blue sc in ea of next 2 sts, ch 2, sc in next st, rep from * around, sl st in first sc. Fasten off brown.

Rnd 5: With blue, sl st into next ch-2 sp, ch 8 for first dc and ch 5, dc in same sp, * dc in next st, ch 1, sk across sc-shell-sc grp, dc in next st, (dc, ch 5, dc) in next ch-2 sp, rep from * around, sl st in 3rd ch of beg ch-8.

Rnd 6: With blue, sl st into next ch-5 sp, ch 1, (2 sc, ch 3,

2 sc) in same sp, * join brown and work a shell in next dc, sk 1 st, with blue work 3 sc in next sp, sk 1 st, with brown work a shell in next dc, with blue work (2 sc, ch 3, 2 sc) in next ch-5 sp, rep from * around, sl st in first sc. Fasten off brown.

Rnd 7: With blue, sl st into next ch-3 sp, ch 4 for first dc and ch 1, dc in same sp, * dc in ea of next 2 sts, ch 1, sk next shell and sc, dc in next sc, ch 1, sk next sc and shell, dc in ea of next 2 sc, (dc, ch 1, dc) in next ch-3 sp, rep from * around, sl st in 3rd ch of beg ch-4.

Rnd 8: Sl st into next ch-1 sp, ch 5 for first tr and ch 1, 2 tr in same sp, * tr in next st, dc in ea of next 2 sts, dc in next sp, hdc in next st, dc in next sp, dc in ea of next 2 sts, tr in next st, (2 tr, ch 1, 2 tr) in next ch-1 sp, rep from * around, end with tr in same sp as beg, sl st in 4th ch of beg ch-5. Fasten off.

Rnd 9: Join brown with sl st in any ch-1 sp, ch 1, * sc in ea of next 13 sts, (sc, ch 1, sc) in next ch-1 sp, rep from * around, sl st in first sc. Fasten off.

Rnd 10: Join green with sl st in any ch-1 sp, ch 6 for first dc and ch 3, dc in same sp, ch 1, * sk 1 st, dc in ea of next 13 sts, ch 1, sk 1 st, (dc, ch 3, dc) in next ch-1 sp, ch 1, rep from * around, end with sl st in 3rd ch of beg ch-4. Fasten off.

2nd motif: Rep rnds 1-9 as for first motif, using colors according to table and placement diagram.

Rnd 10 (joining rnd): Join color for rnd 10 with sl st in any ch-1 sp, ch 6 for first dc and ch 3, dc in same sp, ch 1, * sk 1 st, dc in ea of next 13 sts, ch 1, sk 1 st, (dc, ch 3, dc) in next ch-1 sp, ch 1, rep from * 4 times more, ch 1, sk 1 st, dc in ea of next 13 sts, ch 1, sk 1 st, dc in next ch-1 sp, ch 1, sc in ch-3 sp on first motif, [ch 1, dc in same sp on 2nd motif, ch 1, sk 1 st, dc in ea of next 13 sts, ch 1, sk 1 st], dc in next ch-1 sp, ch 1, sc in next ch-3 sp on first motif, rep bet [ ] once, sl st in 3rd ch of beg ch-6. Fasten off.

Rep rnds 1-10 according to placement diagram and using colors as foll (make the number of ea motif as shown in parentheses):

Motif	Rnds 1-2	Rnd 3	Rnds 4-8	Rnd 9	Rnd 10
A (5)	Blue	Green	Blue/brown shells	Brown	Green
B (6)	Blue	Brown	Green/brown shells	Brown	Blue
C (6)	Blue	Green	Brown/green shells	Green	Blue
D (4)	Green	Brown	Blue/brown shells	Brown	Green
E (4)	Green	Blue	Brown/blue shells	Blue	Green

A	C	E	B	A
C	D	B	E	C
D	B	A	B	D
C	E	B	D	C
A	B	E	C	A

Placement Diagram

Small motif (make 16): *Note:* Small motifs are joined in the openings bet rows of large motifs.

Rnds 1-3: With brown, rep rnds 1-3 of large motif.

Rnd 4 (joining rnd): (Sc, 5 dc, sc) in next st, sl st in next st, * ch 6, sc in joining sc of 2 large motifs, ch 6, sk 2 sts on small motif, sl st in next st, (sc, 5 dc, sc) in next st, sl st in next st, ch 6, sc in center st of 13-dc grp on large motif, ch 6, sk 2 sts on small motif, sl st in next st, (sc, 5 dc, sc) in next st, sl st in next st, rep from * around, sl st in first sc. Fasten off.

Cont to make and join small motifs as est.

RICH ROSE LACE

A lacy crocheted edging highlights this woven-fabric afghan bedecked with a subtly shaded cross-stitch motif.

FINISHED SIZE

Edging: Approximately 6″ wide.

MATERIALS

45″ x 58″ piece of white Anne Cloth 18 (available in cross-stitch shops).

White sewing thread.

Size 20 crochet cotton (440-yd. ball): 4 rose.

Size 8 steel crochet hook, or size to obtain gauge.

5½ yards of blue-green decorative trim.

DMC or Anchor embroidery floss (8-yd. skein): see color key.

GAUGE

Small flower = 2″ diameter.

DIRECTIONS

Note: To hem Anne Cloth, turn under ½″ twice along all raw edges, mitering corners. Slipstitch hem in place.

Edging: **Rnd 1:** With right side facing and afghan turned to work across long edge, join rose with sl st in corner, * 3 sc in corner, 479 sc evenly spaced across to next corner, 3 sc in corner, 383 sc evenly spaced across to next corner, rep from * around, sl st in first sc.

Rnd 2: Sc in same st, ch 7, sc in 4th ch from hook to make a picot, ch 7, picot, ch 3, sk 1 sc, sc in next sc (corner picot-lp made), * (ch 7, picot) twice, ch 3 (picot-lp made), sk 5 sc, sc in next sc **, rep from * 79 times more, [(ch 7, picot) twice, ch 3, sk 1 sc, sc in next sc] for corner, rep from * to ** 64 times, rep bet [ ] once more for corner, rep from * around as est, sl st in first sc.

Rnd 3: Sl st into center of corner picot-lp, sc in same lp, (make a picot-lp, sc in center of next picot-lp) around, end with sl st in first sc.

Rnd 4: Turn to wrong side, sl st into center of next picot-lp, turn back to right side, sc in same lp, (make a picot-lp, sc in center of next picot-lp) around, end with sl st in first sc.

Rnd 5: Sl st into center of next picot-lp, * ch 7, sc in center of next lp, turn, ch 2 for hdc, (7 dc, hdc) in ch-7 lp just made, ch 2 for hdc, turn, dc in ea of 7 dc, hdc in top of first ch-2 (shell made), rep from * around, end with sl st in first ch of beg ch-7.

Rnd 6: Sl st into top of first st of next shell, sc in same st, (make a picot-lp, sc in first st of next shell) around, end with sl st in first sc.

Rnd 7: Sl st into center of next picot-lp, sc in same lp, (make a picot-lp, sc in center of next picot-lp) around, end with sl st in first sc.

Rnds 8 and 9: Rep rnds 4 and 5.

Rnd 10: Sl st into top of first st of next shell, sc in same st, * (make a picot-lp, sc in first st of next shell) to next corner shell, make a picot-lp, sc in first st of corner shell, make a picot-lp, sc in 6th st of same shell, rep from * around, end with sl st in first sc.

Rnd 11: Rep rnd 7.

Rnd 12: Sl st into center of next picot-lp, sc in same lp, * ch 7, picot, ch 16, dc in 8th ch from hook (lp made), ch 3, sk next 3 ch, sc in ea of next 4 ch, ch 6, picot, ch 3, sc in center of next picot-lp, rep from * around, end with sl st in first sc. Fasten off.

Rnd 13: Join rose with sl st in any rnd-12 lp, ch 4 for first tr, (4 tr, ch 4, sc in top of last tr to make a picot, 5 tr) in same lp, * ch 1, (5 tr, picot, 5 tr) in next lp, rep from * around, ch 1, sl st in top of beg ch-4. Fasten off.

Small flower (make 4): Ch 6, join with a sl st to form a ring.

Rnd 1: * (Ch 3, 3 dc, ch 3, sl st) in ring, rep from * 4 times more = 5 petals.

Rnd 2: * (Sc, hdc, dc) in next ch-3 sp, working in bk lps only of next 3 sts, 2 dc in next dc, 3 tr in next dc, 2 dc in next dc, (dc, hdc, sc) in next ch-3 sp, rep from * around, sl st in first sc.

Rnd 3: * Working in bk lps only, ch 3, sk next 2 sts, sl st in next st, (ch 3, sl st in next st) 6 times, ch 3, sk 2 sts, sl st bet next 2 sts (bet petals), rep from * around. Fasten off.

Large flower (make 1): Rep rnds 1-3 of small flower. Do not fasten off.

Rnd 4: * (Ch 3, sl st in next ch-3 sp) 8 times, ch 3, sl st in next sl st, rep from * around.

Rnd 5: * Ch 3, sk next ch-3 sp, sl st in next sp, (ch 3, sl st in next ch-3 sp) 6 times, ch 3, sk next sp, sl st in next sl st, rep from * around. Fasten off.

Finishing: Tack crocheted flowers to 1 corner of edging as desired (see photo). Stitch decorative trim to right side of afghan, ⅜″ from hemmed edge.

Cross-stitch: Working over 1 thread and referring to chart for placement, stitch design in each of 3 squares in 1 corner of afghan (see photo).

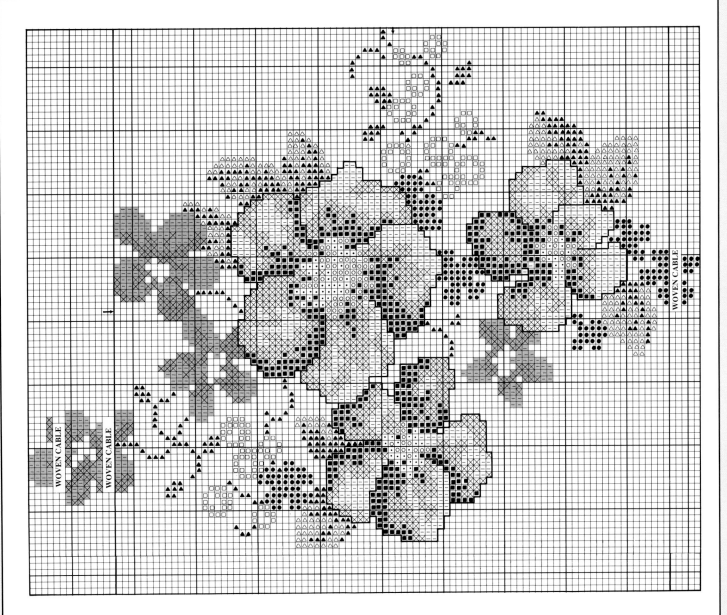

Cross-stitch Chart

(*Note:* Heavy lines on chart indicate inner and outer woven borders of square of Anne Cloth.)

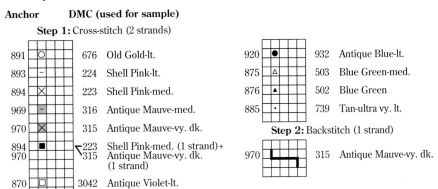

Color Key

Anchor		DMC (used for sample)	

Step 1: Cross-stitch (2 strands)

Anchor		DMC			Anchor		DMC	
891	○	676	Old Gold-lt.		920	●	932	Antique Blue-lt.
893	−	224	Shell Pink-lt.		875	△	503	Blue Green-med.
894	✕	223	Shell Pink-med.		876	▲	502	Blue Green
969	⊟	316	Antique Mauve-med.		885	·	739	Tan-ultra vy. lt.
970	⊠	315	Antique Mauve-vy. dk.					
894 970	■	223 315	Shell Pink-med. (1 strand)+ Antique Mauve-vy. dk. (1 strand)					
870	☐	3042	Antique Violet-lt.					

Step 2: Backstitch (1 strand)

970	▬	315	Antique Mauve-vy. dk.

41

LACY DAFFODILS

For an elegant tablecloth to grace your formal dining room, join damask napkins with a dainty crocheted edging.

FINISHED SIZE

Approximately 55″ square.

MATERIALS

9 (17″) square damask napkins.
Size 20 crochet cotton (440-yd. ball): 4 yellow.
Sizes 5 and 10 steel hooks, or size to obtain gauge.
Size 20 crochet cotton (405-yd. ball): 1 ecru.

GAUGE

Medallion = 4″ diameter with size 5 hook.

DIRECTIONS

Note: If edges of napkins are not hemmed, turn under ¼″ twice along all edges and slipstitch in place.

Square (make 9): **First square: Rnd 1:** With size 10 hook, join yellow with sl st in any corner of napkin, ch 2 for first hdc, hdc in same corner, * work 103 hdc across to next corner, 3 hdc in corner, rep from * around, end with hdc in beg corner, sl st in top of beg ch-2.

Rnd 2: With size 5 hook, ch 3 for first dc, 4 dc in same st, ch 1, * keeping last lp of ea st on hook, work 3 dc in next st, yo and pull through all lps on hook (3-dc cl made), ch 1, sk 1 st, 5 dc in next st, drop last lp from hook, insert hook in first st of grp, pick up dropped lp and pull through (popcorn made), ch 1, sk 1 st, 3-dc cl in next st, ch 2, sk next 3 sts, tr in next st, ch 3, working in front of prev tr, tr in 2nd sk st (cross st made), ch 2, sk 1 st, rep from * across to corner, ch 1, 5 dc in center corner st, ch 1, rep from * around as est, sl st in top of beg ch-3.

Rnd 3: Ch 5, sc in last dc of corner grp, * [ch 5, sc in top of next popcorn, (ch 5, sc in next ch-2 sp) twice] across to 5-dc corner grp, ch 5, sc in first dc of corner, ch 5, sc in last dc of corner, rep from * around, sl st in first ch of beg ch-5.

Rnd 4: Ch 4 for first tr, 2-tr cl in same st, ch 3, (3-tr cl, ch 3) in ea of next 3 ch, 3-tr cl in last ch of corner, * ch 5, sl st in next sc, [ch 3, sl st in center ch of next ch-5 lp, ch 5 for dtr, keeping last lp of ea st on hook, 2 dtr in same ch, 3 dtr in center ch of next ch-5 lp, 2 dtr in center ch of next ch-5 lp, yo and pull through all lps on hook, ch 5, sl st in same ch as last 2 dtr (3-petal cl made), ch 3, sl st in next sc] 10 times, ch 5, 3-tr cl in first ch of corner ch-5, ch 3, (3-tr cl, ch 3) in ea of next 3 ch, 3-tr cl in last ch of corner, rep from * around, sl st in top of beg cl. Fasten off.

2nd square: Rep rnds 1-3 as for first square.

Rnd 4 (joining rnd): Ch 4 for first tr, 2-tr cl in same st, ch 3, 3-tr cl in next ch of corner, ch 3, 3-tr cl in center ch of corner, drop lp from hook, insert hook in center corner cl on first square, pick up dropped lp and pull through, ch 3, 3-tr cl in next ch on 2nd square, ch 3, 3-tr cl in last ch of corner on 2nd square, ch 5, sl st in next sc, ch 3, sl st in center ch of next ch-5 lp, [ch 5 for dtr, keeping last lp of ea st on hook, 2 dtr in same ch, 3 dtr in center ch of next ch-5 lp, 2 dtr in center ch of next ch-5 lp, yo and pull through all lps on hook (3-petal cl made), drop lp from hook, insert hook in center of corresponding 3-petal cl on first square, pick up dropped lp and pull through, ch 5, sl st in same ch as last 2 dtr on 2nd square, ch 3, sl st in next sc, ch 3, sl st in center ch of next ch-5 lp] 10 times, ch 5, 3-tr cl in first ch of corner, ch 3, 3-tr cl in next ch of corner, ch 3, 3-tr cl in center ch of corner, join to corresponding corner on first square as est, ch 3, 3-tr cl in next ch of corner on 2nd square, ch 3, 3-tr cl in last ch of corner, ch 5, complete square same as first square. Fasten off.

Cont to make and join squares as est for a throw 3 squares wide and 3 squares long.

Accent point: *Note:* Accent points are worked across joinings of squares (see photo).

Row 1: With size 5 hook, join yellow with sl st in center of 2nd 3-petal cl before joining of 2 squares, ch 4, 3-tr cl in same st, ch 4, 3-tr cl in top of 3-tr cl just made (2-cl section made), sl st in next sc, make a 2-cl section, sl st in center of next 3-petal cl, make a 2-cl section, sl st in next sc, make a 2-cl section, sl st in joining bet 2 squares, make a 2-cl section, sl st in next sc, make a 2-cl section, sl st in center of next 3-petal cl, make a 2-cl section, sl st in next sc, make a 2-cl section, sl st in center of next 3-petal cl, turn.

Row 2: Ch 4, sl st in center of next 2-cl section, (make a 2-cl section, sl st in center of next 2-cl section) 7 times, turn.

Row 3: Rep row 2, except rep bet ( ) 6 times.
Row 4: Rep row 2, except rep bet ( ) 5 times.
Row 5: Rep row 2, except rep bet ( ) 4 times.
Row 6: Rep row 2, except rep bet ( ) 3 times.
Row 7: Rep row 2, except rep bet ( ) twice. Fasten off.
Rep rows 1-7 across ea joining of 2 squares.

Medallion (make 9): With size 5 hook and yellow, ch 12, join with a sl st to form a ring.

Rnd 1: Ch 3 for first dc, 2-dc cl in ring, ch 3, 4-dc popcorn in ring, (ch 3, 3-dc cl in ring, ch 3, 4-dc popcorn in ring) 3 times, ch 3, sl st in top of beg cl.

Rnd 2: * Ch 6, sl st in 4th ch from hook to make a picot, ch 7, sl st in 4th ch from hook to make a picot, ch 2 (picot-lp made), sc in top of next popcorn, make a picot-lp, sc in top of next cl, rep from * around, end with sl st in first ch of beg picot-lp.

Rnd 3: Sl st into center of next picot-lp, ch 3 for first dc, 2-dc cl in same lp, ch 3, 3-dc cl in same lp, * ch 6, (3-dc cl, ch 3, 3-dc cl) in next picot-lp, rep from * around, ch 6, sl st in top of beg cl.

Rnd 4: * Make a picot-lp, sc in top of next cl, ch 6, sc in top of next cl, rep from * around, sl st in first ch of beg picot-lp.

Rnd 5: Sl st into center of next picot-lp, ch 3 for first dc, 2-dc cl in same lp, ch 5, 3-dc cl in same lp, * ch 4, tr over and around both ch-6 lps of 2 prev rows, ch 4, (3-dc cl, ch 5, 3-dc cl, ch 5, 3-dc cl) in center of next picot-lp, rep from * around, end with 3-dc cl in beg lp, ch 5, sl st in top of beg cl.

Rnd 6: Make a picot-lp, sc in top of next cl, ch 6, * sc in top of next cl, (make a picot-lp, sc in top of next cl) twice, ch 6, rep from * around, sl st in first ch of beg picot-lp. Fasten off.

Stitch 1 medallion to the center of each napkin.

Tassel (make 12): *Note:* See page 141 for tassel diagrams. For each tassel, wind ecru and yellow threads 75 times around a 5″ piece of cardboard. Wrap tassel with yellow thread. Stitch a tassel to each accent point and each corner of throw.

BLOCK PARTY

*Try out new stitch patterns or substitute
your old favorites to craft these
sampler squares using scrap-bag yarns.*

FINISHED SIZE

Approximately 38″ x 45″.

MATERIALS

Sportweight wool (124-yd. ball): 1 each dark rust, light rust, medium rust, medium red, dark red, coral.

Worsted-weight acrylic (110-yd. ball): 1 each dark blue, dark green, lavender; scraps of orchid.

Sportweight mercerized cotton (154-yd. ball): 1 light brown, scraps of purple.

Sportweight cotton (115-yd. ball): 1 each blue, orange, medium orange, red.

Fingering-weight mercerized cotton (190-yd. ball): 1 gold.

Worsted-weight wool (137-yd. skein): 3 black.

Size F crochet hook, or size to obtain gauge.

GAUGE

9 hdc and 7 rows = 2″.

DIRECTIONS

Blackberry st block (make 5 using colors as foll):

	Rows 1-7	Rows 8-12	Rows 13-15
A	Dark rust	Medium rust	Light rust
B	Blue	Light brown	Dark green
C	Orange	Medium orange	Red
D	Light brown	Dark blue	Lavender
E	Coral	Medium red	Dark red

Row 1 (right side): Ch 23, dc in 4th ch from hook and ea ch across, turn = 21 dc (including beg ch-3).

Row 2: Ch 1, sc in same st as tch and in next st, * keeping last lp of ea st on hook, work 5 dc in next st, yo and pull through all lps on hook (bobble made), ch 1, sc in ea of next 3 sts, rep from * across, sc in last st and in tch, turn.

Row 3: Ch 3 for first dc, dc in ea sc and bobble across, turn = 21 dc.

Row 4: Ch 1, sc in same st as tch and ea of next 3 sts,

* bobble in next st, sc in ea of next 3 sts, rep from * across, sc in tch, turn.

Row 5: Rep row 3.

Rows 6-15: Rep rows 2-5, ending after row 3. Fasten off after row 15.

Border: Rnd 1: With right side facing, join black with a sl st in any corner, ch 2 for first hdc, 2 hdc in same st for corner, * work 19 hdc across to next corner, 3 hdc in corner st, rep from * around, sl st in top of beg ch-2.

Rnd 2: Sl st into center corner st, ch 2 for first hdc, 2 hdc in same st for corner, * hdc in ea st to corner, 3 hdc in center corner st, rep from * around, sl st in top of beg ch-2.

Rnds 3-6: Rep rnd 2. Fasten off after rnd 6 = 31 sts bet corner sts.

Puff cables block (make 2 using colors as foll):

	Rows 1-3	Rows 4-7	Rows 8-11
A	Dark blue	Light brown	Lavender
B	Dark green	Light brown	Blue

Row 1: Ch 15, dc in 4th ch from hook and ea ch across, turn = 13 dc (including beg ch-3).

Row 2: Ch 3 for first dc, * yo twice, insert hook from back to front around post of next dc, complete st as a tr (tr/rb made), keeping last lp of ea st on hook, work 5 hdc in next st, yo and pull through all lps on hook (puff made), tr/rb around post of next dc, dc in next st, rep from * twice more, turn.

Row 3: Ch 3 for first dc, * keeping last lp of ea st on hook, dc in next st, sk puff, yo twice, insert hook from front to back around post of row-2 tr/rb after puff, complete st as a tr (tr/rf made), dc in sk puff working in front of prev tr/rf, yo and pull through all lps on hook, keeping last lp of ea st on hook, tr/rf around post of row-2 tr/rb before puff, dc in st after puff, yo and pull through all lps on hook, dc in next dc, rep from * twice more, turn.

Row 4: Ch 3 for first dc, * tr/rb around row-3 cabled tr, puff in next st, tr/rb around post of next dc, dc in next dc, rep from * twice more, turn.

Rows 5-11: Rep rows 3 and 4 alternately, ending after row 3. Fasten off after row 11.

Border: Row 1: With right side facing, join black in top of last dc of row 11, ch 2 for first hdc, work 22 hdc across side edge of block, turn.

Rows 2-5: Ch 2 for first hdc, hdc in ea st across, turn. Do not turn after row 5.

Rnd 1: With right side facing and working across bottom edge of block, ch 2 for first hdc, 2 hdc in same st, * work 21 hdc across to next corner, 3 hdc in corner st, rep from * around, sl st in top of beg ch-2.

Rnds 2-5: Rep rnd 2 of border as for blackberry st block.

Fasten off after rnd 5 = 31 sts bet corner sts.

Ripple block (make 6 using colors as foll):

	Rows 1-6	Rows 7-8	Row 9
A	Dark blue	Purple (2 strands)	Orchid
B	Light brown	Dark green	Blue
C	Coral	Dark red	Medium red
D	Orange	Medium orange	Red
E	Dark rust	Medium rust	Light rust
F	Dark blue	Lavender	Light brown

Note: For rows 7 and 8 of block A, use 2 strands of purple held tog as 1.

Row 1: Ch 23, dc in 4th ch from hook and ea ch across, turn = 21 dc (including beg ch-3).

Row 2: Ch 1, sc in ea st across, turn.

Row 3: Ch 3 for first dc, * yo twice, insert hook from front to back around post of next row-1 dc, complete st as a tr (tr/rf made), sk st behind tr/rf, dc in next sc, rep from * across, turn.

Row 4: Rep row 2.

Row 5: Ch 3 for first dc, * dc in next sc, tr/rf around post of next row-3 dc, sk st behind tr/rf, rep from * across, turn.

Rows 6-9: Rep rows 2-5. Fasten off after row 9.

Border: Row 1: With wrong side facing, join black in last st of row 9, ch 2 for first hdc, hdc in ea st across, turn = 21 hdc.

Rows 2-7: Ch 2 for first hdc, hdc in ea st across, turn.

Rnd 1: Ch 2 for first hdc, work 2 hdc in same st for corner, * work 19 hdc across to next corner, 3 hdc in corner st, rep from * around, sl st in top of beg ch-2.

Rnds 2-5: Rep rnd 2 of border as for blackberry st block. Fasten off after rnd 5 = 31 sts bet corner sts.

Shell pockets block (make 5 using colors as foll):

	Rows 1-4	Rows 5-8	Rows 9-12
A	Red	Gold (2 strands)	Medium orange
B	Light brown	Lavender	Dark blue
C	Dark rust	Medium rust	Light rust
D	Light brown	Dark green	Blue
E	Coral	Medium red	Dark red

Note: For rows 5-8 of block A, use 2 strands of gold held tog as 1.

Row 1 (wrong side): Ch 24, dc in 4th ch from hook and ea ch across, turn = 22 dc (including beg ch-3).

Row 2 (right side): Ch 1, (sc, hdc, 3 dc) around post of next dc (shell pocket made), sk 2 sts, sl st in next st, * shell pocket around post of same st as sl st, sk 2 sts, sl st in next st, rep from * 5 times more, end with sl st in tch, turn = 7 shell pockets.

Row 3: Ch 3 for first dc, work 3 dc in top of row-1 dc

behind ea shell pocket, dc in last st, turn = 24 dc.

Row 4: Ch 1, * shell pocket around post of next dc, sk 2 sts, sl st in next st, rep from * across, turn.

Rows 5-12: Rep rows 3 and 4 alternately. Fasten off after row 12.

Border: **Row 1:** With right side facing and block turned to work across top edge, join black in corner, ch 2 for first hdc, work 18 hdc across, turn = 19 hdc.

Rows 2-8: Ch 2 for first hdc, hdc in ea st across, turn. Fasten off after row 8.

Rep rows 1-8 across bottom edge of block = 19 hdc.

Rep rows 1-8 across ea side edge = 29 hdc.

Rnd 1: Join black in corner, ch 2 for first hdc, 2 hdc in same st, * hdc in ea st to next corner, 3 hdc in corner st, rep from * around, sl st in top of beg ch-2. Fasten off.

Spike cl block (make 1): With dark red, ch 22.

Row 1: Sc in 2nd ch from hook and ea ch across, turn = 21 sc.

Rows 2 and 3: Ch 1, sc in same st as tch and ea st across, turn.

Row 4: Ch 1, sc in same st as tch and ea of next 3 sts, * keeping all lps on hook, yo, insert hook and pull up 1 lp ea as foll: 2 sts to right of next st and 1 row below, 1 st to right of next st and 2 rows below, 3 rows below next st, 1 st to left of next st and 2 rows below, 2 sts to left of next st and 1 row below (6 lps on hook), insert hook in next row-3 st, yo and pull up a lp, yo and pull through all lps on hook (spike cl made), sc in ea of next 7 sts, rep from * once more, sc in last st, turn.

Rows 5-7: Ch 1, sc in ea st across, turn = 21 sc. Fasten off after row 7.

Row 8: Join medium red, ch 1, sc in same st as tch and ea of next 7 sts, spike cl in next st, sc in ea of next 7 sts, spike cl in next st, sc in ea of last 4 sts, turn.

Row 9: Ch 1, sc in ea st across, turn = 21 sc.

Rows 10-15: Rep rows 2-7. Fasten off after row 15.

Rows 16 and 17: Join coral and rep rows 8 and 9.

Rows 18-22: Rep rows 2-6. Fasten off after row 22.

Border: With right side facing, join black in corner of block and rep rnds 1-5 of border as for blackberry st block. Fasten off after rnd 5 = 31 sts bet corner sts.

Diagonal spike st block (make 1): With red, ch 15.

Row 1: Dc in 4th ch from hook and ea of next 2 ch, yo and pull up a lp in same st as first dc, complete st as a dc (spike dc made), sk next ch, * dc in ea of next 3 ch, spike dc in same st as first st of 3-dc grp, sk next ch, rep from * once more, dc in last ch, turn.

Row 2: Ch 3 for first dc, * dc in ea of next 3 sts, turn,

spike dc in same st as first st of 3-dc grp, turn, sk next st, rep from * twice more, dc in tch, turn.

Row 3: Ch 3 for first dc, * dc in ea of next 3 sts, spike dc in same st as first st of 3-dc grp, sk next st, rep from * twice more, dc in tch, turn. Fasten off.

Rows 4 and 5: Join medium orange, rep rows 2 and 3. Fasten off after row 5.

Note: For rows 6-9, use 2 strands of light brown held tog as 1.

Rows 6-9: Join light brown, rep rows 2 and 3 alternately. Fasten off after row 9.

Border: **Row 1:** With right side facing and block turned to work across side edge, join black in corner, work 20 hdc across to corner, turn.

Rows 2 and 3: Ch 2 for first hdc, hdc in ea st across = 21 hdc. Fasten off.

Rep rows 1-3 across rem side edge of block. Do not fasten off after row 3.

Rnd 1: Ch 2 for first hdc, 2 hdc in same st for corner, * work 19 hdc across to next corner, 3 hdc in corner st, rep from * around, sl st in top of beg ch-2.

Rnds 2-6: Rep rnd 2 of border as for blackberry st block. Fasten off after rnd 6 = 31 sts bet corner sts.

Assembly: Arrange blocks as desired for a throw 4 blocks wide and 5 blocks long. Holding 2 blocks with wrong sides facing and working through both pieces, join black with sc in corner, sc in ea st across. Make 4 rows of 5 blocks ea. Join rows as est.

Edging: **Rnd 1:** With right side facing, join blue with sc in corner, working in ft lps only, sc in same st, * (sc in ea st across block, 2 sc across joining st) across edge to corner, 3 sc in corner, rep from * around, sc in beg corner, sl st in first sc. Fasten off.

Rnd 2: Join black in corner st, ch 2 for first hdc, working in unworked lps behind rnd-1 sts, 2 hdc in same st for corner, * [hdc in ea of next 15 sts, keeping last lp of ea st on hook, hdc in ea of next 2 sts, yo and pull through all lps (hdc dec over 2 sts made), hdc in ea of next 16 sts, dc in ea of 2 joining sts] across to corner, 3 hdc in center corner st, rep from * around, sl st in top of beg ch-2.

Rnd 3: Sl st into center corner st, ch 2 for first hdc, 2 hdc in same st for corner, * hdc in ea st to corner, 3 hdc in center corner st, rep from * around, sl st in top of beg ch-2.

Rnds 4-6: Sl st into center corner st, ch 2 for first hdc, 2 hdc in same st for corner, * hdc in ea st to corner, except work 1 hdc dec per square, evenly spaced across edge, 3 hdc in center corner st, rep from * around, end with sl st in top of beg ch-2. Fasten off after rnd 6.

BLUE HEATHER

*The quiet beauty of this afghan
comes from heathery hues of blue and green
worked in puff stitches.*

FINISHED SIZE

Approximately 60″ x 68″.

MATERIALS

Worsted-weight wool-mohair blend (150-yd. ball): 18 dark green, 18 green, 6 blue.

Size F crochet hook, or size to obtain gauge.

GAUGE

Puff, V-st, puff = 2″.

2 rows in pat = 1″.

DIRECTIONS

Small panel (make 2): With dark green, ch 30.

Row 1: * (Dc, ch 2, dc) in 4th ch from hook (V-st made), sk 2 ch, (yo and pull up a lp) 4 times in next ch, yo and pull through all lps on hook (puff made), ch 1, sk 2 ch, rep from * 3 times more, V-st in next ch, sk 1 ch, dc in last ch, turn.

Row 2: Ch 3 for first dc, * puff in ch-2 sp of V-st, ch 1, V-st in puff, rep from * 3 times more, puff in last V-st, ch 1, dc in tch, turn.

Row 3: Ch 3 for first dc, V-st in puff, * puff in ch-sp of V-st, ch 1, V-st in puff, rep from * across, dc in tch, turn.

Rep rows 2 and 3 alternately for a total of 151 rows. Fasten off.

Border: With right side facing and panel turned to work across long edge, join dark green with sc in corner, work 2 sc in side of ea row to corner, sc in corner = 304 sts. Fasten off. Rep border across rem long edge.

Side panel (make 2): With dark green, ch 14, rep directions for small panel for a total of 151 rows.

Border: With right side facing and panel turned to work across long edge, rep small panel border across the foll edges: work across right-hand edge only of 1 panel and left-hand edge only of rem panel.

Large panel (make 3): With dark green, ch 60.

Rows 1-6: Work as for small panel. Fasten off after row 6. Turn.

Row 7: Join green with sl st in top of last dc, ch 3 for first dc, dc in ea st and ch across, end with dc in tch = 59 sts (including beg ch-3), turn.

Rows 8-10: Ch 3 for first dc, dc in ea st across. Fasten off after row 10.

Note: Work rows 11-17 with right side facing and do not turn.

Row 11: Join dark green with sl st in top
for first dc, sk 1 dc, * sc in next dc, puff in
2 dc, rep from * across, end with sk 1 dc, s
puffs. Fasten off.

Row 12: Join green with sl st in top of beg ch-3 on prev row, ch 3 for first dc, puff in same st, * ch 1, sc in next puff, puff in same st, rep from * across, end with sc in last sc = 20 puffs. Fasten off.

Row 13: Join blue with sl st in top of beg ch-3 on prev row, ch 3 for first dc, * sc in puff, puff in same st, ch 1, rep from * across to last puff, sk last puff, sc in last sc = 19 puffs. Fasten off.

Row 14: With green, rep row 12.

Row 15: With dark green, rep row 13.

Row 16: With blue, rep row 12.

Row 17: Join green with a sl st in top of beg ch-3 on prev row, ch 3 for first dc, rep row 7 = 59 sts (including beg ch-3), turn.

Rows 18-20: Ch 3 for first dc, dc in ea st across, turn. Fasten off after row 20.

Rows 21-26: Rep rows 11-16, changing colors as specified.

Rep rows 17-26 as est 13 times.

With green, rep rows 17-20.

With dark green, rep rows 1-6. Fasten off.

Border: With panel turned to work across long edge, join dark green with sc in corner, 2 sc in side of ea of 6 rows, * 2 sc in ea dc row, sc in first puff row, 2 sc in ea of next 4 puff rows, sc in next puff row, rep from * across to last 6 rows, 2 sc in ea of last 6 rows, sc in corner = 304 sts. Fasten off.

Rep border across rem long edge.

Assembly: With dark green, whipstitch panels tog in the foll order: side panel (with sc border on right-hand edge), large panel, small panel, large panel, small panel, large panel, side panel (with sc border on left-hand edge).

Edging: With right side facing and afghan turned to work across short edge, join dark green with sc in corner, sc in same corner, [(2 sc in ch-sp of V-st, sc in next sp, sc in puff, sc in next sp) across to joining, 2 sc in joining] to corner, 3 sc in corner, 2 sc in side of ea row to corner, 3 sc in corner, [(sc in puff, 2 sc in next sp, sc in base of V-st, 2 sc in next sp) across to joining, 2 sc in joining] to corner, 3 sc in corner, 2 sc in side of ea row to corner, sc in beg corner, sl st in first sc. Fasten off.

RUFFLED COMFORT

Soft seashell colors ripple in waves of ruffles across this inviting afghan, ready to soothe away your tension.

FINISHED SIZE

Approximately 43″ x 66″.

MATERIALS

Sportweight acrylic (190-yd. ball): 4 pink.
Sportweight brushed acrylic (135-yd. skein): 28 pastel ombre.
Size F crochet hook, or size to obtain gauge.

GAUGE

5 dc = 1″.

DIRECTIONS

Base grid: With pink, ch 192.

Row 1: Dc in 6th ch from hook, (ch 2, sk 2 ch, dc in next ch) across, turn = 63 sps.

Row 2: Ch 5 for first dc and ch 2, dc in next dc, (ch 2, dc in next dc) across, end with dc in 3rd ch of tch, turn.

Rows 3-97: Rep row 2. Fasten off after row 97.

Ruffle: *Note:* Work ruffle over bars of ea square of grid. Ruffle is worked from outer edge to center of grid.

Rnd 1: With grid turned to work across short edge, join pastel ombre with sl st in corner, ch 3 for first dc, 3 dc across top edge of corner square, * 4 dc down side of same square, 4 dc across bottom of next square, 4 dc up side of same square, 4 dc across top of next square, rep from * around outer edge of grid, working across both outer edges of ea corner square, sl st in top of beg ch-3. Fasten off.

Rnd 2: Join pastel ombre with sl st around unworked bar of any square just inside rnd-1 ruffle, ch 3 for first dc, 2 dc across same side of square, * 3 dc down side of same square, 3 dc across bottom of next square, 3 dc up side of same square, 3 dc across top of next square, rep from * around, do not join at end of rnd. Cont working ruffle in a spiral as est until grid is completely covered. Fasten off.

Border: Join pastel ombre with sl st in any unworked bar of outer edge of grid, (sc, hdc, dc, 2 tr, dc, hdc, sc) across same bar (shell made), * sc around next bar on edge of grid bet 2nd and 3rd dc of ruffle, shell across next unworked bar, rep from * to corner square, sc bet 2nd and 3rd dc of ruffle on side of square before corner, shell in corner of grid, rep from * around, end with sl st in first sc. Fasten off.

SUNSHINE KISSES

*For baby's first throw, a white yarn
dotted with hints of yellow and green
is the perfect selection.*

FINISHED SIZE
Approximately 47″ square, including ruffle.

MATERIALS
Worsted-weight acrylic-cotton blend bouclé (344-yd. ball): 5 white with yellow accents, 6 white with green accents.

Size F crochet hook, or size to obtain gauge.

GAUGE
2 shells and 4 rows = 2″.
Square = 12½″.

DIRECTIONS
Square (make 4 yellow, 5 green): **First square: Row 1:** With green, ch 40, dc in 4th ch from hook, 2 dc in same st, * sk 2 ch, sc in next st, ch 3, 3 dc in same st as sc (3-dc shell made), rep from * across to last 3 sts, sk 2 ch, sc in last st, turn = 13 shells.

Row 2: Ch 3 for first dc, 3 dc in first sc, (sc in next ch-3 lp, ch 3, 3-dc shell in same lp) across, sc in last ch-3 lp, turn.

Rows 3-26: Rep row 2.

Border ch-lps: Work around square as foll: * (ch 7, sc in base of next shell) 13 times to next corner, rep from * twice more, (ch 7, sc in ch-3 lp) 12 times, ch 7, sl st in base of beg ch-7 = 52 lps. Fasten off.

2nd square: With yellow, rep rows 1-26 as for first square.

Border ch-lps (joining rnd): Work as for first square across 2 edges of 2nd square, (ch 3, sl st in center ch of corresponding lp on first square, ch 3, sc in base of next shell on 2nd square) 13 times, complete 2nd square border as est for first square. Fasten off.

Cont to make and join squares in a checkerboard pat as est for a throw with 3 rows of 3 squares ea.

Ruffle: **Rnd 1:** Join green with sl st in any sc, ch 3, 3-dc shell in same st, * (sc, ch 3, 3-dc shell) in 3rd ch of next lp, (sc, ch 3, 3-dc shell) in 5th ch of same lp, (sc, ch 3, 3-dc shell) in next sc, rep from * around, end with sc in base of beg ch-3, turn. Fasten off.

Rnd 2: Join yellow with sl st in ch-3 lp of first rnd-1 shell, ch 3, 3-dc shell in same lp, (sc, ch 3, 3-dc shell) in ea ch-3 lp around, end with sc in base of beg ch-3, sl st into next ch-3 lp, turn.

Rnd 3: Ch 3, 3-dc shell in same lp, (sc, ch 3, 3-dc shell) in ea ch-3 lp around, end with sc in base of beg ch-3, turn. Fasten off.

Rnd 4: Join green with sl st in ch-3 lp of any shell, ch 3, 3-dc shell in same lp, (sc, ch 3, 3-dc shell) in ea ch-3 lp around, end with sc in base of beg ch-3, sl st into next ch-3 lp, turn.

Rnds 5 and 6: Rep rnd 4. Fasten off after rnd 6.

Rnds 7-9: Join yellow, rep rnd 4. Fasten off after rnd 9.

Rnd 10: Join green, rep rnd 4. Fasten off.

Flower (make 4): With green, ch 6, join with a sl st to form a ring.

Rnd 1: Ch 1, (sc, hdc, dc, hdc, sc) in ea ch around, sl st in beg ch-1 = 6 petals.

Rnd 2: Sl st in back of next sc, holding petals to front of work, (ch 3, sl st in back of first sc of next petal) 5 times, ch 3, sl st in beg sl st, sl st into next ch-3 lp = 6 lps.

Rnd 3: (Sc, hdc, 2 dc, hdc, sc) in ea lp around, sl st in first sc, sl st in back of same sc = 6 petals.

Rnd 4: Holding petals to front of work, (ch 3, sc in next rnd-2 sc bet petals) 6 times. Fasten off.

Rnd 5: Join yellow with sl st in any ch-3 lp, (sc, hdc, dc, tr, dc, hdc, sc) in ea lp around, sl st in back of first sc = 6 petals.

Rnd 6: Holding petals to front of work, (ch 4, sc in next rnd-4 sc bet petals) 6 times, sl st into next ch-4 lp.

Rnd 7: (Sc, hdc, dc, 2 tr, dc, hdc, sc) in ea lp around, sl st in first sc.

Rnd 8: Sl st into 2nd tr on next petal, sc in same st, (ch 5, keeping last lp of ea st on hook, tr in ea of next 2 sts, sk next 3 sts, tr in ea of next 2 sts on next petal, yo and pull through all lps on hook, ch 5, sc in 2nd tr on same petal) around, end with sl st in first sc. Fasten off.

Whipstitch flowers to afghan at corners of center square (see photo).

ROSE MEDALLIONS

*Remember Grandmother's garden with
an afghan of pale green lace studded with roses
in a variety of colors.*

FINISHED SIZE

Approximately 44″ x 66″.

MATERIALS

Size 5 pearl cotton (27-yd. skein): 10 each yellow, mauve; 59 pistachio green.

Size 5 pearl cotton (53-yd. ball): 5 each peach, rose.

Size 7 steel hook, or size to obtain gauge.

GAUGE

Square = 5½″.

DIRECTIONS

Flower (make 24 ea yellow, mauve, peach, rose): With yellow, ch 6, join with a sl st to form a ring.

Rnd 1: Ch 1, sc in ring, (3 dc, sc) 7 times in ring, 3 dc in ring, sl st in first sc = 8 petals.

Rnd 2: Ch 1, sc in same st, (ch 3, holding petals to front of work, sc in back of next sc bet petals) around, end with sl st in first sc.

Rnd 3: (Sc, 5 dc) in ea lp around, end with sl st in first sc = 8 petals.

Rnd 4: Ch 1, sc in same st, (ch 4, holding petals to front of work, sc in back of next sc bet petals) around, end with sl st in first sc.

Rnd 5: (Sc, 6 dc) in ea lp around, end with sl st in first sc.

Rnd 6: Ch 1, sc in same st, (ch 5, holding petals to front of work, sc in back of next sc bet petals) around, end with sl st in first sc.

Rnd 7: (Sc, 7 dc) in ea lp around, end with sl st in first sc.

Rnd 8: Ch 1, sc in same st, (ch 6, holding petals to front of work, sc in back of next sc bet petals) around, end with sl st in first sc.

Rnd 9: (Sc, dc, 6 tr, dc) in ea lp around, end with sl st in first sc. Fasten off.

Square: Work around ea flower as foll. **First square: Rnd 1:** Working behind rnd-9 petals of flower, join green with sc in any rnd-8 sc bet petals, (ch 5, sc in back of next rnd-8 sc bet petals) around, end with sl st in first sc.

Rnd 2: Sl st into next ch-5 lp, ch 4 for first dc and ch 1, (dc, ch 1 in same lp) 3 times, * (dc, ch 1 in next lp) 4 times, rep from * around, end with sl st in 3rd ch of beg ch-4.

Rnd 3: Sc in next ch-1 sp, (ch 5, sc in next sp) around, end with ch 5, sl st in first sc.

Rnd 4: Sc in next lp, * ch 5, sk next 2 lps, (4 tr, ch 3, 4 tr) in next lp for corner, ch 5, sk next 2 lps, sc in next lp **, ch 5, sk next lp, sc in next lp, rep from * around, end last rep at **, ch 2, dc in first sc.

Rnd 5: Sc in lp just made, * ch 3, sc in next lp, ch 5, keeping last lp of ea st on hook, tr in ea of next 4 tr, yo and pull through all lps on hook (4-tr cl made), ch 5, sl st in top of cl to make a picot, ch 5, sl st in corner ch-3 sp, ch 5, 2-tr cl in same sp, picot, ch 5, sl st in same sp, ch 5, 4-tr cl over next 4 tr, picot, ch 5, sc in next lp, ch 3, sc in next lp, rep from * around, end with sl st in first sc.

Rnd 6: Ch 5 for first dtr, 4 dtr in same st, * ch 5, sc in next picot, ch 5, (2-dc cl, ch 5, 2-dc cl) in next picot for corner, ch 5, sc in next picot, ch 5, sk next sc, 5 dtr in next sc, rep from * around, end with sl st in top of beg ch-5.

Rnd 7: Ch 3 for first dc, dc in ea of next 4 dtr, * 3 dc in next lp, ch 5, dc in next lp, ch 5, (3 dc, ch 5, 3 dc) in corner ch-5 sp, ch 5, dc in next lp, ch 5, 3 dc in next lp, dc in ea of next 5 dtr, rep from * around, end with sl st in top of beg ch-3.

Rnd 8: Ch 3 for first dc, dc in ea of next 5 dc, * ch 5, dc in next lp, ch 5, 3 dc in next lp, dc in ea of next 3 dc, (3 dc, ch 5, 3 dc) in corner ch-5 sp, dc in ea of next 3 dc, 3 dc in next lp, ch 5, dc in next lp, ch 5, sk next 2 dc **, dc in ea of next 7 dc, rep from * around, end last rep at **, dc in next dc, sl st in top of beg ch-3.

Rnd 9: Sl st in next dc, ch 3 for first dc, 2-dc cl over next 2 dc, * (ch 5, dc in next lp) twice, ch 5, sk 3 dc, dc in ea of next 6 dc, (3 dc, ch 5, 3 dc) in corner ch-5 sp, dc in ea of next 6 dc, (ch 5, dc in next lp) twice, ch 5 **, sk 2 dc, 3-dc cl over next 3 dc, rep from * around, end last rep at **, sl st in top of beg cl. Fasten off.

2nd square: Rep rnds 1-8 as for first square.

Rnd 9 (joining rnd): Sl st in next dc, ch 3 for first dc, 2-dc cl over next 2 dc, (ch 5, dc in next lp) twice, ch 5, sk 3 dc, dc in ea of next 6 dc, 3 dc in corner sp, ch 2, sc in corresponding corner sp on first square, ch 2, 3 dc in same corner sp on 2nd square, dc in ea of next 6 dc, * (ch 2, sc in corresponding lp on first square, ch 2, sc in next lp on 2nd square) twice, ch 2, sc in corresponding lp on first square, ch 2 **, sk 2 dc on 2nd square, 3-dc cl over next 3 dc on 2nd square, rep from * to ** once more, sk 3 dc on 2nd square, dc in ea of next 6 dc, 3 dc in corner sp, ch 2, sc in corresponding corner sp on first square, ch 2, 3 dc in same corner sp on 2nd square, complete square as est for first square. Fasten off.

Cont to make and join squares as est, arranging flower colors as desired, for an afghan 8 squares wide and 12 squares long.

VIVID WAVES

Create a stunning home accessory by crocheting jewel-colored yarns in a geometric design.

FINISHED SIZE

Approximately 48″ x 57″.

MATERIALS

Worsted-weight wool-mohair blend (150-yd. ball): 5 aqua.
Worsted-weight wool (110-yd. ball): 4 plum.
Worsted-weight wool (137-yd. skein): 10 teal, 4 black.
Size H crochet hook, or size to obtain gauge.

GAUGE

Square = 6″.

DIRECTIONS

Note: Work with 2 strands of aqua held tog as 1. For ea hdc, pull up ⅝″ lps.

Square A (make 18): **Row 1:** With 2 strands of aqua held tog as 1, ch 8, hdc in 3rd ch from hook and ea ch across = 7 sts, turn.

Rows 2-4: Ch 2 for first hdc, hdc in ea of next 6 sts, turn. Fasten off after row 4.

Note: Work foll rows across 2 edges of small square.

Row 5: Join plum in top of last row-4 st, ch 2 for first hdc, hdc in ea of next 5 sts, (hdc, ch 2, hdc) in next st for corner, work 6 hdc across to corner of square, turn.

Rows 6-8: Ch 2 for first hdc, hdc in ea st to corner, (dc, ch 2, dc) in corner ch-2 sp, hdc in ea st across, turn. Fasten off after row 8.

Rows 9-12: Join teal with sl st in last st, rep row 6. Fasten off after row 12.

Rows 13-16: Join black with sl st in last st, rep row 6 = 17 hdc across ea edge after row 16. Fasten off after row 16.

Square B (make 22): Work as for square A, using colors as foll: **Rows 1-4:** Black.
Rows 5-8: Teal.
Rows 9-12: Plum.
Rows 13-16: Aqua (2 strands).

Square C (make 31): With teal, rep rows 1-16 as for square A.

Assembly: Referring to diagram for placement, whipstitch squares together.

Placement Diagram

GYPSY PATHS AFGHAN

*For an afghan appropriate to many settings,
garnish earth-tone panels
with crocheted motifs and embroidery.*

FINISHED SIZE

Approximately 50″ square.

MATERIALS

Size 20 crochet cotton (440-yd. ball): 7 each tan, taupe; 4 each blue, brown; 1 each ecru, rose, green, blue-green, yellow, pink, periwinkle.

Sizes 1 and 7 steel crochet hooks, or size to obtain gauge. Assorted acrylic mirrors and acrylic jewels.

GAUGE

24 dc and 11 rows = 4″ with size 1 hook.

DIRECTIONS

Panel 1 (make 2 tan, 1 blue): **Row 1** (wrong side): With size 1 hook and 2 strands of thread held tog as 1, ch 40, dc in 4th ch from hook and ea ch across, turn = 38 dc.

Row 2: Ch 1, (dc in next st, sc in next st) across, dc in last st, turn.

Rows 3-30: Ch 1, (dc in ea sc, sc in ea dc) across, dc in last st, turn.

Rows 31-51: Ch 3 for first dc, dc in ea st across, turn.

Rows 52 and 53: Ch 1, sc in ea st across, turn.

Row 54: Ch 1, sc in ea of next 2 sts, ch 3 loosely, sk next 2 sts, sc in next st, turn, sc loosely in ea ch of ch-3, sl st in sc before ch-3, turn, working behind ch-3 lp, sc in ea of 2 sk sts, * ch 3 loosely, sk joining st of prev ch, sk next 2 sts, sc in next st, turn, sc loosely in ea ch of ch-3, sl st in sc before ch-3, turn, working behind ch-3 lp, sc in ea of 2 sk sts, rep from * across to last 2 sts, sc in ea of last 2 sts, turn = 11 lps.

Row 55: Working behind ch-3 lps, ch 3 for first dc, dc in ea of next 3 sc, (dc in next sl st, dc in ea of next 2 sc) 11 times, dc in last st, turn = 38 sts.

Rows 56-59: Rep rows 52-55.

Row 60: Ch 3 for first dc, dc in ea st across, turn.

Row 61: Ch 3 for first dc, dc in ft lp only of ea st across, turn.

Rows 62-72: Rep rows 60 and 61 alternately, ending after row 60, turn.

Rows 73-75: Rep rows 53-55.

Rows 76-79: Rep rows 52-55.

Rows 80 and 81: Ch 3 for first dc, dc in ea st across, turn.

Rows 82-161: Rep rows 2-81.

Rows 162-191: Rep rows 2-31. Do not fasten off after last row.

Border: With right side facing, work * 3 sc in corner, sc across to next corner, rep from * around = 309 sc across ea long edge and 36 sc across ea short edge (not including corner grps). Fasten off.

Panel 2 (make 2 taupe, 1 brown): **Row 1** (wrong side): With size 1 hook and 2 strands of thread held tog as 1, ch 40, dc in 4th ch from hook and ea ch across, turn = 38 dc.

Rows 2-21: Ch 3 for first dc, dc in ea st across, turn.

Rows 22-29: (Rep rows 52-55 of panel 1) twice.

Rows 30-42: Rep rows 60-72 of panel 1.

Rows 43-45: Rep rows 53-55 of panel 1.

Rows 46-49: Rep rows 52-55 of panel 1.

Rows 50-78: Rep rows 2-30 of panel 1.

Rows 79-99: Ch 3 for first dc, dc in ea st across, turn.

Rows 100-107: (Rep rows 52-55 of panel 1) twice.

Rows 108-120: Rep rows 60-72 of panel 1.

Rows 121-123: Rep rows 53-55 of panel 1.

Rows 124-127: Rep rows 52-55 of panel 1.

Rows 128-157: Rep rows 2-30 of panel 1.

Rows 158-182: Ch 3 for first dc, dc in ea st across, turn.

Border: With right side facing, work border as for panel 1.

Assembly: *Note:* Use size 1 hook and 2 strands of thread held tog as 1. Work rows 1-3 across left-hand edge of 1 tan panel, blue panel, brown panel, and both taupe panels.

Row 1: With right side facing and panel turned to work across long edge, join 2 strands of matching thread with sc in corner, (ch 7, sk next 3 sts, sc in next st) to corner, turn = 78 lps.

Rows 2 and 3: (Ch 7, sc in next lp) across to last lp, ch 4, tr in last lp, turn. Fasten off after row 3.

Rep to work rows 1 and 2 across right-hand edge of both tan panels, blue panel, brown panel, and 1 taupe panel.

Work joining row 3 to join panels in the foll order: tan, taupe, blue, brown, tan, taupe.

Joining row 3: With panels right side up and side-by-side, ch 3, sc in corresponding lp on first panel, * ch 3, sc in next lp on 2nd panel, ch 3, sc in next lp on first panel, rep from * across. Fasten off.

Round motif (make 2 ea rose, green; make 1 ea brown, blue-green, pink, yellow): **Rnd 1:** With size 7 hook and 1 strand of thread, ch 2, work 16 sc in 2nd ch from hook, sl st in top of beg ch-2.

Rnd 2: Ch 7 for first tr and ch 3, (tr in next sc, ch 3) 15 times, sl st in 4th ch of beg ch-7, sl st in next ch.

Rnd 3: Sc in same sp, (ch 4, sc in next sp) 15 times, ch 3, sl st in first sc, sl st into next sp.

Rnd 4: Ch 4 for first tr, 3 tr in same sp, (ch 7, 4 tr in next sp) 15 times, ch 4, tr in top of beg ch-4.

Rnd 5: Ch 3 for first dc, (dc, ch 3, 2 dc) in same lp, * ch 3, (sc, ch 5, sc in next lp), ch 3, (2 dc, ch 3, 2 dc) in next lp, rep from * around, end with ch 1, dc in top of beg ch-3.

Rnd 6: Sc in sp just made, * ch 3, (sc, ch 3, sc) in next ch-3 sp, ch 3, sc in next ch-3 sp, rep from * around, end with sl st in first sc. Fasten off.

Square motif (make 3 ea taupe, brown, ecru): With size 7 hook and 1 strand of thread, ch 4, join with a sl st to form a ring.

Rnd 1: Ch 1, 8 sc in ring, sl st in first sc.

Rnd 2: Ch 3 for first dc, 2 dc in same st, (ch 5, 3 dc in next st) 7 times, ch 5, sl st in top of beg ch-3.

Rnd 3: Ch 1, sc in same st, * ch 3, sk next dc, sc in next dc, ch 3, 3 dc in next sp, ch 3, sc in next dc, rep from * around, end with sl st in first sc.

Rnd 4: Work 3 sc in next ch-3 sp, * ch 3, sk next (ch-3, 3-dc, ch-3) grp, 3 sc in next ch-3 sp, rep from * around, end with sl st in first sc.

Rnd 5: Ch 3 for first dc, * (2 dc, ch 1, 2 dc) in next sc (shell made), dc in next sc of same grp, ch 5, dc in next sc, rep from * around, end with sl st in top of beg ch-3.

Rnd 6: Sl st into ch-1 sp of next shell, ch 1, sc in same sp, * ch 11, sc in ch-1 sp of next shell, ch 5, sc in next ch-5 lp, ch 5, sc in ch-1 sp of next shell, rep from * around, end with sl st in first sc.

Rnd 7: Ch 1, sc in same st, * ch 5, (sc, ch 7, sc) in next ch-11 lp, ch 5, sc in next sc, 5 sc in ea of next 2 ch-5 lps, sc in next sc, rep from * around, end with sl st in first sc.

Rnd 8: Sc in next lp, ch 7, sc in same lp, * ch 5, (shell, ch 3, shell) in next lp for corner, (ch 5, sc, ch 7, sc) in next lp, (ch 5, sc in center st of next 5-sc grp) twice, ch 5, (sc, ch 7, sc) in next lp, rep from * around, end with sl st in first sc.

Rnd 9: Sl st into next lp, sc in same lp, ch 5, sc in next

lp, ch 5, 2 dc in ch-1 sp of next shell, ch 5, 2 dc in corner ch-3 sp, ch 5, 2 dc in ch-1 sp of next shell, (ch 5, sc in next lp) 7 times, rep from * around, end with sl st in first sc. Fasten off.

Finishing: Attach embellishments as specified below or as desired. Refer to a dictionary of embroidery stitches or a book about needle lace or needleweaving for instructions on working detached buttonhole filling stitch, buttonhole cups, and filet stitch. *Panel 1:* Stitch 1 brown square in 2nd section; work detached buttonhole filling stitch with 4 strands of periwinkle in 3rd section; stitch yellow round in 5th section; stitch 3 blocks of running stitch using 4 strands of brown (see photo), and make 3 leaf-shaped buttonhole cups (1 with a jewel) using 2 strands of blue in 6th section.

Panel 2: Stitch 1 green round and 1 ecru square in first section; work 2 rows of chainstitch in a circle using 4 strands of rose in 3rd section; stitch 1 brown square on point in 4th section; stitch 1 ecru square in 6th section; make a butterfly with buttonhole cups using 2 strands of tan and using 1 jewel for body and 4 mirrors for wings in 7th section (see photo).

Panel 3: Stitch 1 green round in 2nd section; work filet stitch over upper left ¼ of 3rd section using 2 strands of rose; work a buttonhole cup with rays around 1 mirror using 2 strands of yellow in lower right corner of 3rd section; stitch 1 taupe square in 5th section; stitch pink round in 6th section.

Panel 4: Make buttonhole cups around 3 jewels and 2 mirrors using 2 strands of periwinkle in first section; make buttonhole cups around 4 jewels using 2 strands of brown in 3rd section; stitch 1 ecru square on point in 4th section; stitch 1 taupe square on point in 7th section.

Panel 5: Whipstitch 4 strands of blue through cables at top and bottom of 2nd section; make 1 buttonhole cup around 1 mirror with a knotted grid or web radiating out from it using 4 strands of blue in 2nd section (see photo); stitch 1 taupe square in 3rd section; stitch buttonhole net over 3 jewels and 3 mirrors using 2 strands of blue in 5th section; stitch brown round in 6th section.

Panel 6: Stitch 1 brown square on point in first section; make buttonhole cups around 5 jewels and 1 mirror using 2 strands of periwinkle in 3rd section; stitch both rose rounds in 4th section; work detached buttonhole filling stitch over ⅔ of 6th section using 2 strands of pink; stitch blue-green round in 7th section.

BUNNIES 'N CARROTS

*Cross-stitch a garden of
bright orange carrots and fluffy white bunnies
to delight the child in your heart.*

FINISHED SIZE

Approximately 42″ x 49″.

MATERIALS

Worsted-weight wool-mohair blend (150-yd. ball): 4 green, 10 light blue.

Sizes F and G crochet hooks, or size to obtain gauge.

Sportweight brushed acrylic (156-yd. ball): 1 white (for cross-stitch).

Sportweight brushed acrylic (170-yd. skein): 1 each pink, gray (for cross-stitch).

Paternayan Persian wool (8-yd. skein): see color key.

GAUGE

8 sc and 9 rows = 2″ with size G hook.

DIRECTIONS

Throw: **Row 1:** With size G hook and green, ch 148, sc in 2nd ch from hook and ea ch across, turn = 148 sts.

Rows 2-63: Ch 1, sc in ea st across, turn. Fasten off.

Row 64: Join light blue with sl st in last st of row 63, ch 1, sc in ea st across, turn.

Rows 65-199: Ch 1, sc in ea st across, turn. Do not turn or fasten off after last row.

Edging: **Rnd 1:** (Sc, ch 1, sc) in corner, work 201 sc across long edge to next corner, (sc, ch 1, sc) in corner, work 147 sc across to next corner, (sc, ch 1, sc) in next corner, work 201 sc across to first st of last row, sc in corner, ch 1, sl st in next sc.

Rnd 2: Sl st backward into corner ch-1 sp, ch 3 for first dc, dc in ea of next 2 sts, * (ch 1, sk next st, dc in ea of next 3 sts) 36 times, ch 1, sk next st, dc in ea of next 2 sts, (dc, ch 1, dc) in corner sp, dc in ea of next 2 sts, (ch 1, sk next st, dc in ea of next 3 sts) 49 times, ch 1, sk next st, dc in ea of next 2 sts, (dc, ch 1, dc) in corner sp, dc in ea of next 2 sts, rep from * around, sl st in top of beg ch-3.

Rnds 3 and 4: Sl st backward into corner ch-1 sp, ch 3 for first dc, dc in same sp, dc in next dc, * (ch 1, sk next dc, dc in ea of next 3 sts) to 2 sts before corner sp, ch 1, sk next st, dc in next dc, (2 dc, ch 1, 2 dc) in corner sp, dc in next dc, rep from * around, sl st in top of beg ch-3.

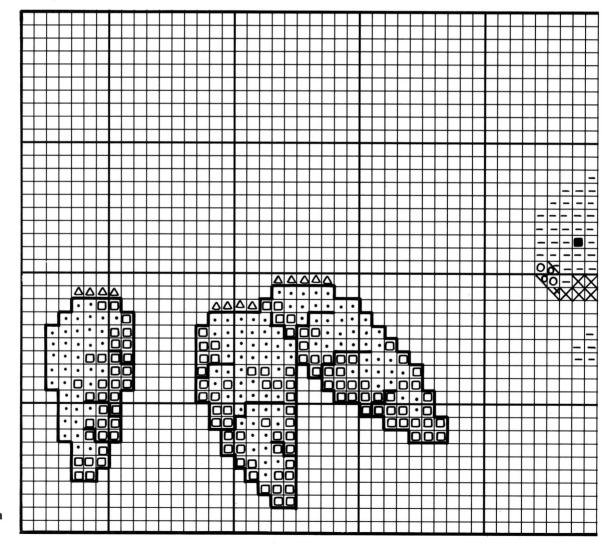

Cross-stitch Chart

Rnd 5: Sl st backward into corner ch-1 sp, ch 3 for first dc, 2 dc in same sp, * sk next st, dc in next st, (dc, ch 1, dc) in next ch-1 sp (V-st made), rep from * across to corner ch-1 sp, (3 dc, ch 1, 3 dc) in corner sp, rep from * around, sl st in top of beg ch-3.

Rnd 6: With size F hook, ch 1, working in bk lps only, sc in ea st to corner sp, (sc, ch 1, sc) in corner sp, rep from * around, sl st in beg ch-1. Fasten off.

Cross-stitch: Referring to photo for placement, cross-stitch carrots and bunnies according to color key and chart. Bottom row of each bunny is worked on row 55 of crochet. Skip 13 row-55 stitches between bunnies. Cross-stitch a row of 10 carrots across afghan below bunnies, beginning bottom of each carrot on row 10 of crochet and skipping 12 row-10 stitches between carrots.

For carrot tops, use 1 strand of Pine Green-dk. to make 15-18 loops in a variety of sizes, secured with backstitches at top of each carrot. Tack some of the larger loops to afghan (see photo).

Color Key

Step 1: Cross-stitch

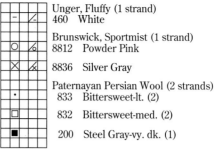

−	⟋	Unger, Fluffy (1 strand) 460 White
O	⟋	Brunswick, Sportmist (1 strand) 8812 Powder Pink
X	⟋	8836 Silver Gray

Paternayan Persian Wool (2 strands)
·		833 Bittersweet-lt. (2)
□		832 Bittersweet-med. (2)
■		200 Steel Gray-vy. dk. (1)

Step 2: Backstitch (1 strand)

831 Bittersweet-dk. (1)

Step 3: Loops (1 strand)

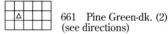

661 Pine Green-dk. (2)
(see directions)

Note: The number of 8-yd. skeins required for each color of Persian wool is indicated in parentheses.

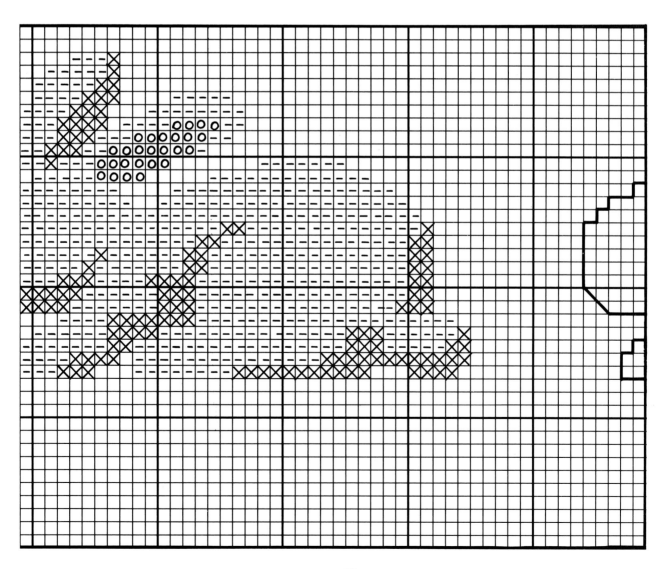

MEMORY LANE

*A rich purple yarn with flecks of gold
is perfect for making this lap rug patterned
after those of yesteryear.*

FINISHED SIZE

Approximately 40″ x 52″, not including edging.

MATERIALS

Sportweight mohair-acrylic-wool blend (137-yd. ball): 8 each purple, brown.

Size J crochet hook, or size to obtain gauge.

GAUGE

3 cl = 2″.

DIRECTIONS

Throw: **Row 1** (right side): With purple, ch 112, dc in 4th ch from hook and ea ch across = 110 sts, turn.

Row 2: Ch 3 for first dc, * keeping last lp of ea st on hook, dc in ea of next 2 sts, yo and pull through all lps on hook (cl made), ch 1, rep from * across, dc in last st, turn = 54 cl.

Rows 3-61: Ch 3 for first dc, work cl over ch-1 sp and cl as foll: * keeping last lp of ea st on hook, dc in ch-1 sp, dc in cl, yo and pull through all lps on hook, ch 1, rep from * across, dc in last st, turn. Fasten off after row 61.

Edging: **Rnd 1:** Join brown in top of last st on row 61, ch 1, * 2 sc in side of ea row to corner, sc in corner, sc in ea st across to next corner, sc in corner, rep from * around, end with sl st in beg ch-1 = 122 sc across ea long edge and 108 sc across ea short edge (not including corner sts).

Rnd 2: Ch 3 for first dc, dc in same st, * (ch 1, sk next st, dc in ea of next 3 sts) to corner, ch 1, 3 dc in corner st

(shell made), rep from * around, end with dc in beg corner, sl st in top of beg ch-3 = 30 (3-dc) grps across ea long edge and 27 (3-dc) grps across ea short edge (not including corner shells). Turn.

Rnd 3: Sl st into next ch-1 sp, ch 3 for first dc, (dc, ch 3, 2-dc cl) in same sp, [dc in ea of next 3 dc, 2-dc cl in next sp] 26 times, * dc in ea of next 3 dc, (2-dc cl, ch 3, 2-dc cl) in next sp (cl shell made), ch 1, sk next dc, cl shell in center st of corner, ch 1, sk next dc, cl shell in next sp, ch 1 **, rep bet [ ] 29 times, rep from * to ** once for corner, cont around as est, end with sl st in top of beg ch-3.

Rnd 4: Sl st backward into ch-1 sp, ch 3 for first dc, 2 dc in same sp, ch 1, 3-dc shell in next sp, * (ch 1, sk next cl, dc in ea of next 3 dc) across to corner, ch 1, sk next cl, (3-dc shell, ch 1) in ea of next 5 sps at corner, sk cl, dc in ea of next 3 dc, rep from * around, end with sl st in top of beg ch-3.

Rnd 5: Sc backward in next sp, (ch 5, sc in next sp) around, end with ch 2, dc in first sc.

Rnd 6: Sc in lp just made, (ch 5, sc in next lp) around, end with ch 2, dc in first sc.

Rnd 7: Sc in lp just made, (ch 5, sc in next lp) around, end with ch 5, sl st in first sc.

Rnd 8: Ch 1, sc in same sc, (7 dc in next lp, sc in next sc) around, end with sl st in first sc.

Rnd 9: Ch 1, sc in same sc, * (dc, ch 3, dc) in ea of next 2 dc, (dc, ch 4, dc) in next dc, (dc, ch 5, dc) in next dc, (dc, ch 4, dc) in next dc, (dc, ch 3, dc) in ea of next 2 dc, sc in next sc, rep from * around, end with sl st in first sc. Fasten off.

LUXURIOUS LACE

*Soft shades of peach and green
are artfully blended in this dressy
and timeless design.*

FINISHED SIZE

Approximately 56″ x 62″.

MATERIALS

Worsted-weight cotton (93-yd. skein): 13 light green, 7 peach.

Bulky-weight mohair-silk blend (70-yd. skein): 13 variegated green/gray/peach.

Size G crochet hook, or size to obtain gauge.

GAUGE

Square = 8½″.

DIRECTIONS

Square (make 32): **First square:** With light green, ch 10, join with a sl st to form a ring.

Rnd 1: Ch 1, 5 sc in ring, (ch 5, 9 sc in ring) 3 times, ch 5, 4 sc in ring, sl st in first sc = 4 lps.

Rnd 2: * Ch 15, sc in center sc bet next 2 lps, rep from * twice more, ch 15, sl st in first ch of beg ch-15. Fasten off.

Rnd 3: Join variegated yarn with sl st in any ch-15 lp, (sc, hdc, 17 dc, hdc, sc) in ea ch-15 lp around, sl st in first sc. Fasten off.

Rnd 4: Join peach with sl st in 2nd dc of any grp, sc in same st, * ch 7, sk next 6 dc, (3 dc, ch 3, 3 dc) in next dc for corner, ch 7, sk next 6 dc, sc in next dc, ch 5, sc in 2nd dc of next grp, rep from * around, end with sl st in first sc. Fasten off.

Rnd 5: Join variegated yarn with sl st in any ch-5 lp, ch 3 for first dc, * dc in next ch-7 lp, ch 5, dc in first dc of corner, 4 dc in next dc, drop last lp from hook, insert hook in first st of grp, pick up dropped lp and pull through, ch 1 (popcorn made), dc in next dc, (2 dc, ch 3, 2 dc) in ch-3 corner sp, dc in next dc, popcorn in next dc, dc in next dc, ch 5, dc in next ch-7 lp, (dc, ch 5, dc) in ch-5 lp, rep from * around, end with dc in beg ch-5 lp, ch 5, sl st in top of beg ch-3. Fasten off.

Rnd 6: Join light green with sc in first popcorn after any corner, * (ch 5, sc in next lp) 3 times, ch 5, sc in next popcorn, ch 5, sc in corner sp, ch 5, sc in next popcorn, rep from * around, end with sl st in first sc.

Rnd 7: Sl st into next ch-5 lp, ch 2 for first hdc, (2 hdc, ch 3, 3 hdc) in same lp, * 6 hdc in next lp, ch 3, 6 hdc in next lp, (3 hdc, ch 3, 3 hdc) in next lp, 6 hdc in next lp for beg of corner section, 3 hdc in next lp, ch 6, drop lp from hook, insert hook in 4th hdc of prev 6-hdc grp, pick up dropped lp and pull through, (2 sc, ch 3, 2 sc, ch 3, 2 sc, ch 3, 2 sc) in ch-6 lp, 3 hdc in ch-5 lp to complete corner section, (3 hdc, ch 3, 3 hdc) in next lp, rep from * around, end with sl st in top of beg ch-2. Fasten off.

2nd square: Rep rnds 1-6 as for first square.

Rnd 7 (joining rnd): Sl st into next ch-5 lp, ch 2 for first

hdc, 2 hdc in same lp, ch 1, sc in corresponding ch-3 lp on first square, ch 1, 3 hdc in same ch-5 lp on 2nd square, 6 hdc in next lp, ch 1, sc in corresponding ch-3 lp on first square, ch 1, 6 hdc in next lp on 2nd square, 3 hdc in next lp on 2nd square, ch 1, sc in corresponding ch-3 lp on first square, ch 1, 3 hdc in same lp on 2nd square, 6 hdc in next lp on 2nd square for beg of corner section, 3 hdc in next lp, ch 6, drop lp from hook, insert hook in 4th hdc of prev 6-hdc grp, pick up dropped lp and pull through, 2 sc in ch-6 lp, (ch 1, sc in corresponding ch-3 corner lp on first square, ch 1, 2 sc in ch-6 lp on 2nd square) twice, ch 3, 2 sc in same ch-6 lp on 2nd square, 3 hdc in ch-5 lp to complete corner section on 2nd square, complete 2nd square as est for first square. Fasten off.

Referring to placement diagram for positioning, cont to make and join squares as est.

Tassel (make 14): *Note:* See page 141 for tassel diagrams. For each tassel, wind peach and light green yarns 5 times each and variegated yarn 15 times around a 9″ piece of cardboard. Wrap tassel with light green yarn. Attach tassels to afghan at inside points as indicated on placement diagram.

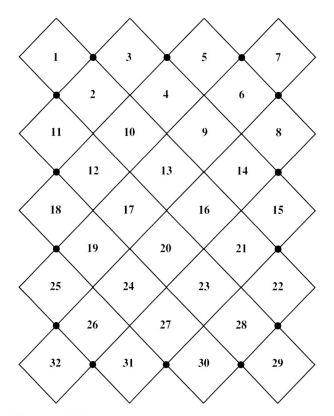

Placement Diagram

CHAMPAGNE TOAST

*Salute someone near and dear with
a throw made from a caramel-colored yarn
with silver lamé accents.*

FINISHED SIZE

Approximately 40"x 60".

MATERIALS

Bulky-weight acrylic-polyamide ribbon blend (75-yd. skein): 20 beige.

Worsted-weight viscose-lamé-cotton blend (80-yd. skein): 2 variegated caramel/silver/white.

Sizes G and I crochet hooks, or size to obtain gauge.

GAUGE

Large motif = 10" with size I hook.

DIRECTIONS

Large motif (make 24): **First motif:** With beige and size I hook, ch 6, join with a sl st to form a ring.

Rnd 1: Ch 2 for first hdc, 15 hdc in ring, sl st in top of beg ch-2 = 16 sts.

Rnd 2: Ch 3 for first dc, dc in same st, (ch 3, sk 1 st, 2 dc in next st) 7 times, ch 3, sl st in top of beg ch-3.

Rnd 3: Ch 3 for first dc, dc in sp before next dc, dc in next dc, (ch 4, dc in next dc, dc bet 2 dc, dc in next dc) 7 times, ch 4, sl st in top of beg ch-3.

Rnd 4: Ch 3 for first dc, * dc before next st, dc after next st, dc in last st of same grp, ch 5, dc in first dc of next grp, rep from * around, end with sl st in top of beg ch-3.

Rnd 5: Ch 3 for first dc, * (dc bet next 2 dc) 3 times, dc in last dc of same grp, ch 6, dc in first dc of next grp, rep from * around, end with sl st in top of beg ch-3.

Rnd 6: Ch 3 for first dc, * (dc bet next 2 dc) twice, ch 3, (dc bet next 2 dc) twice, dc in last dc of same grp, ch 4, dc in first dc of next grp, rep from * around, end with sl st in top of beg ch-3.

Rnd 7: Sl st in ea of next 2 sts and into ch-3 sp, ch 4 for first tr, * (tr in same sp, ch 3, sl st in top of tr to make a picot) 8 times, tr in same sp, sc in next ch-4 sp, tr in next ch-3 sp, rep from * around, end with sl st in top of beg ch-4. Fasten off.

2nd motif: Rep rnds 1-6 as for first motif.

Rnd 7 (joining rnd): Rep rnd 7 of first motif to last 2 scallops, * (tr, 3 tr with picots) in next ch-3 sp, (tr in same sp, ch 1, sl st in corresponding picot on first motif, ch 1, sl st in top of last tr on 2nd motif) twice, (3 tr with picots, tr) in same sp, sc in next ch-4 sp, rep from * once more, sl st in top of beg ch-4. Fasten off.

Cont to make and join motifs as est for a throw 4 motifs wide and 6 motifs long.

Small motif (make 15): *Note:* Small motifs are worked in the openings bet rows of large motifs.

With size G hook, join variegated yarn with sc in center picot just beyond joining on large motif, (ch 18, sc in center picot on next scallop) 7 times, ch 18, drop lp from hook and cut yarn, leaving a 7" tail. To weave ch-18 lps tog, use crochet hook to pull 6th lp through 7th lp, 5th lp through 6th lp, 4th lp through 5th lp, 3rd lp through 4th lp, 2nd lp through 3rd lp, first lp through 2nd lp. Thread unfinished end of last lp up through first lp, around both halves of 7th ch-18 lp, and back down through first lp, pick up dropped lp of last ch-18 and sl st in first sc. Fasten off.

Trim: With right side facing and size G hook, join variegated yarn with sc in top of any sk hdc on rnd 1 of large motif, (ch 5, sc in next rnd-1 sk hdc) 7 times, ch 5, sl st in first sc. Fasten off.

Rep to work trim on ea large motif.

FALLING STARS

*Gold stars stitched on a
background of blue and white stripes
make a bold statement.*

FINISHED SIZE

Approximately 32″ x 42″.

MATERIALS

Bulky-weight wool (105-yd. skein): 7 navy.
Worsted-weight mercerized cabled cotton (185-yd. ball):
3 white.
Soft-twist metallic thread (300m spool): 1 gold.
Size H crochet hook, or size to obtain gauge.
Size 4 steel crochet hook.

GAUGE

2 sts and 2 rows = 1″ in pat with size H hook.

DIRECTIONS

Throw: With size H hook and navy, ch 112.

Row 1: Sc in 4th ch from hook, (ch 1, sk next st, sc in next st) across, turn = 55 sps.

Row 2: Ch 3 for first dc, keeping last lp of ea st on hook, work 2 dc in next ch-1 sp, yo and pull through all lps on hook (cl made), ch 1, cl in ea sp across, end with dc in last st, turn = 55 cl.

Row 3: (Ch 1, sc in next ch-1 sp) across, end with sc in tch, turn.

Rows 4-8: Rep rows 2 and 3 alternately. Fasten off after row 8.

Rows 9-16: Join white in last st of row 8, rep rows 3 and 2 alternately. Fasten off after row 16.

Note: Work with 2 strands of gold held tog as 1.

Row 17: Join 2 strands of gold in last st of row 16, rep row 3.

Row 18: Ch 3 for first dc, 3-dc cl in ea ch-1 sp across, end with dc in last st, turn. Fasten off.

Rows 19-26: Join navy, rep rows 3 and 2 alternately. Fasten off after row 26.

Rows 27-34: Join white, rep rows 3 and 2 alternately. Fasten off after row 34.

Rows 35 and 36: Join 2 strands of gold, rep rows 17 and 18. Fasten off after row 36.

Rows 37-68: Join navy, rep rows 3 and 2 alternately. Fasten off after row 68.

Rows 69 and 70: Join white, rep rows 3 and 2. Fasten off after row 70.

Rows 71 and 72: Join 2 strands of gold, rep rows 17 and 18. Fasten off after row 72.

Rows 73 and 74: Join navy, rep rows 3 and 2. Fasten off after row 74.

Rows 75 and 76: Join white, rep rows 3 and 2. Fasten off after row 76.

Row 77: Join 2 strands of gold, rep row 3. Fasten off.

Row 78: Join navy, rep row 2. Fasten off.

Rows 79-91: Rep rows 3 and 2 alternately as est, working 2 rows ea with white and navy, ending after row 3. Do not fasten off after row 91.

Edging: **Rnd 1:** Ch 2 for first sc and ch 1, sc in same st, * (2 sc in side of next dc row, sc in side of next sc row) to next corner, (sc, ch 1, sc) in corner st, sc in ea st to next corner, (sc, ch 1, sc) in corner st, rep from * around, sl st in first ch of beg ch-2.

Rnd 2: Sl st into next ch-1 sp, ch 2 for first sc and ch 1, sc in same sp, * (ch 1, sk 1 st, sc in next st) to corner ch-1 sp, ch 1, (sc, ch 1, sc) in corner sp, rep from * around, end with sl st in first ch of beg ch-2. Fasten off.

Rnd 3: Join white in corner ch-1 sp, ch 3 for first dc, (dc, ch 3, 2-dc cl) in same sp, * 2-dc cl in ea ch-1 sp to corner, (2-dc cl, ch 3, 2-dc cl) in corner sp, rep from * around, end with sl st in top of beg ch-3 = 69 cl across ea long edge and 56 cl across ea short edge (not including corner grps). Fasten off.

Star (make 5): *Note:* Work with 2 strands of gold held tog as 1. **Rnd 1:** With size 4 hook, ch 2, 5 sc in 2nd ch from hook, sl st in first sc.

Rnd 2: Ch 3 for first dc, 2 dc in same st, 3 dc in ea of next 4 sc, sl st in top of beg ch-3.

Rnd 3: * Ch 10, working back down ch-10, sl st in 2nd ch from hook, sc in ea of next 2 ch, hdc in ea of next 2 ch, dc in ea of next 2 ch, tr in ea of next 2 ch, sk next 2 sts on rnd 2, sl st in next st, rep from * 4 times more, end with sl st in last sl st of rnd 2. Fasten off.

Stitch stars to afghan as desired (see photo).

TOUCHES OF GOLD

*A diamond-patterned afghan and
matching pillow trimmed with gold are
sophisticated bedroom adornments.*

FINISHED SIZE

Afghan: Approximately 54″ square.

Pillow: Approximately 22″ square, not including ruffle.

MATERIALS

Worsted-weight acrylic (110-yd. ball): 37 white for afghan; 4 white for pillow.

Fingering-weight metallic (163-yd. ball): 4 gold for afghan; 1 gold for pillow.

Sizes F and G crochet hooks, or size to obtain gauge.

3¼ yards of white satin.

2½ yards of gold lamé.

White sewing thread.

24″-square pillow form.

GAUGE

4 sc and 4 rows = 1″ with size G hook.

DIRECTIONS

Afghan: **Row 1:** With size G hook and white, ch 2, 2 sc in 2nd ch from hook, turn.

Row 2: Ch 1, sc in first st, 2 sc in next st, turn.

Row 3: Ch 1, sc in ea of first 2 sts, 2 sc in next st, turn.

Row 4: Ch 1, sc in ea of first 3 sts, 2 sc in next st, turn.

Rows 5-13: Ch 1, sc in ea st to last st, 2 sc in last st, turn = 14 sts plus beg ch-1 after row 13.

Row 14 (right side): Ch 1, sc in ea of 5 sts, yo twice, insert hook from front to back around post of center st on row 11, complete st as a tr (tr/rf made), sk 1 sc (center st of prev row), sc in ea of next 3 sc, tr/rf around same st as last tr/rf (bottom point of diamond made), sk 1 sc, sc in ea of next 3 sc, 2 sc in last st, turn.

Rows 15-17: Ch 1, sc in ea st to last st, 2 sc in last st, turn = 18 sts after row 17.

Row 18: Ch 1, sc in ea of 5 sts, tr/rf around first row-14 tr/rf, sk 1 sc, sc in ea of next 3 sc, working behind prev tr/rf, work tr/rf around same row-14 tr/rf, tr/rf around next row-14 tr/rf (top point of diamond made), sk 1 sc (center st of prev row), sc in ea of next 3 sc, working in front of prev tr/rf, work tr/rf around same row-14 tr/rf, sk 1 sc, sc in ea of next

3 sc, 2 sc in last st, turn.

Rows 19-21: Rep row 15 = 23 sts after row 21.

Row 22: Ch 1, sc in ea of 5 sts, tr/rf around first row-18 tr/rf, sk 1 sc, sc in ea of next 3 sc, working behind prev tr/rf, work tr/rf around same tr/rf, work tr/rf around both row-18 tr/rf at top point of next diamond, sk 2 sc, sc in ea of next 3 sc, working behind prev tr/rf, work tr/rf around same top point of diamond, tr/rf around next row-18 tr/rf, sk 1 sc, sc in ea of next 3 sc, working in front of prev tr/rf, work tr/rf around same tr/rf, sk 1 sc, sc in ea of next 3 sc, 2 sc in last st, turn.

Rows 23-25: Rep row 15 = 28 sts after row 25.

Row 26 (diamond row): Ch 1, sc in ea of 5 sts, tr/rf around first tr/rf, sk 1 sc, sc in ea of next 3 sc, working behind prev tr/rf, work tr/rf around same tr/rf, (tr/rf around both tr/rf at top point of next diamond, sk 2 sc, sc in ea of next 3 sc, working behind prev tr/rf, work tr/rf around same top point of diamond) across to last tr/rf of row, tr/rf around next tr/rf, sk 1 sc, sc in ea of next 3 sc, working in front of prev tr/rf, work tr/rf around same tr/rf, sk 1 sc, sc in ea of next 3 sc, 2 sc in last st, turn.

Rows 27-29: Rep row 15 = 33 sts after row 29.

Row 30 and foll rows: Work as est in rows 26-29, inc 1 st at end of ea row and working 3 rows sc bet diamond rows until there are 76 tr/rf across.

Next row (beg dec): Cont working in pat as est in rows 26-29, dec 1 sc at end of ea row until only 1 st rem. Work sc dec as foll: pull up a lp in ea of last 2 sts of row, yo and pull through all lps on hook. Do not fasten off after last row. Piece should measure approximately 44″ square.

Border: With right side facing, ch 1, * sc in ea st to corner, (sc, ch 1, sc) in corner, rep from * around, end with sc in beg corner, ch 1, sl st in beg ch-1. Fasten off.

Edging: **Rnd 1:** With size F hook, join 1 strand ea of white and gold with sl st in last sl st, working with both yarns held tog as 1, ch 5 for first dc and ch 2, dc in same st, * ch 2, (sk 2 sts, dc in next st, ch 2) to corner, (dc, ch 2, dc, ch 2, dc) in corner, rep from * around, end with dc in beg corner, ch 2, sl st in 3rd ch of beg ch-5 = 55 dc bet corner grps. Fasten off gold.

Rnd 2: With size G hook and white, ch 1, sc in same st, * (2 sc in next sp, sc in next dc) to corner, 3 sc in corner dc, rep from * around, end with sc in beg corner, sl st in beg ch-1, turn.

Rnds 3-5: Ch 1, sc in same st, (sc in ea st to corner, 3 sc in corner st) around, end with sc in beg corner, sl st in beg ch-1, turn = 179 sc across ea edge after rnd 5.

Rnd 6 (right side): With size F hook, join gold and working with both yarns held tog as 1, rep rnd 1, sk only 1 st before ea corner, turn = 60 dc bet corners. Fasten off gold.

Rnd 7: With size G hook and white, ch 1, sc in same st, rep rnd 2, turn.

Rnds 8-11: Ch 1, sc in same st, (sc in ea st to corner, 3 sc in corner) around, turn = 197 sc bet corners after rnd 11.

Rnd 12: Ch 1, sc in same st, * sc in ea of next 2 sts, sk 1 sc, tr/rf around post of sc 3 rows below next st, (sc in ea of next 3 sc, tr/rf around same sc as prev tr/rf, sk 1 sc, tr/rf around sc 3 rows below next st) across to 3 sts before corner, sc in ea of next 3 sc, 3 sc in corner, rep from * around, end with sc in beg corner, sl st in beg ch-1 = 48 V-sts across ea edge, turn.

Rnds 13-15: Rep rnd 8 = 249 sts bet corners after rnd 15.

Rnd 16 (right side): With size F hook, join gold and working with both yarns held tog as 1, ch 3 for first dc, keeping last lp of ea st on hook, work 2 dc in next st, yo and pull through all lps on hook (2-dc cl made), ch 2, * (3-dc cl in next st, ch 2, sk 3 sts) across to corner, (3-dc cl, ch 2) in ea of 3 corner sts, rep from * around, sl st in top of beg ch-3 = 62 cl bet corners. Do not turn. Fasten off gold.

Rnd 17: With size G hook and white, ch 6 for first dc and ch 3, dc in same st, * (dc, ch 3, dc) in ea ch-2 sp to center corner cl, (dc, ch 3, dc) in center corner cl, rep from * around, sl st in 3rd ch of beg ch-6. Fasten off.

Pillow: **Rows 1-42:** With size G hook and white, rep rows 1-42 as for afghan.

Next row (beg dec): Cont working in pat as est for afghan, dec 1 sc at end of ea row until only 1 st rem. Do not fasten off after last row. Piece should measure approximately 9½″ square.

Border: With right side facing, work border as for afghan. Fasten off.

Edging: **Rnd 1:** With size F hook, join 1 strand ea of white and gold with sl st in last sl st, rep rnd 1 of afghan edging = 16 dc bet corner grps. Fasten off.

Flower and leaf sprays (make 4): With size G hook and white, ch 12, join with a sl st to form a ring.

Rnd 1: Work 24 sc in ring, sl st in first sc.

Rnd 2: (Ch 8, sk 3 sts, sc in next st) 5 times, ch 8, sk 3 sts, sl st in base of beg ch-8.

Rnd 3: (*Note:* Leaf sprays are worked with white and gold held tog as 1. To work flower sts, use white only and carry gold across by working over it.) Work 7 sc in next ch-8 lp, join gold and work spray as foll with both yarns held tog as 1, ch 9, sl st in 6th ch from hook to make a picot, (ch 11, sl st in 6th ch from hook to make a picot) twice, ch 5, sl st in 3rd ch-sp from corner on edge of diamond square, sl st in ea of next 3 ch on ch-5, ch 7, picot, ch 1, sl st in ea of next 3 ch on ch-11 bet picots, ch 7, picot, ch 1, sl st in ea of 3 ch on ch-11 bet picots, ch 7, picot, ch 1, sl st in ea of 2 ch to flower (long leaf spray made), working with white only and carrying gold along, work 7 sc in same ch-8 lp of flower, 7 sc in next ch-8 lp, ch 9, picot, ch 4, sl st in 4th sp from joining of prev leaf spray on same edge of diamond square, sl st in next 2 ch of ch-4, ch 7, picot, ch 1, sl st in ea of 2 ch to flower (short leaf spray made), 7 sc in same ch-8 lp, 7 sc in next ch-8 lp, make a short leaf spray and join in 4th sp from last joining on diamond square, 7 sc in same ch-8 lp, 7 sc in next ch-8 lp, make a long leaf spray and join in 4th sp from last joining, 7 sc in same ch-8 lp, (7 sc in next lp, make a short spray without joining, 7 sc in same ch-8 lp) twice, sl st in first sc. Fasten off.

Rep to join a flower and accompanying leaf sprays on ea side of diamond square.

Border: **Rnd 1:** With size F hook, join 1 strand ea of white and gold in center dc of any corner of diamond square, working with both yarns held tog as 1, ch 8 for first dc and ch 5, dc in same st, * ch 10, sk 2 picots on next long leaf spray, tr in center sl st bet picots closest to flower on long spray, ch 10, sl st in center ch bet picots on next short spray, ch 21 for corner, sl st in center ch bet picots on next short spray, ch 10, sk 1 picot on next long spray, sl st in center sl st bet picots closest to flower on long spray, ch 10, (dc, ch 5, dc) in center dc of next corner of diamond square, rep from * around, sl st in 3rd ch of beg ch-8. Fasten off.

Rnd 2: With size F hook, join 1 strand ea of white and gold in center ch of any ch-21 corner, working with both yarns held tog as 1, ch 5 for first dc and ch 2, dc in same st, * (ch 2, sk 2 sts, dc in next st) to corner, (dc, ch 2, dc, ch 2, dc) in center corner st, rep from * around, end with dc in beg corner, ch 2, sl st in 3rd ch of beg ch-5. Fasten off gold.

Rnd 3: With size G hook and white, rep rnd 2 of afghan edging.

Rnds 4-8: Rep rnd 3 of afghan edging.

Rnd 9: Rep rnd 12 of afghan edging.

Rnds 10 and 11: Rep rnd 3 of afghan edging. Fasten off.

Finishing: Use ¼″ seam. From satin, cut 22½″ squares for front and back, and cut 6½″-wide bias strips, piecing as needed to make 2 (140″) bias strips. From lamé, cut 6½″-wide strips, piecing as needed to make 2 (140″) bias strips.

With right sides facing, stitch short ends of 1 bias strip together at a 45° angle. Repeat with remaining bias strips. With right sides facing, stitch 1 satin strip to 1 lamé strip along 1 long edge. Turn. Repeat to stitch remaining satin and lamé strips together. Turn. With raw edges aligned and lamé sides facing, run a row of gathering threads through all layers, ¼″ from long raw edge. Gather ruffle to fit pillow front. With raw edges aligned, baste ruffle to right side of pillow front. With right sides facing, raw edges aligned, and ruffle to center, stitch pillow front to back around 3 sides. Turn, insert pillow form, and slipstitch opening closed.

Place crochet right side up on pillow front and slipstitch to pillow at seam.

DIAMONDS

*To complement a modern decor, frame
brilliant purple and green
diamonds with black.*

FINISHED SIZE

Approximately 44″ x 65″.

MATERIALS

Worsted-weight acrylic-mohair blend (185-yd. skein): 9 black; 4 each purple, dark green.

Size H crochet hook, or size to obtain gauge.

GAUGE

Block = 6″ x 6½″.

DIRECTIONS

Black block A (make 28): **Row 1:** With black, ch 20, hdc in 3rd ch from hook and ea ch across, turn = 19 sts.

Rows 2-18: Ch 2 for first hdc, hdc in ea st across, turn. Do not fasten off.

Border: Work * 18 sc across edge of block to corner, 3 sc in corner, rep from * around, sl st in first sc. Fasten off.

Color block B (make 30): *Note:* To change colors, work last st of prev color with both colors held tog as 1. **Row 1:** With purple, ch 20, hdc in 3rd ch from hook and ea of next 15 ch, join dark green and hdc in next ch with both yarns, drop purple, hdc in last ch with dark green, turn = 19 sts.

Row 2: With dark green, ch 2 for first hdc, hdc in next st, pick up purple and hdc in next st with both yarns, drop dark green, hdc in ea of next 16 sts with purple, turn.

Row 3: With purple, ch 2 for first hdc, hdc in ea of next 14 sts, pick up dark green and hdc in next st with both yarns, drop purple, hdc in ea of last 3 sts with dark green, turn.

Rows 4-18: Cont as est working 1 fewer st with purple and 1 more st with dark green ea row. Fasten off after row 18.

Border: Join black with sl st in any corner and work as for black block border.

Black triangle C (make 14): **Row 1:** With black, ch 3, hdc in 3rd ch from hook, turn = 2 sts.

Row 2: Ch 2 for first hdc, 2 hdc in next st, turn.

Row 3: Ch 3, hdc in 3rd ch from hook and ea of next 3 sts, turn.

Row 4: Ch 2 for first hdc, hdc in ea of 3 sts, 2 hdc in last st, turn.

Row 5: Ch 3, hdc in 3rd ch from hook and ea st across, turn.

Row 6: Ch 2 for first hdc, hdc in ea st across, turn.

Rows 7-12: Rep rows 5 and 6 alternately = 14 sts after row 12.

Row 13: Ch 2 for first hdc, keeping last lp of ea st on hook, hdc in ea of next 2 sts, yo and pull through all lps on hook (hdc dec made), hdc in ea st across, turn.

Row 14: Ch 2 for first hdc, hdc in ea st across to last 2 sts, hdc dec over last 2 sts, turn.

Rows 15-23: Rep rows 13 and 14 alternately.

Row 24: Ch 2 for first hdc, hdc dec over last 2 sts. Do not fasten off.

Border: * Sc across to point of triangle, 3 sc in point, rep from * around, sl st in first sc. Fasten off.

Color triangle D (make 10): Work as for black triangle, using colors as foll: **Rows 1-12:** Purple.

Rows 13-24: Dark green.

Border: Join black with sl st in any point and work as for black triangle border.

Assembly: Referring to diagram for placement, use black to whipstitch blocks and triangles together.

Border: With right side facing and afghan turned to work across short edge, join black with sl st in corner, ch 1, sc in same corner, [sc across to next corner, (sc, ch 1, sc) in corner] around, end with 2 sc in beg corner, turn.

* Ch 3 for first dc, dc in ea st across to next corner, turn, rep from * across same edge. Fasten off. With wrong side facing and afghan turned to work across rem short edge, join black in corner and rep from * to work 2 rows of dc as est. Fasten off.

Placement Diagram

HOLIDAY PLAID

*Weave strands of gold and red
through green crochet stitches to produce
a special Christmas throw.*

FINISHED SIZE

Approximately 44" x 59".

MATERIALS

Worsted-weight acrylic (110-yd. ball): 23 dark green.

Paternayan Persian wool (8-yd. skein): 3 Red #968.

Rainbow Gallery's Metallic Plastic Canvas Yarn (8-yd. skein): 6 Gold #PC1.

Size I crochet hook, or size to obtain gauge.

GAUGE

7 hdc and 6 rows = 2".

DIRECTIONS

Afghan: **Row 1:** With dark green, ch 156, hdc in 3rd ch from hook and ea ch across, turn = 155 hdc.

Rows 2-177: Ch 2 for first hdc, hdc in ea st across, turn.

Border: Ch 1, * sc in ea st to corner, (sc, ch 1, sc) in corner, rep from * around, sl st in beg ch-1. Fasten off.

Finishing: Use 3 strands of Paternayan Persian wool and 1 strand of Rainbow Gallery metallic yarn. Cut all lengths 4"

longer or wider than afghan as necessary. Weave strands over 4 stitches or rows and under 1 stitch or row, leaving 2" at each edge of afghan. Fold excess to back and tack to secure.

Weave 1 gold length across width of afghan through each of the following rows: 3, 13, 17, 39, 43, 51, 55, 80, 84, 108, 112, 122, 126, 150, 154, 164.

Weave 1 red length across width of afghan through each of the following rows: 1, 15, 41, 53, 82, 110, 124, 152, 166.

Weave 1 gold length across length of afghan working between each of the following stitches: 4 and 5, 15 and 16, 22 and 23, 58 and 59, 65 and 66, 74 and 75, 82 and 83, 92 and 93, 99 and 100, 133 and 134, 140 and 141, 151 and 152.

Weave 1 red length across length of afghan working between each of the following stitches: 1 and 2, 18 and 19, 61 and 62, 77 and 78, 95 and 96, 137 and 138, 154 and 155.

Fringe: Knot 2 (15") strands of dark green through each stitch across both short edges of afghan.

SPRING DAWN

*Capture the pure colors of dawn in
these bobble-stitch squares of
lavender, peach, and orchid.*

FINISHED SIZE

Approximately 41″ x 70″.

MATERIALS

Worsted-weight acrylic (110-yd. ball): 2 willow, 8 pink, 6 orchid, 12 lavender, 7 variegated gray/magenta/purple.

Size G crochet hook, or size to obtain gauge.

GAUGE

Square = 5½″.

DIRECTIONS

Square A (make 50): **Rnd 1:** With willow, ch 2, 7 sc in 2nd ch from hook, sl st in top of beg ch-2.

Rnd 2: Ch 1, sc in same st, * (hdc, dc, hdc) in next st, sc in next st, rep from * around, sl st in first sc. Fasten off.

Note: Work foll rows across 2 edges of small willow square.

Row 1: With right side facing, join pink with sl st in any corner dc, ch 1, sc in same st, sc in ea st to next dc, (2 sc, ch 1, 2 sc) in next dc for corner, sc in ea st to next dc, 2 sc in next dc, turn.

Row 2: Ch 3 for first dc, (sc in next st, dc in next st) 7 times, turn.

Row 3: Ch 1 for first sc, (dc in next st, sc in next st) 3 times, (dc, sc, dc) in next st for corner, (sc in next st, dc in next st) 3 times, dc in last st, turn.

Row 4: Ch 3 for first dc, (sc in next dc, dc in next sc) 3 times, sc in next dc, (dc, sc, dc) in corner, (sc in next st, dc in next st) 4 times, turn.

Row 5: Ch 1 for first sc, sc in ea of next 8 sts, 3 sc in corner st, sc in ea of next 9 sts. Fasten off. Do not turn.

Row 6: With right side facing, join orchid with sl st in beg ch-1 of row 5, ch 3 for first dc, dc in ea of next 9 sts, (dc, ch 1, dc) in corner st, dc in ea of next 10 sts, turn.

Row 7: Ch 1 for first sc, working in ft lps only, sc in ea of next 10 sts, (sc, ch 1, sc) in corner ch-1, sc in ea of next 11 sts, turn.

Row 8: Ch 3 for first dc, dc in same st, (sk next st, 2 dc in next st) 5 times, sk next st, (2 dc, ch 1, 2 dc) in corner ch-1 sp, (sk next st, 2 dc in next st) 6 times. Fasten off. Do not turn.

Row 9: With right side facing, join lavender with sl st in top of beg ch-3 of row 8, ch 1 for first sc, working in bk lps only, sc in ea of next 13 sts, (sc, ch 1, sc) in corner ch-1 sp, sc in ea of next 14 sts, turn.

Row 10: Ch 1 for first sc, sc in next st, * keeping last lp of ea st on hook, 4 dc in next st, yo and pull through all lps on hook, ch 1 (bobble made), sc in ea of next 2 sts, rep from * 3 times more, bobble in next st, sc in corner ch-1 sp, (bobble in next st, sc in ea of next 2 sts) 5 times, turn.

Row 11: Ch 3 for first dc, dc in next st, (sk next bobble, 2 dc in ea of next 2 sc) 4 times, (dc, 3 tr, dc) in corner sc, (sk next bobble, 2 dc in ea of next 2 sc) 4 times, sk next bobble, dc in ea of last 2 sc, turn.

Row 12: Ch 1 for first sc, sc in ea of next 19 sts, (sc, ch 1, sc) in corner st, sc in ea of next 20 sts, turn. Fasten off.

Row 13: With right side facing, join variegated yarn with sl st in top of last st on row 12, ch 3 for first dc, dc in ea of next 20 sts, (dc, ch 1, dc) in corner ch-1 sp, dc in ea of next 21 sts, turn.

Rows 14 and 15: Ch 1 for first sc, sc in ea st to corner ch-1 sp, (sc, ch 1, sc) in corner ch-1 sp, sc in ea rem st, turn. Fasten off after row 15.

Square B (make 36): Work as for square A, using colors as foll: **Rnds 1 and 2:** Willow.

Rows 1-5: Lavender.

Rows 6-8: Orchid.

Rows 9-12: Pink.

Rows 13-15: Lavender.

Assembly: With right sides facing and referring to placement diagram (on page 82), whipstitch squares together.

Edging: **Row 1:** With right side facing, join variegated yarn with sl st in st indicated on placement diagram, ch 3 for first dc, work 2 dc in side of ea dc row and 1 dc in side of ea sc row to point = 24 dc, (dc, ch 1, dc) in dc at point, * work 22 dc across edge of square to inside point, keeping last lp of ea st on hook, dc in next sc on same square, sk 2 sts, dc in

next sc on next square, yo and pull through all lps on hook (dc dec made), work 22 dc across edge of square to point, (dc, ch 1, dc) in st at point, rep from * 3 times more, work 24 dc across edge of last square, turn.

Row 2: Ch 1, sc in ea of next 24 dc, * (sc, ch 1, sc) in ch-1 sp at point, sc in ea of next 22 dc, sk 2 dc, sc in ea of next

22 dc to point, rep from * 3 times more, (sc, ch 1, sc) in ch-1 sp at point, sc in ea of last 24 dc, turn.

Rnd 1: Ch 1 for first sc, * sc in ea st to st at point, (sc, ch 1, sc) in st at point, sc in ea st to 1 st before inside point, sk 2 sts, rep from * around as est, end with sl st in beg ch-1. Fasten off.

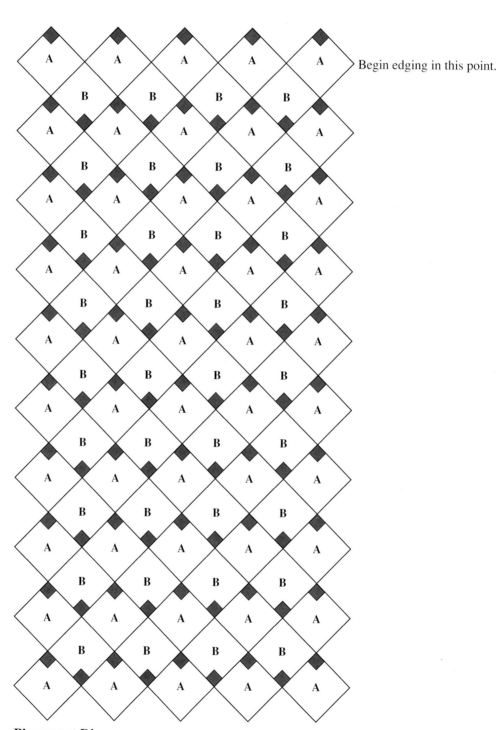

Begin edging in this point.

Placement Diagram

SNOWMEN

*These cross-stitched snowmen with
their colorful hats and scarves
will keep out winter's chill.*

FINISHED SIZE
Approximately 37″ x 43″.

MATERIALS
Worsted-weight acrylic (110-yd. ball): 18 navy.

Size F crochet hook, or size to obtain gauge.

Paternayan Persian wool (8-yd. skein): 2 each Green #681, Red #970, Blue #502, Yellow #726 (for scarves and cross-stitch).

Size 5 steel crochet hook.

Sportweight brushed acrylic (156-yd. ball): 3 white (for cross-stitch and Smyrna crosses).

8 (½″) round black shank buttons (for buttons).

8 (¼″) round black shank buttons (for eyes).

GAUGE
8 sc and 11 rows = 2″ with size F hook.

DIRECTIONS
Throw: With size F hook and navy, ch 147.

Row 1 (wrong side): Dc in 4th ch from hook and ea ch across = 145 dc, turn.

Row 2 (right side): Ch 3 for first dc, dc in next dc, * (yo and insert hook from front to back around post of dc 1 row below prev st, yo and pull up a lp) twice, yo and pull through 4 lps on hook (post-cl made), sk next dc, post-cl around dc 1 row below next st, yo and pull through rem 3 lps on hook, dc in top of dc above last post-cl, dc in ea of next 2 dc, rep from * across, end with dc in last st, turn.

Row 3: Ch 3 for first dc, dc in ea st across, turn.

Row 4: Ch 3 for first dc, dc in ea of next 3 dc, * post-cl around post of dc 1 row below prev st, sk next dc, post-cl around post of dc 1 row below next st, yo and pull through rem 3 lps on hook, dc in top of dc above last post-cl, dc in ea of next 2 dc, rep from * across, dc in last st, turn.

Row 5: Ch 3 for first dc, dc in ea st across, turn.

Row 6: Rep row 2.

Rows 7-9: Ch 1, sc in ea st across, turn.

Row 10: Ch 1, sc in ea of next 4 sc, (post-cl around sc 3 rows below prev st, sk next sc of same prev row, post-cl around next sc of same prev row, yo and pull through rem 3 lps on hook, sk next sc of current row, sc in ea of next 3 sc) 3 times, sc in ea of next 115 sc, rep bet ( ) 3 times, sc in last st, turn.

Rows 11-13: Ch 1, sc in ea st across, turn.

Row 14: Ch 1, sc in ea of next 2 sc, (post-cl around sc 3 rows below prev st, sk next sc of same prev row, post-cl around next sc of same prev row, yo and pull through rem 3 lps on hook, sk next sc of current row **, sc in ea of next 3 sc) 3 times, sc in ea of next 119 sc, rep bet ( ) 3 times, ending last rep at **, sc in ea of last 2 sts, turn.

Rows 15-54: Rep rows 7-14 for pat.

Row 55 (wrong side): Ch 3 for first dc, dc in ea st across = 145 dc.

Rows 56-132: Rep rows 4, 5, 2, and 3 for pat, ending after row 4. Do not fasten off after last row. Work * 3 sc in corner, sc in ea st to next corner, rep from * around, sl st in first sc. Fasten off.

Scarf (make 4 using colors as specified): **Row 1:** With size 5 hook and 1 strand of Paternayan Persian wool, ch 7, hdc in 3rd ch from hook and ea ch across, turn = 6 hdc.

Rows 2-34: Ch 2 for first hdc, hdc in ea of next 5 hdc, turn. Fasten off after row 34.

Fringe: Knot 2 (3″) strands of wool in ea st across 1 end of scarf.

Scarf for Snowman A: **Rows 1-18:** Green.

Rows 19, 21, 27, 29: Yellow.

Rows 20, 22-26, 28, 30-34: Green.

Scarf for Snowman B: **Rows 1-34:** Yellow. **Trim:** With red, ch 80. Fasten off. Tack chain to scarf in zigzag pattern.

Scarf for Snowman C: **Rows 1-34:** Red. **Trim:** Weave 3 strands of blue through stitches of scarf as desired.

Scarf for Snowman D: **Rows 1-34:** Blue. **Trim:** With 1 strand of yellow, make French knots on scarf as desired.

Cross-stitch: Beginning 6 stitches from last cluster on row 8 of throw and using 2 strands of yarn, cross-stitch 4 snowmen according to chart and color key. Skip 12 stitches on row 8 between snowmen. Cross-stitch hats and hatbands with 2 strands of Paternayan Persian wool according to chart and using colors as follows: red hat and green hatband for snowman A, blue hat and yellow hatband for snowman B, green hat and blue hatband for snowman C, yellow hat and red hatband for snowman D.

Referring to photo, attach scarves to snowmen. For each snowman, stitch black shank buttons as indicated on chart. For snowflakes, add Smyrna crosses to throw as desired.

Color Key

△	White (Unger, Fluffy)
▲	Hat (see directions and photo)
✕	Hatband (see directions and photo)
✳	White Smyrna Cross (Unger, Fluffy)

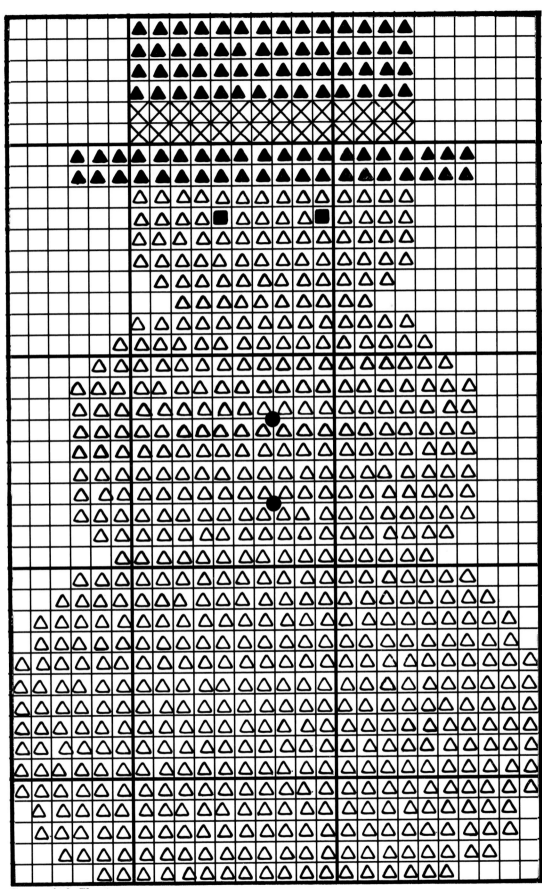

Cross-stitch Chart

BUTTERCUP BLANKET

*Choose a pretty cotton yarn to best display
the texture of the front post cluster stitches
used in this blanket.*

FINISHED SIZE

Approximately 36″ x 34″, not including edging.

MATERIALS

Sportweight cotton (120-yd. ball): 20 yellow.
Size G crochet hook, or size to obtain gauge.

GAUGE

5 front post cl and 12 rows = 6″.

DIRECTIONS

Afghan: **Row 1:** Ch 123, dc in 4th ch from hook and ea ch across = 121 sts, turn.

Row 2: Ch 3 for first dc, dc in next st, * (yo and insert hook from front to back around post of st below dc just made, yo and pull up a lp) twice, yo and pull through 4 lps on hook, sk 1 dc, (yo and insert hook around post of next st on prev row, yo and pull up a lp) twice, yo and pull through 4 lps on hook, yo and pull through all rem lps on hook (front post cl made), dc in top of same st as 2nd leg of cl, dc in ea of next 2 dc, rep from * across, turn.

Row 3: Ch 3 for first dc, dc in ea st across = 121 dc, turn.

Row 4: Ch 3 for first dc, dc in ea of next 3 sts, * first leg of cl around post of st below dc just made, sk 1 dc, 2nd leg of cl around post of next st on prev row, dc in top of same st as 2nd leg of cl, dc in ea of next 2 dc, rep from * across, end with dc in last st, turn.

Row 5: Rep row 3.

Rows 6-68: Rep rows 2-5 for pat, ending after row 4. Do not fasten off after last row.

Edging: **Rnd 1:** Ch 1, * 2 sc in side of ea row to corner, 3 sc in corner, sk 1 st, sc in ea st to next corner, 3 sc in corner, rep from * around, sl st in first sc = 136 sts across ea long edge and 119 sts across ea short edge.

Rnd 2: Ch 3 for first dc, (yo and pull up a lp) 3 times in same st, yo and pull through all lps on hook (puff made), ch 2, puff in next st, sk 2 sts, * 6 dc in next st, ch 1, sk 3 sts **, (puff, ch 2, puff) in next st, sk 3 sts, rep from * to 3-sc corner grp, ending last rep at **, [puff in next st, ch 2, (puff, ch 2, puff) in center corner st, ch 2, puff in next st], sk 3 sts, rep from * to next corner grp, sk only 2 sts before corner, rep bet [ ] once for corner section, cont around as est, end with sl st in top of first puff.

Rnd 3: Sl st backward into corner ch-2 sp, ch 3 for first dc, puff in same sp, ch 2, (puff, ch 2, puff) in next ch-2 sp, [* dc in ea of next 6 dc, ch 1, (puff, ch 2, puff) in next ch-2 sp, rep from * to corner ch-2 sp, ch 2, (puff, ch 2, puff) in corner sp, ch 2, (puff, ch 2, puff) in next ch-2 sp] around, end with sl st in top of first puff.

Rnd 4: Sl st backward into corner ch-2 sp, ch 3 for first dc, puff in same sp, [ch 2, (puff, ch 2, puff) in next ch-2 sp] twice, [* ch 1, sk 1 dc, dc in ea of next 4 dc **, (puff, ch 2, puff, ch 2, puff, ch 2, puff) in next ch-2 sp, rep from * to corner section, ending last rep at **, (puff, ch 2, puff, ch 2) in ea of next 5 ch-2 sps, omit last ch 2] around, end with sl st in top of first puff.

Rnd 5: Sl st backward into corner ch-2 sp, ch 3 for first dc, puff in same sp, ch 1, puff in next sp, [ch 1, (puff, ch 2, puff) in next sp] twice, [* ch 1, sk 1 dc, dc in ea of next 2 dc **, (ch 1, puff, ch 2, puff) in next ch-2 sp, ch 1, puff in next sp, (ch 1, puff, ch 2, puff) in next sp, rep from * to corner section, ending last rep at **, ch 1, (puff, ch 2, puff) in next ch-2 sp, ch 1, sk next sp, (puff, ch 2, puff) in next sp, ch 1, puff in next ch-2 sp, ch 1, (puff, ch 2, puff) in corner ch-2 sp, ch 1, puff in next sp, (ch 1, puff, ch 2, puff) in next sp, ch 1, sk next sp, (puff, ch 2, puff) in next sp] around, end with sl st in top of first puff.

Rnd 6: Sl st backward into corner ch-2 sp, ch 3 for first dc, puff in same sp, (ch 1, puff in next sp) twice, (ch 1, puff, ch 2, puff) in next sp, ch 1, sk next sp, (puff, ch 2, puff) in next sp, [* ch 1, dc bet next 2 dc **, (ch 1, puff, ch 2, puff) in ea of next 4 ch-2 sps, rep from * to corner section, ending last rep at **, ch 1, (puff, ch 2, puff) in next ch-2 sp, sk next sp (puff, ch 2, puff) in next sp, (ch 1, puff in next sp) twice, (ch 1, puff, ch 2, puff) in corner sp, (ch 1, puff in next sp) twice, (ch 1, puff, ch 2, puff) in next sp, ch 1, sk next sp, (puff, ch 2, puff) in next sp] around, end with sl st in top of first puff.

Rnd 7: Ch 4 for first dc and ch 1, (dc in next sp, ch 1) 6 times, [* (sc in next sp, ch 1) twice **, (dc in next sp, ch 1)

7 times, rep from * to corner section, ending last rep at **, (dc in next sp, ch 1) 13 times] around, end with sl st in 3rd ch of beg ch-4.

Rnd 8: Sl st backward into corner ch-1 sp, ch 3 for first dc, puff in same sp, (ch 1, puff, ch 2, puff) in next sp, [(ch 1, puff in next sp) 5 times, ch 1, * sk next sp, 4 dc in sp bet next 2 sc, sk next sp **, (puff in next sp, ch 1) twice, (puff, ch 2, puff, ch 1) in ea of next 2 sps, (puff in next sp, ch 1) twice, rep from * to corner section, ending last rep at **, (puff in next sp, ch 1) 5 times, (puff, ch 2, puff) in ea of next 2 sps] around, end with sl st in top of first puff.

Rnd 9: Sl st into next sp, ch 3 for first dc, puff in same sp, [(ch 1, dc in next sp) 5 times, (ch 1, puff, ch 2, puff) in next sp, * sk 1 dc, dc in ea of next 2 dc, ch 1, (puff, ch 2, puff) in next sp **, (ch 1, dc in next sp) twice, ch 1, (puff, ch 2, puff) in next sp, (ch 1, dc in next sp) twice, ch 1, (puff, ch 2, puff) in next sp, ch 1, rep from * to corner section, ending last rep at **, (ch 1, dc in next sp) 5 times, (ch 1, puff, ch 2, puff) in corner sp] around, end with sl st in top of first puff.

Rnd 10: Sc backward in corner sp, (ch 3, sc in next sp) 8 times, [* ch 3, sk 2 dc, sc in next sp **, (ch 3, sc in next sp) 10 times, rep from * to corner section, ending last rep at **, (ch 3, sc in next sp) 16 times] around, end with sl st in first sc. Fasten off.

FALL WREATH

*Cross-stitch a richly colored wreath depicting
the fruits of fall on a background of
single crochet stitches.*

FINISHED SIZE

Approximately 40″ x 61″.

MATERIALS

Sportweight acrylic (175-yd. ball): 17 ecru.

Size H crochet hook, or size to obtain gauge.

Paternayan Persian wool (8-yd. skein): 2 each Forest Green #604, Ginger #886, Tobacco #744 (for fringe).

DMC or Anchor embroidery floss (8-yd. skein): see color key.

GAUGE

5 sc and 6 rows = 1″.

DIRECTIONS

Afghan: **Row 1:** With ecru, ch 172, sc in 2nd ch from hook and ea ch across, turn.

Rows 2-342: Ch 1, sc in ea st across, turn = 172 sc. Do not fasten off.

Edging: **Rnd 1:** With right side facing, ch 1, * sc in ea st to corner, (sc, ch 1, sc) in corner, sc across to next corner, dec as necessary to have 256 sts across long edge, (sc, ch 1, sc) in corner, rep from * around, end with sc in beg corner, ch 1, sl st in beg ch-1 = 170 sc across ea short edge and 256 sc across ea long edge (not including corner sts).

Rnd 2: Sl st into corner ch-1 sp, ch 4 for first dc and ch 1, 2 dc in same sp, * dc in ea st to next corner, (2 dc, ch 1, 2 dc) in corner sp, rep from * around, end with dc in beg corner, sl st in 3rd ch of beg ch-4 = 172 dc across ea short edge and 258 dc across ea long edge (not including corner sts).

Rnd 3: Sl st into corner ch-1 sp, ch 4 for first dc and ch 1, 2 dc in same sp, * (ch 2, sk next 2 sts, dc in ea of next 2 sts) across to corner, ch 2, (2 dc, ch 1, 2 dc) in corner ch-1 sp, rep from * around, end with dc in beg corner, sl st in 3rd ch of beg ch-4.

Rnd 4: Sl st into corner ch-1 sp, ch 4 for first dc and ch 1, 2 dc in same sp, * (ch 2, 2 dc in next ch-2 sp) across to corner, ch 2, (2 dc, ch 1, 2 dc) in corner ch-1 sp, rep from * around, end with dc in beg corner, sl st in 3rd ch of beg ch-4.

Rnd 5: Sl st into corner ch-1 sp, ch 4 for first dc and ch 1, 2 dc in same sp, * (dc in ea of next 2 dc, 2 dc in next ch-2 sp) across to corner ch-1 sp, (2 dc, ch 1, 2 dc) in corner sp, rep from * around, end with dc in beg corner, sl st in 3rd ch of beg ch-4.

Fringe: For each tassel, cut 4 (10½″) lengths of ecru or 3 (10½″) lengths of Paternayan Persian wool. Knot 1 tassel through every other stitch across each short edge of afghan, arranging colors as desired.

Cross-stitch: Use 12 strands of floss for cross-stitching and 2 strands for backstitching. Referring to photo for positioning, cross-stitch wreath design on each end of afghan according to chart.

Color Key

Anchor		DMC (used for sample)	
Step 1: Cross-stitch (12 strands)			
881	·	945	Peach Beige (4)
307	+	977	Golden Brown-lt. (4)
308	∴	976	Golden Brown-med. (4)
324	O	922	Copper-lt. (4)
339	●	920	Copper-med. (4)
11	−	3328	Salmon-dk. (4)
20	✕	498	Christmas Red-dk. (4)
871	△	3041	Antique Violet-med. (4)
872	▲	3740	Antique Violet-dk. (2)
859	⊟	523	Fern Green-lt. (4)
373	□	422	Hazel Nut Brown-lt. (4)
375	■	420	Hazel Nut Brown-dk. (4)
903	◎	3032	Mocha Brown-med. (2)
382	⊠	3021	Brown Gray-vy. dk. (2)
Step 2: Backstitch (2 strands)			
341		918	Red Copper-dk. (2) (outline of leaves)
382		3021	Brown Gray-vy. dk. (2) (acorns)

Note: The number of 8-yd. skeins required for each color is indicated in parentheses.

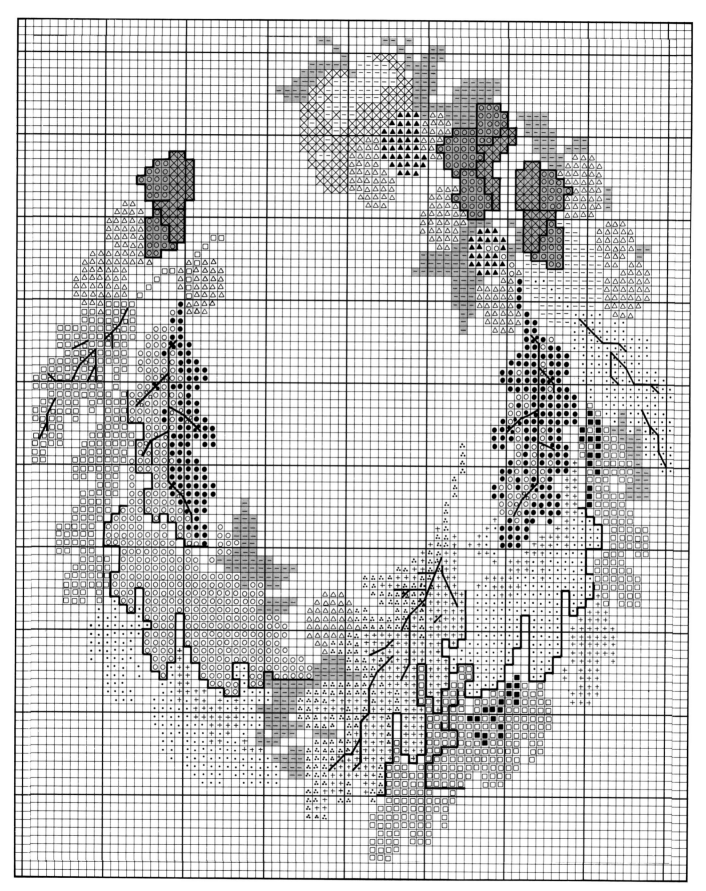

Cross-stitch Chart

VINTAGE ARAN

*Crossed stitches and cables are among the traditional
Irish fisherman crochet patterns used
in making this burgundy afghan.*

FINISHED SIZE

Approximately 55" x 65".

MATERIALS

Worsted-weight acrylic (110-yd. ball): 32 burgundy.
Size H crochet hook, or size to obtain gauge.

GAUGE

4 dc and 2 rows = 1".

DIRECTIONS

Afghan: Ch 207. **Row 1** (right side): Dc in 4th ch from hook, dc in next st, ch 1, sk next st, (yo and pull up a lp) 7 times in next st, yo and pull through all lps on hook (lg puff made), ch 3, lg puff in same st, ch 1, sk 1 st, work *first pat section* as foll: * dc in ea of next 3 sts, (yo and pull up a lp) 5 times in next st, yo and pull through all lps on hook (sm puff made), ch 1, sk next st, rep from * 5 times more, dc in next st, ch 1, sk next st, (lg puff, ch 3, lg puff) in next st (puff braid made), ch 1, sk 1 st, work *2nd pat section* as foll: dc in next st, * ch 1, sk 2 sts, dc in next st, working in front of dc just made, dc in 2nd sk st (cross st made), rep from * 8 times more, ch 1, sk 1 st, dc in next st, ch 1, sk 1 st, puff braid in next st, ch 1, sk 1 st, work *3rd pat section* as foll: * dc in ea of next 3 sts, pull up a lp in next st, ch 4, yo and pull through all 3 lps on hook (ch-st made), rep from * 13 times more, dc in ea of next 3 sts, ch 1, sk 1 st, puff braid in next st, ch 1, sk 1 st, work *4th pat section* as for 2nd pat section, work *5th pat section* as for first pat section, except beg section with 1 dc in next st and end with dc in ea of next 3 sts before puff braid, dc in ea of last 3 sts after puff braid, turn.

Row 2 (wrong side): Ch 3 for first dc, dc in ea of next 2 dc, ch 1, puff braid in sp of puff braid, ch 1, (dc in ea of next 3 dc, dc in ch-1, dc in puff) 6 times, dc in next dc, ch 1, puff braid in sp of puff braid, ch 1, dc in next dc, (dc in ch-1, dc in ea of next 2 dc) 9 times, dc in ch-1, dc in next dc, ch 1, puff braid in sp of puff braid, ch 1, (dc in ea of next 3 dc, dc in top of ch-st) 14 times, dc in ea of next 3 dc, ch 1, puff braid in sp of puff braid, ch 1, dc in next dc, (dc in ch-1, dc in ea of next 2 dc) 9 times, dc in ch-1, dc in next dc, ch 1, puff braid in sp of puff braid, ch 1, dc in next dc, (dc in ch-1, dc in puff, dc in ea of next 3 dc) 6 times, ch 1, puff braid in sp of puff braid, ch 1, dc in ea of last 3 sts, turn.

Row 3: Ch 3 for first dc, dc in ea of next 2 dc, ch 1, puff braid, ch 1, *first pat section:* dc in next dc, (puff in next dc, ch 1, sk 1 dc, dc in ea of next 3 dc) 6 times, ch 1, puff braid, ch 1, *2nd pat section:* dc in next dc, [ch 1, sk 2 dc, dc in next dc, working in front of dc just made, dc in 2nd sk dc (cross st made)] 9 times, ch 1, sk 1 dc, dc in next dc, ch 1, puff braid, ch 1, *3rd pat section:* dc in next dc, ch-st in next dc, dc in next dc, yo twice and insert hook from front to back around post of st 2 rows below dc just made, (yo and pull through 2 lps on hook) twice, yo twice and insert hook from front to back around post of center dc bet next 2 ch-sts 2 rows below, (yo and pull through 2 lps on hook) twice, yo and pull through rem lps on hook (ftptr-2-tog made), sk next dc, * dc in next dc, ch-st in next dc, dc in next dc, ftptr-2-tog around post of same st as 2nd leg of prev ftptr-2-tog and around post of center dc bet next 2 ch-sts 2 rows below, sk next dc, rep from * 12 times more, dc in next dc, ch-st in next dc, dc in next dc, ch 1, puff braid, ch 1, *4th pat section:* dc in next dc, (ch 1, sk 2 dc, cross st) 9 times ch 1, sk 1 dc, dc in next dc, ch 1, puff braid, ch 1, *5th pat section:* dc in ea of next 3 dc, (puff in next st, ch 1, sk 1 dc, dc in ea of next 3 dc) 5 times, puff in next dc, ch 1, sk 1 dc, dc in next dc, ch 1, puff braid, ch 1, dc in ea of last 3 sts, turn.

Row 4: Rep row 2 working 1 dc in top of ea ftptr-2-tog.

Row 5: Ch 3 for first dc, dc in ea of next 2 dc, ch 1, puff braid, ch 1, work first and 2nd pat sections as est in row 1, dc in next dc, yo twice and insert hook from front to back around top of ftptr-2-tog 2 rows below, complete st as a tr (ftptr made), * sk next dc, dc in next dc, ch-st in next dc, dc in next dc, ftptr-2-tog around same prev ftptr-2-tog and next ftptr-2-tog 2 rows below, rep from * 12 times more, sk next dc, dc in next dc, ch-st in next dc, dc in next dc, ftptr around same prev ftptr-2-tog 2 rows below, sk next dc, dc in next dc, ch 1, puff braid, ch 1, work 4th and 5th pat sections as est in row 1, turn.

Row 6: Rep row 4.

Row 7: Ch 3 for first dc, dc in ea of next 2 dc, ch 1, puff braid, ch 1, work first and 2nd pat section as est in row 3, dc in next dc, ch-st in next dc, dc in next dc, ftptr-2-tog around first ftptr and next ftptr-2-tog 2 rows below, * sk next dc, dc in next dc, ch-st in next dc, dc in next dc, ftptr-2-tog around same prev ftptr-2-tog and next ftptr-2-tog 2 rows below, rep from * 11 times more, sk next dc, dc in next dc, ch-st in next dc, dc in next dc, ftptr-2-tog around same prev ftptr-2-tog and last ftptr 2 rows below, sk next dc, dc in next dc, ch-st in next dc, dc in next dc, ch 1, puff braid, ch 1, work 4th and 5th pat sections as est in row 3, turn.

Row 8: Rep row 4.

Rows 9-135: Rep rows 5-8 for pat as est. Do not fasten off after last row.

Border: Ch 1, * sc evenly across to next corner, (sc, ch 1, sc) in corner, rep from * around, sl st in first sc. Fasten off.

FANCY FILIGREE

*Interchange tweed and mohair yarns to crochet
these lacy floral motifs reminiscent of
intricate ornamental openwork.*

FINISHED SIZE

Approximately 46″ x 64″.

MATERIALS

Worsted-weight wool (175-yd. skein): 4 light blue tweed.

Bulky-weight mohair-blend (70-yd. skein): 5 variegated blue.

Sizes G and H crochet hooks, or size to obtain gauge.

GAUGE

Square = 8″ with size H hook.

DIRECTIONS

First square A: With size H hook and light blue tweed, ch 12, join with a sl st to form a ring.

Rnd 1: Ch 3 for first dc, 23 dc in ring, sl st in top of beg ch-3.

Rnd 2: Ch 1, sc in same st, * ch 10, sk 2 dc, keeping last lp of ea st on hook, 5 dtr in next st, yo and pull through all lps on hook (5-dtr cl made), ch 10, sk 2 dc, sc in next dc, rep from * around, sl st in first sc.

Rnd 3: Ch 1, (5 sc, ch 5, 5 sc) in next lp, [ch 5, (5 sc, ch 5, 5 sc) in ea of next 2 ch-10 lps] 3 times, ch 5, (5 sc, ch 5, 5 sc) in next lp, sl st in first sc.

Rnd 4: Sl st in ea st to next ch-5 lp, sl st into center of lp, ch 4 for first tr, keeping last lp of ea st on hook, 2 tr in same lp, yo and pull through all lps on hook (3-tr cl made), * ch 7, (4-tr cl, ch 7, 4-tr cl, ch 7, 4-tr cl) in next ch-5 lp for corner, ch 7, 3-tr cl in ea of next 2 ch-5 lps, rep from * around, sl st in top of beg ch-4.

Rnd 5: Sc in same st, * (ch 5, sc in ch-7 lp, ch 5, sc in next cl) 3 times, ch 5, sc in next lp, ch 5, sc bet next 2 cl, rep from * around, sl st in first sc. Fasten off.

2nd square: Rep rnds 1-4 as for first square.

Rnd 5 (joining rnd): Sc in same st, (ch 5, sc in next lp, ch 5, sc in next cl) twice, * ch 2, sc in corresponding lp on first square, ch 2, sc in next lp on 2nd square, ch 2, sc in corresponding lp on first square, ch 2, sc in next cl on 2nd square, ch 2, sc in corresponding lp on first square, ch 2, sc in next lp on 2nd square, ch 2, sc in corresponding lp on first square, ch 2 **, sc bet next 2 cl on 2nd square, rep from * to ** once, sc in next cl on 2nd square, complete square as est for first square. Fasten off.

Cont to make and join squares as est, using colors as specified below. Arrange squares as desired for an afghan 5 squares wide and 8 squares long.

Square A (make 14)**:** Rnds 1-5 light blue tweed.

Square B (make 12)**:** Rnds 1-3 light blue tweed, rnd 4 variegated blue, rnd 5 light blue tweed.

Square C (make 14)**:** Rnd 1 variegated blue, rnds 2 and 3 light blue tweed, rnd 4 variegated blue, rnd 5 light blue tweed.

Border: **Rnd 1:** With right side facing and afghan turned to work across long edge, use size G hook to join variegated blue with sl st in center sc of corner, ch 4 for first tr, keeping last lp of ea st on hook, 3 tr in same st, yo and pull through all lps on hook (4-tr cl made), * ch 5, (4-tr cl, ch 5, 4-tr cl) in next ch-5 lp, [sk next 2 lps, (4-tr cl, ch 5, 4-tr cl) in next lp, ch 5, (4-tr cl, ch 5, 4-tr cl) in next lp, sk next 2 lps, (4-tr cl, ch 5, 4-tr cl) in next lp **, sk 2 joining lps, (4-tr cl, ch 5, 4-tr cl) in next lp] across to corner, end last rep at **, ch 5, 4-tr cl in corner sc, rep from * around, sl st in top of beg ch-4.

Rnd 2: Sc in same st, ch 5, sc in ea ch-5 lp and cl around, end with ch 5, sl st in first sc. Fasten off.

SHADES OF CORAL

*Assemble panels shaded from light coral to
dark rust and then apply tassels, fringe, and beads
for a throw to accent a southwestern decor.*

FINISHED SIZE
Approximately 58″ x 45″.

MATERIALS
Sportweight wool (124-yd. ball): 9 dark rust, 7 light coral,
3 medium rust, 9 dark red, 1 light rust, 3 light red, 9 coral.
Size J crochet hook, or size to obtain gauge.

GAUGE
3 dc = 1″.

DIRECTIONS
Note: Use 2 strands of yarn held tog as 1.

Panel pat: Ch 30. **Row 1** (right side): Dc in 3rd ch from
hook, dc in ea of next 12 ch, (dc, ch 1, dc) in next ch (V-st
made), dc in ea of next 12 ch, keeping last lp of ea st on
hook, dc in ea of next 2 ch, yo and pull through all lps on
hook (dc dec over 2 sts made), turn.

Row 2: Ch 2, working in ft lps only, sk dc dec, dc in ea
of next 13 dc, V-st in next ch-1 for point, dc in ea of next 12
dc, dc dec over next 2 dc, turn.

Row 3: Ch 2, working in bk lps only, sk dc dec, dc in ea
of next 13 dc, V-st in next ch-1 for point, dc in ea of next 12
dc, dc dec over next 2 dc, turn.

Rep rows 2 and 3 alternately, using colors as specified
below.

Panel 1: Rows 1-8 light coral, rows 9 and 10 dark rust,
rows 11-14 light coral, rows 15 and 16 dark red, rows 17-26
light coral, rows 27 and 28 medium rust, rows 29-34 light
coral, rows 35 and 36 light red, rows 37-44 light coral, rows
45 and 46 medium rust, rows 47-52 light coral, rows 53 and
54 light red, rows 55-58 light coral, rows 59 and 60 dark
red, rows 61-66 light coral.

Panel 2: Rows 1-10 coral, rows 11 and 12 light rust, rows
13-18 coral, rows 19 and 20 medium rust, rows 21-24 coral,
rows 25 and 26 light coral, rows 27-38 coral, rows 39 and
40 dark red, rows 41-48 coral, rows 49 and 50 dark rust,
rows 51-54 coral, rows 55 and 56 dark red, rows 57 and 58
light rust, rows 59-66 coral.

Panel 3: Rows 1-6 dark red, rows 7 and 8 medium rust,
rows 9-20 dark red, rows 21 and 22 coral, rows 23-30 dark
red, rows 31 and 32 light coral, rows 33 and 34 dark rust,
rows 35-40 dark red, rows 41 and 42 medium rust, rows 43-
50 dark red, rows 51 and 52 coral, rows 53-62 dark red,
rows 63 and 64 light coral, rows 65 and 66 dark red.

Panel 4: Rows 1-4 dark rust, rows 5 and 6 light coral, rows
7-18 dark rust, rows 19 and 20 medium rust, rows 21-24
dark rust, rows 25 and 26 dark red, rows 27-32 dark rust,
rows 33 and 34 light coral, rows 35-40 dark rust, rows 41
and 42 medium rust, rows 43-46 dark rust, rows 47 and 48
dark red, rows 49-60 dark rust, rows 61 and 62 light coral,
rows 63-66 dark rust.

Panel 5: Rows 1 and 2 dark rust, rows 3 and 4 dark red,
rows 5-10 dark rust, rows 11 and 12 dark red, rows 13-16
dark rust, rows 17 and 18 medium rust, rows 19-28 dark
rust, rows 29 and 30 light red, rows 31-36 dark rust, rows
37 and 38 coral, rows 39-42 dark rust, rows 43 and 44 dark
red, rows 45-52 dark rust, rows 53 and 54 light red, rows
55-58 dark rust, rows 59 and 60 medium rust, rows 61-66
dark rust.

Assembly: Arrange panels in order from left to right.
Holding 2 panels with wrong sides facing and working
through both pieces, join dark red with sl st in corner, (ch 2,
sl st through both panels at top of next row) across to next
corner. Fasten off. Rep to join rem panels in same manner.

Edging: With right side facing and afghan turned to work
across long edge, join dark red with sl st in corner, (ch 2, sl
st in top of next row) across to next corner. Fasten off. Rep
to work edging across rem long edge.

Finishing: If desired, decorate afghan with fringe, tassels,
and other trims, referring to photo for inspiration.

CROCHET TOUCHÉ

*Crocheted hearts and flowers and other trims
are artfully arranged on a pure white throw
filled with everything nice.*

FINISHED SIZE

Approximately 39″ x 52″.

MATERIALS

Size 5 crochet cotton (141-yd. ball): 21 white.

Sizes 2 and 7 steel crochet hooks, or size to obtain gauge.

Size 5 pearl cotton (53-yd. ball): 1 each peach, pink, blue, violet, green; 2 yellow.

Size 5 pearl cotton (27-yd. skein): 2 each light blue, lavender, light pink; 4 light green.

Assorted buttons, ribbons, trims, and lace.

GAUGE

6 dc = 1″ with size 2 hook.

DIRECTIONS

Afghan: **Row 1** (right side): With size 2 hook and white, ch 249, dc in 4th ch from hook and ea ch across = 247 sts, turn.

Row 2 and foll even-numbered rows: Ch 1, working in ft lps only, sc in ea st across, turn.

Row 3: Ch 3 for first dc, working in both lps, dc in next st, * sk 2 dc of row 1, yo twice, insert hook from front to back around post of next row-1 dc, complete st as a tr (fptr made), fptr around post of 2nd sk dc, fptr around post of first sk dc (cable made), sk 3 sc on prev row, dc in ea of next 2 sc, rep from * across = 49 cables across, turn.

Rows 5-27 (odd-numbered rows only): Ch 3 for first dc, dc in next st, * sk 2 fptr sts, fptr around next fptr 2 rows below, fptr around 2nd sk fptr, fptr around first sk fptr, sk next 3 sc on prev row, dc in ea of next 37 sc, rep from * across, dc in ea of last 2 sc, turn.

Row 29: Ch 3 for first dc, dc in next st, * sk 2 fptr sts, fptr around next fptr 2 rows below, fptr around 2nd sk fptr, fptr around first sk fptr, sk next 3 sc on prev row, (dc in ea of next 2 sc, sk next 2 dc 2 rows below, fptr around next dc 2 rows below, fptr around 2nd sk dc, fptr around first sk dc, sk next 3 sc on prev row) 7 times, dc in ea of next 2 sts, rep from * across, turn.

Rows 30-211: (Rep rows 4-29) 7 times.

Row 212: Ch 1, working through both lps, sc in ea st across. Fasten off.

Square motif (make 1 ea peach, light green, yellow): With size 7 hook, ch 6, join with a sl st to form a ring.

Rnd 1: Ch 4 for first dc and ch 1, dc in ring, (ch 1, dc in ring) 14 times, ch 1, sl st in 3rd ch of beg ch-4.

Rnd 2: Ch 3 for first dc, 5 dc in same st, drop last lp from hook, insert hook in first st of grp, pick up dropped lp and pull through (popcorn made), ch 3, popcorn in next dc, * (ch 3, dc in next dc) twice, (ch 3, popcorn in next dc) twice, rep from * around, end with ch 3, sl st in top of beg ch-3.

Rnd 3: Ch 6 for first dc and ch 3, * dc in sp bet next 2 popcorns, ch 3, 5 dc in next sp, popcorn in next sp, ch 1, 5 dc in next sp, ch 3, rep from * around, end with 4 dc in last sp, sl st in 3rd ch of beg ch-6.

Rnd 4: Sl st into next sp, ch 5 for first dc and ch 2, * (dc, ch 3, dc) in next dc for corner, ch 2, dc in next sp, ch 3, dc in 3rd st of 5-dc grp, ch 3, dc in ch-1 of popcorn, ch 3, dc in 3rd st of 5-dc grp, ch 3, dc in next sp, ch 2, rep from * around, sl st in 3rd ch of beg ch-5.

Rnd 5: Sl st into corner ch-3 sp, ch 6 for first dc and ch 3, dc in same sp, * (ch 5, sc in next sp) 6 times, ch 5, (dc, ch 3, dc) in next corner sp, rep from * around, sl st in 3rd ch of beg ch-6.

Rnd 6: Sl st into corner sp, ch 6 for first dc and ch 3, dc in same sp, * ch 3, (sc in 3rd ch of next sp, ch 3, 3 dc in same sp) 6 times, sc in 3rd ch of next sp, ch 3, (dc, ch 3, dc) in next corner sp, rep from * around, sl st in 3rd ch of beg ch-6.

Rnd 7: Sl st into corner sp, ch 6 for first dc and ch 3, dc in same sp, * sk next sp, (ch 5, sc in next ch-3 sp) 6 times, ch 5, sk next sp, (dc, ch 3, dc) in next corner sp, rep from * around, sl st in 3rd ch of beg ch-6.

Rnd 8: Sl st into corner sp, ch 6 for first dc and ch 3, dc in same sp, * ch 3, 5 dc in next sp, ch 5, sc in next sp, (ch 7, sc in next sp) 4 times, ch 5, 5 dc in next sp, ch 3, (dc, ch 3, dc) in next corner sp, rep from * around, sl st in 3rd ch of beg ch-6.

Rnd 9: Sl st into corner sp, ch 6 for first dc and ch 3, dc in same sp, * ch 3, 3 dc in next sp, ch 5, sk 5-dc grp, 3 dc in next sp, (ch 3, dc in next lp) 4 times, ch 3, 3 dc in next sp, ch 5, sk 5-dc grp, 3 dc in next sp, ch 3, (dc, ch 3, dc) in next corner sp, rep from * around, sl st in 3rd ch of beg ch-6. Fasten off.

Shell st motif (make 1 ea using colors as foll): Rows 1-17 light blue. Rows 1, 3, 5, 7, 9, 11, 13, and 15 yellow; rows 2,

4, 6, 8, 10, 12, 14, 16, and 17 green. Rows 1-2, 5-6, 9-10, and 13-14 lavender; rows 3-4, 7-8, 11-12, and 15-17 pink.

Row 1: With size 7 hook, ch 47, dc in 4th ch from hook and ea ch across = 45 sts, turn.

Row 2: Ch 4, * 4 dc in same st, sk next 4 sts, sc in next st, ch 7, sk next 4 sts, sc in next st, ch 3, rep from * 3 times more, 4 dc in same st, sk next 3 sts, sc in next st, turn.

Row 3: Ch 10, sk next 4-dc grp, * sc in next ch-3 sp, ch 3, 4 dc in same sp, sc in 4th ch of next ch-7 lp, ch 7, sk next 3 ch and 4-dc grp, rep from * 3 times more, dc in last ch-3 sp, turn.

Row 4: Ch 4, 4 dc in dc just made, * sc in 4th ch of next lp, ch 7, sk next 3 ch and 4-dc grp, sc in next ch-3 sp, ch 3, 4 dc in same sp, rep from * 3 times more, sc in 4th ch of next lp, turn.

Rows 5-15: Rep rows 3 and 4 alternately, ending after row 3.

Row 16: Ch 6, * sc in 4th ch of next lp, ch 4, sc in next ch-3 sp, ch 4, rep from * 3 times more, sc in 4th ch of next lp, turn.

Row 17: Ch 3 for first dc, dc in ea ch and sc across = 45 sts. Fasten off.

Heart motif (make 1 ea yellow, pink, blue): With size 7 hook, ch 121, sl st in 3rd ch from hook for picot, sk next 2 ch, (hdc in ea of next 3 ch, ch 3, sl st in top of last hdc for picot) twice, (2 hdc in next ch, hdc in next ch, picot) 7 times, (hdc in ea of next 3 ch, picot, 2 hdc in next ch, hdc in next ch, picot) twice, (hdc in ea of next 3 ch, picot) 7 times, hdc in next ch, (2 hdc, picot, hdc) in next ch for bottom point of heart, hdc in ea of next 2 ch, picot, (hdc in ea of next 3 ch, picot) 7 times, (hdc in next ch, 2 hdc in next ch, picot, hdc in ea of next 3 ch, picot) twice, (hdc in next ch, 2 hdc in next ch, picot) 7 times, (hdc in ea of next 3 ch, picot) 5 times, hdc in last ch. Fasten off.

Small flower (make 1 light blue; 2 ea light green, yellow, pink, lavender): **Rnd 1:** With size 7 hook, ch 2, 8 sc in first ch, sl st in first sc.

Rnd 2: Ch 3, 3 dc in same st, ch 3, sl st in same st, * (sl st, ch 3, 3 dc, ch 3, sl st) in next st, rep from * around, sl st in first sl st. Fasten off.

Large flower (make 1 ea using colors as foll): Rnds 1-11 violet, rnd 12 and rows 1-7 green. Rnds 1-11 yellow, rnd 12 and rows 1-7 green. Rnds 1-11 light pink, rnd 12 and rows 1-7 light green.

Rnd 1: With size 7 hook, ch 2, 8 sc in first ch, sl st in first sc.

Rnd 2: Ch 3, working in ft lps only, (3 dc, ch 3, sl st) in same st, [sl st in next st, (sl st, ch 3, 3 dc, ch 3, sl st) in next st] 3 times, sl st in next st, sl st in base of beg ch-3 = 4 petals.

Rnd 3: (Ch 1, sc in unworked bk lp of same st as petal, ch 1, sc in sl st bet petals) around, sl st in first sc.

Rnd 4: Rep rnd 2.

Rnd 5: (Ch 1, 2 sc in unworked bk lp of same st as petal, sc in sl st bet petals) around, sl st in first sc = 12 sts.

Rnd 6: Ch 3, working in ft lps only, (3 dc, ch 3, sl st) in same st, [(sl st, ch 3, 3 dc, ch 3, sl st) in next st] 11 times, sl st in first sl st.

Rnd 7: Ch 1, (2 sc in unworked bk lp of same st as petal, sc in bk lp of ea of next 2 sc) around, sl st in first sc = 16 sts.

Rnd 8: Ch 4, working in ft lps only, (3 tr, ch 4, sl st) in same st, [sl st in next st, (sl st, ch 4, 3 tr, ch 4, sl st) in next st] around, sl st in next st, sl st in first sl st.

Rnd 9: Ch 1, (2 sc in unworked bk lp of same st as petal, sc in bk lp of ea of next 3 sc) around, sl st in first sc = 20 sts.

Rnd 10: Ch 4, working in ft lps only, (3 tr, ch 4, sl st) in same st, [sl st in next st, (sl st, ch 4, 3 tr, ch 4, sl st) in same st] around, sl st in next st, sl st in first sl st.

Rnd 11: Ch 1, sc in unworked bk lp of ea st around, sl st in first sc. Fasten off.

Leaves: Rnd 12: With size 7 hook, join yarn with sl st in any sc of last rnd of flower, ch 3 for first dc, dc in same st, 2 dc in ea of next 19 sts, sl st in top of beg ch-3.

Row 1: Ch 3 for first dc, 2 dc in next st, dc in ea of next 4 sts, 2 dc in next st, dc in next st, turn.

Row 2: Ch 3 for first dc, dc in ea of next 9 sts, turn.

Row 3: Ch 2 for first hdc, keeping last lp of ea st on hook, dc in ea of next 2 sts, yo and pull through all lps on hook (dc dec made), dc in ea of next 4 sts, dc dec over next 2 sts, hdc in last st, turn.

Row 4: Ch 2 for first hdc, dc dec over next 2 sts, dc in ea of next 2 sts, dc dec over next 2 sts, hdc in last st, turn.

Row 5: Ch 2 for first hdc, (dc dec over next 2 sts) twice, hdc in last st, turn.

Row 6: Ch 2 for first hdc, dc dec over next 2 sts, hdc in last st, turn.

Row 7: Ch 2 for first hdc, hdc in last st. Fasten off.

(Join yarn in next rnd-12′st of flower and rep rows 1-7) 4 times.

Finishing: Referring to photo, stitch crocheted motifs and other trims to afghan as desired.

PASTEL PATCHWORK

To make this quilt-like afghan, follow the color placement shown in the crochet chart or work the pink, aqua, and yellow patches as desired.

FINISHED SIZE

Approximately 38" x 58", not including edging.

MATERIALS

Sportweight mercerized cotton (109-yd. ball): 21 aqua, 8 pink, 6 yellow.

Size G crochet hook, or size to obtain gauge.

GAUGE

5 shells and 7 rows = 4".

DIRECTIONS

Note: Afghan is worked diagonally according to chart. Read odd-numbered rows from right to left and even-numbered rows from left to right, beginning in lower right-hand corner of chart. Each symbol on chart represents 1 shell.

Afghan: **Row 1:** With aqua, ch 4, 2 dc in 4th ch from hook, turn.

Row 2: Ch 3 for first dc, 2 dc in first st, ch 1, 3 dc in last st (shell made), turn.

Row 3: Ch 3 for first dc, 2 dc in first st, ch 1, 3-dc shell in ch-1 sp, ch 1, 3-dc shell in last st, turn.

Row 4: Ch 3 for first dc, 2 dc in first st, (ch 1, 3-dc shell in next sp) twice, ch 1, 3-dc shell in last st, turn.

Row 5: Ch 3 for first dc, 2 dc in first st, (ch 1, 3-dc shell in next sp) across, ch 1, 3-dc shell in last st, turn.

Rows 6-62: Work according to chart, rep row 5 for pat and changing colors as indicated = 62 shells after row 62.

Row 63: Ch 3 for first dc, 2 dc in first st, (ch 1, 3-dc shell in next sp) across to last sp, ch 1, keeping last lp of ea st on hook, work 2 dc in last sp, yo and pull through all lps on hook (2-dc dec made), tr in next st, turn = 62 shells.

Row 64: Ch 4 for first tr, 2-dc dec in next sp, (ch 1, 3-dc shell in next sp) across, 3-dc shell in last st, turn = 62 shells.

Rows 65-92: Rep rows 63 and 64 alternately.

Row 93: Ch 4 for first tr, 2-dc dec in next sp, (ch 1, 3-dc shell in next sp) across to last sp, 2-dc dec in last sp, tr in next st, turn = 61 shells.

Rows 94-152: Rep row 93.

Row 153: Ch 3 for first dc, keeping last lp of ea st on hook, dc in next sp, dc in next tr, yo and pull through all lps on hook. Fasten off.

Edging: **Rnd 1:** With right side facing and afghan turned to work across short edge, join pink with sl st in corner, ch 3 for first dc, 2 dc in same st, * (ch 1, 3-dc shell in side of next row) to corner, ch 1, 3-dc shell in corner st, rep from * around, end with sl st in top of beg ch-3 = 61 shells across ea short edge and 91 shells across ea long edge.

Rnd 2: Ch 6 for first dc and ch 3, dc in next sp, * (ch 3, dc in next sp) to next corner shell, ch 3, (dc, ch 3, dc) in center st of corner shell (V-st made), rep from * around, end with sl st in 3rd ch of beg ch-6 = 63 sps across ea short edge and 93 sps across ea long edge. Fasten off.

Rnd 3: Join aqua with sl st in corner sp, ch 3 for first dc, 2 dc in same sp, (sc in next sp, 6-dc shell in next sp) around, end with 3 dc in beg corner, sl st in top of beg ch-3 = 31 shells across ea short edge and 46 shells across ea long edge.

Rnd 4: Ch 6 for first dc and ch 3, dc in same st, V-st in next st, dc in next st, * sc in next sc, dc in next st, V-st in ea of next 4 sts, dc in next st (scallop made), rep from * around, end with V-st in ea of 2 sts, sl st in 3rd ch of beg ch-6, sl st into next dc.

Rnd 5: Sc bet next 2 dc, * (ch 5, sk across to center of next scallop, sc bet center 2 dc of scallop) to corner scallop, ch 5, sk 3 dc of corner scallop, sc bet next 2 dc, sk next 4 dc, sc bet next 2 dc on same scallop, rep from * around, end with sl st in first sc.

Rnd 6: Ch 1, (8 dc in next lp, sc in next sc) around, sl st in beg ch-1.

Rnd 7: Ch 1, * dc in next dc, V-st in ea of next 6 sts, dc in next dc, sc in next sc, rep from * around, end with sl st in beg ch-1.

Rnd 8: Turn to wrong side, sl st in ea of next 6 sts, sl st bet next 2 dc, turn back to right side, ch 1, sc in same st, * (ch 5, sk across to center of next scallop, sc bet center 2 dc of scallop) to corner scallop, ch 5, sk 3 dc of corner scallop, sc bet next 2 dc, (sk 4 dc, sc bet next 2 dc on same scallop) twice, rep from * around, end with sl st in first sc.

Rnds 9 and 10: Rep rnds 6 and 7. Fasten off after rnd 10.

Color Key

●	Aqua
○	Pink
·	Yellow

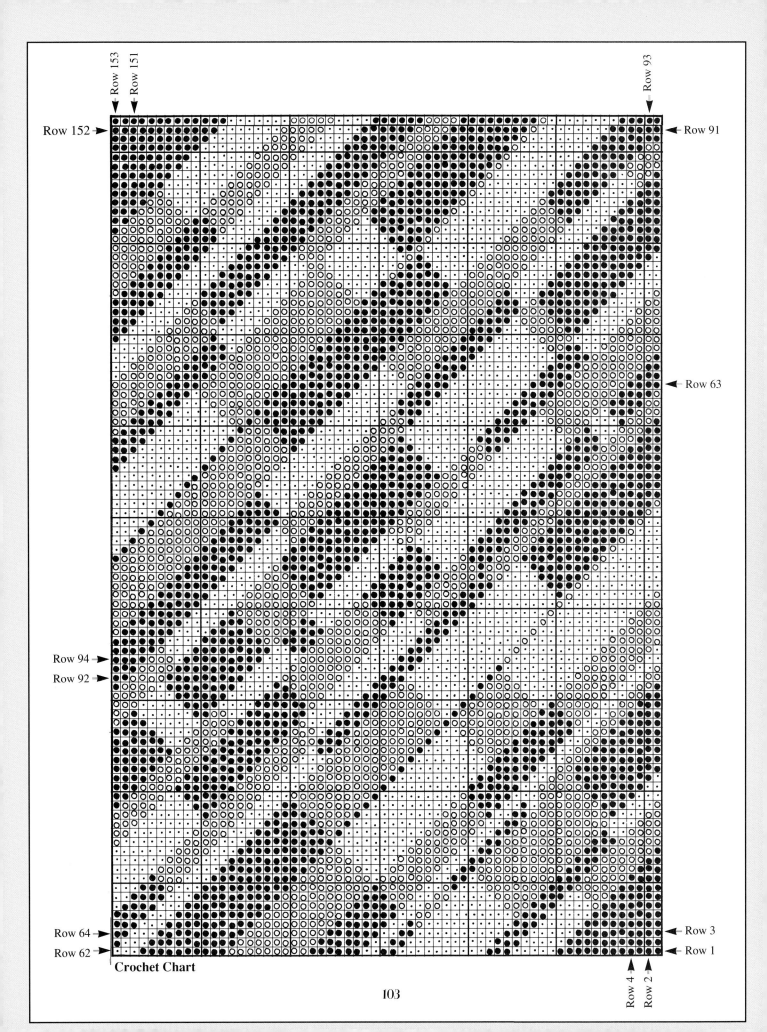

Crochet Chart

WISTERIA ARBOR

*Display this flower-filled arbor done in
cross-stitch and transform any room into
a peaceful and graceful setting.*

FINISHED SIZE
Approximately 55″ x 78″.

MATERIALS
Sportweight acrylic (175-yd. ball): 20 white.
Size I (14″-long) afghan hook, or size to obtain gauge.
Paternayan Persian wool (8-yd. skein): see color key on page 107.
Size G crochet hook.

GAUGE
8 sts and 7 rows = 2″ in afghan st.

DIRECTIONS
Note: See page 141 for afghan st instructions.

Center panel (make 1): With white, ch 111, work 155 rows afghan st. Sl st in ea vertical bar across. Do not fasten off last lp.

Border: With size G crochet hook, ch 1, work 2 sc in same st, * sc in ea st to next corner, 3 sc in corner, rep from * around, sc in beg corner, sl st in first sc. Fasten off.

Side panel (make 2): With white, ch 44, work 155 rows afghan st. Sl st in ea vertical bar across. Work border as for center panel. Fasten off.

End panel (make 2): With white, ch 111, work 44 rows afghan st. Sl st in ea vertical bar across. Work border as for center panel. Fasten off.

Corner panel (make 4): With white, ch 44, work 44 rows afghan st. Sl st in ea vertical bar across. Work border as for center panel. Fasten off.

Assembly: With last row of afghan stitch at top of each panel, whipstitch panels together.

Edging: **Rnd 1:** With wrong side facing and afghan turned to work across short edge, use size G crochet hook to join white with sl st in corner, * sc in ea st to next corner, (sc, ch 1, sc) in corner, rep from * around, sl st in first sc, turn.

Rnd 2 (right side): Sl st into ch-1 sp, ch 4 for first dc and ch 1, (dc, ch 1, dc) in same sp, * (ch 1, sk next st, dc in next st) across to next corner, (dc, ch 1) 4 times in corner sp, dc in same sp, rep from * around, ch 1, (dc, ch 1) twice in beg corner sp, sl st in 3rd ch of beg ch-4 = 86 dc across ea short edge and 126 dc across ea long edge (not including corner grps).

Rnd 3: Sl st into next ch-1 sp, ch 2, (yo and pull up a lp) 4 times in next st, yo and pull through all lps on hook (puff made), * ch 1, puff in next sp, rep from * around, end with ch 1, sl st in top of beg puff.

Rnd 4: Sl st backward into prev sp, ch 4 for first dc and ch 1, (dc, ch 1, dc) in same sp, ch 1, * (dc in ch-1 sp bet puffs, ch 1) to next corner sp, (dc, ch 1) 5 times in corner sp, rep from * around, end with (dc, ch 1) twice in beg corner sp, sl st in 3rd ch of beg ch-4.

Rnd 5: Sl st into next sp, ch 2, (puff, ch 3, puff) in same sp, ch 3, * sc in next sp, ch 3, sk next sp, (puff, ch 3, puff) in next sp, ch 3, sk next sp, rep from * across to corner section, sc in first sp of corner section, ch 3, [(puff, ch 3, puff) in next sp, ch 3] twice, rep from * around as est, end with sl st in top of beg puff.

Rnd 6: Sl st into next sp, ch 2, (puff, ch 3, puff, ch 3, puff) in same sp, * ch 3, sc in next sc, ch 3, (puff, ch 3, puff, ch 3, puff) in sp bet next 2 puffs, rep from * to center corner sp, sk center ch-3 sp of corner, ch 1, (puff, ch 3, puff, ch 3, puff) in next sp bet puffs, rep from * around as est, end with sl st in top of beg puff.

Rnd 7: Sl st into next sp, ch 2, (puff, ch 3, puff) in same sp, ch 3, (puff, ch 3, puff) in next sp bet puffs, ch 3, sc in next sc, * [ch 3, (puff, ch 3, puff) in next sp bet puffs] twice **, ch 3, sc in next sc, rep from * to corner ch-1 sp, ending last rep at **, sk ch-1 sp, [(puff, ch 3, puff) in next sp bet puffs, ch 3] twice, sc in next sc, rep from * around, sl st in top of beg puff.

Rnd 8: Sl st into next sp, (sc, 5 dc, sc) in same sp, (sc, 5 dc, sc) in ea of next 2 sps, * sc in ea of next 2 ch-3 sps, (sc, 5 dc, sc) in ea of next 3 sps, rep from * around, end with sl st in first sc. Fasten off.

Cross-stitch: Stitch design with 2 strands of wool. Referring to photo and charts on pages 106-113 for positioning, stitch designs on panels as specified.

Top

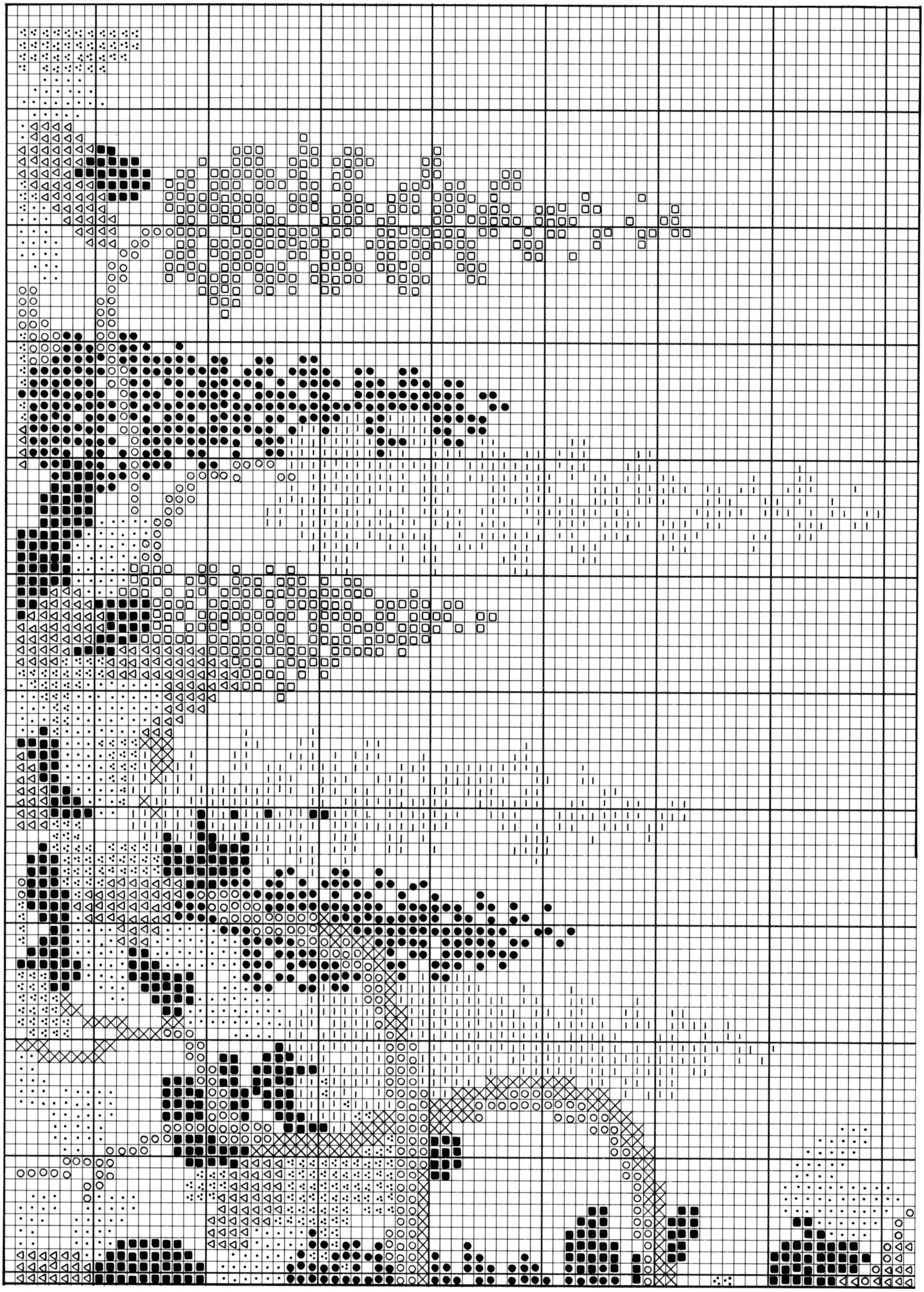

Color Key

Paternayan Persian Wool
(used for sample)

–	303	Violet (9)
□	322	Plum (4)
●	312	Grape (6)
∴	662	Pine Green (12)
•	612	Hunter Green-lt. (11)
△	611	Hunter Green-med. (7)
■	610	Hunter Green-dk. (11)
○	463	Beige Brown-lt. (7)
✕	462	Beige Brown-med. (4)

Note: The number of 8-yd. skeins required for each color is indicated in parentheses.

Cross-stitch Chart
Center Panel

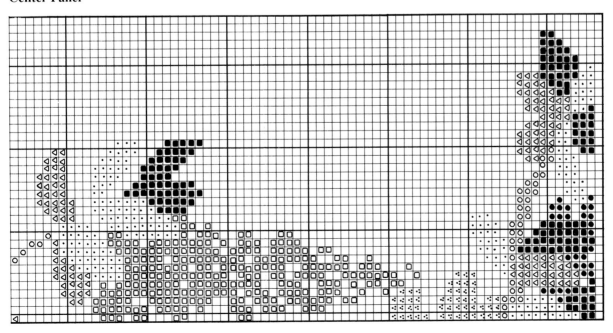

Top

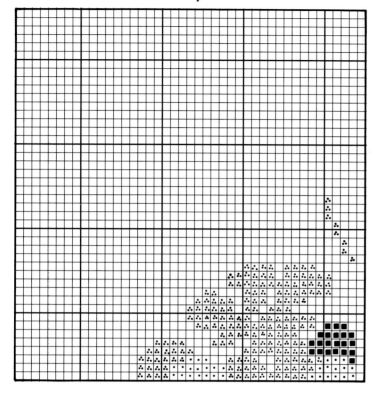

Cross-stitch Chart
Top Left Corner Panel

Top

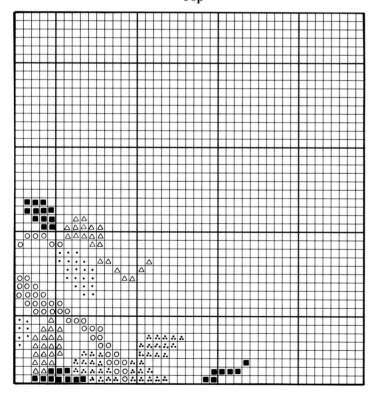

Cross-stitch Chart
Top Right Corner Panel

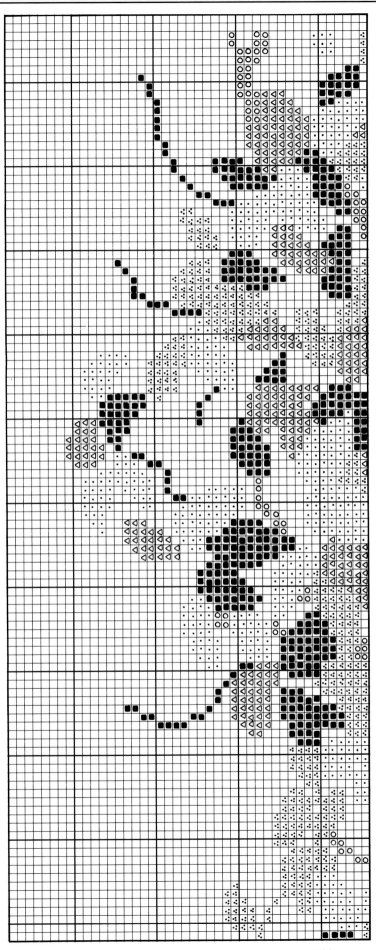

Color Key

Paternayan Persian Wool (used for sample)

−	303	Violet (9)
□	322	Plum (4)
●	312	Grape (6)
∴	662	Pine Green (12)
·	612	Hunter Green-lt. (11)
△	611	Hunter Green-med. (7)
■	610	Hunter Green-dk. (11)
O	463	Beige Brown-lt. (7)
X	462	Beige Brown-med. (4)

Note: The number of 8-yd. skeins required for each color is indicated in parentheses.

**Cross-stitch Chart
Top End Panel**

Top

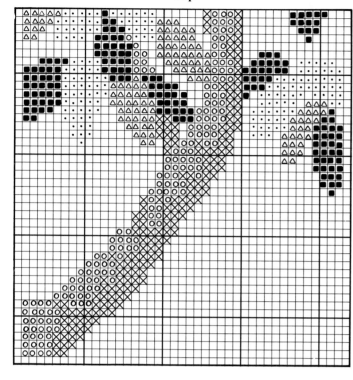

**Cross-stitch Chart
Bottom Left Corner Panel**

Top

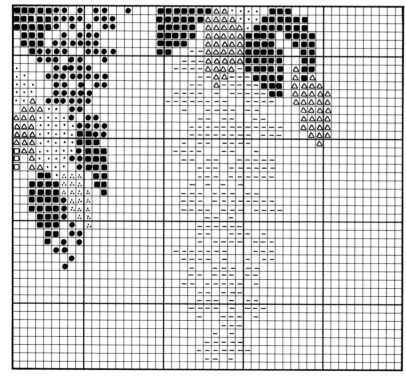

**Cross-stitch Chart
Bottom End Panel**

110

Top

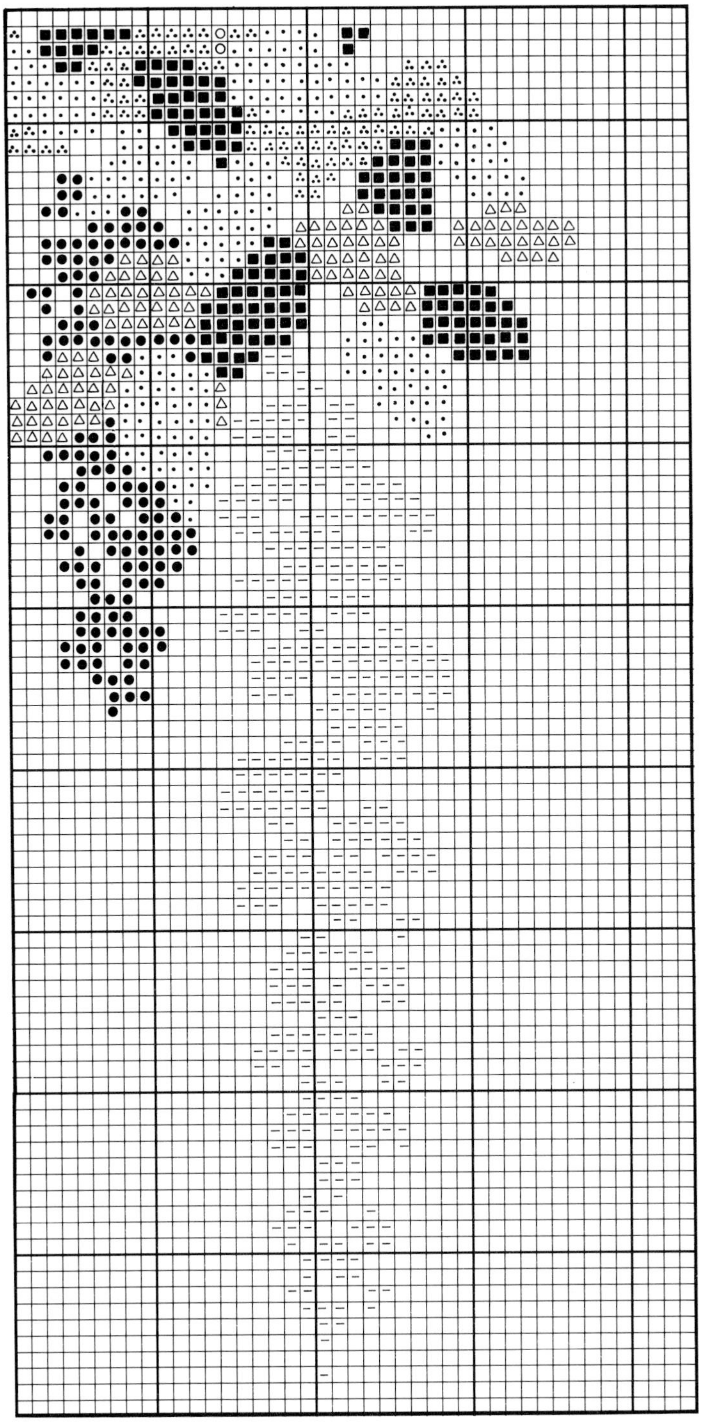

Color Key

**Paternayan Persian Wool
(used for sample)**

−	303	Violet (9)
□	322	Plum (4)
●	312	Grape (6)
∴	662	Pine Green (12)
·	612	Hunter Green-lt. (11)
△	611	Hunter Green-med. (7)
■	610	Hunter Green-dk. (11)
○	463	Beige Brown-lt. (7)
⊠	462	Beige Brown-med. (4)

Note: The number of 8-yd. skeins required for each color is indicated in parentheses.

**Cross-stitch Chart
Right Side Panel**

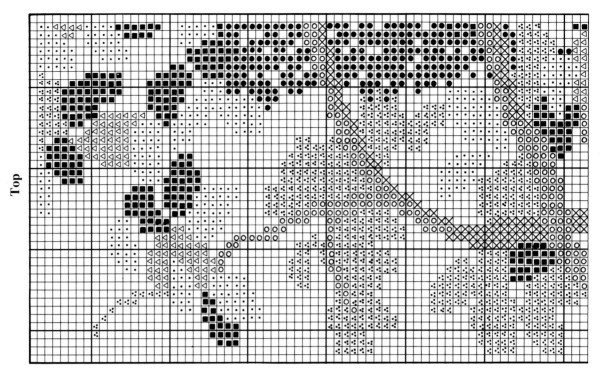

Cross-stitch Chart
Left Side Panel

Top

Color Key

Paternayan Persian Wool
(used for sample)

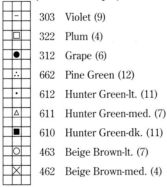

–	303	Violet (9)
▫	322	Plum (4)
●	312	Grape (6)
∴	662	Pine Green (12)
•	612	Hunter Green-lt. (11)
△	611	Hunter Green-med. (7)
■	610	Hunter Green-dk. (11)
○	463	Beige Brown-lt. (7)
✕	462	Beige Brown-med. (4)

Note: The number of 8-yd. skeins required for each color is indicated in parentheses.

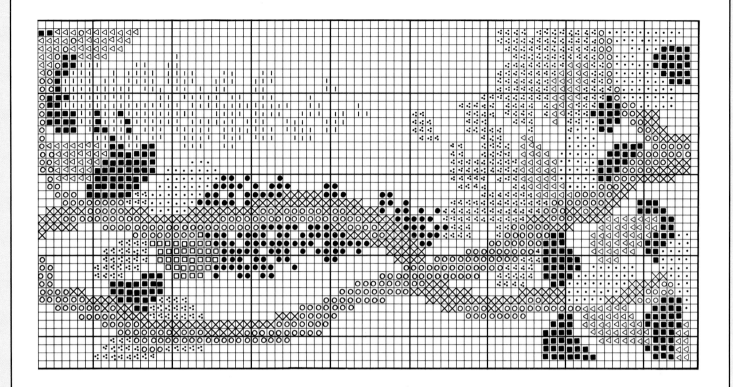

113

HINTS OF AUTUMN

The yarns in this lovely throw display all the rich reds, golds, and greens that herald the coming of fall.

FINISHED SIZE

Approximately 48″ x 70″.

MATERIALS

Worsted-weight cotton (70-yd. skein): 4 brown, 6 gold, 10 green.

Sportweight mohair-acrylic-wool blend (137-yd. ball): 10 dark green with gold accents.

Size G crochet hook, or size to obtain gauge.

GAUGE

Square = 9″.

DIRECTIONS

Square (make 24): **First square:** With brown, ch 4, join with a sl st to form a ring.

Rnd 1: Ch 1, 7 sc in ring, sl st in beg ch-1.

Rnd 2: Ch 4 for first sc and ch 3, sc in next st, (ch 3, sc in next st) 6 times, tr in first ch of beg ch-4.

Rnd 3: Ch 3 for first dc, 4 dc in same lp, ch 3, sl st in 3rd ch from hook to make a picot, (5 dc in next lp, ch-3 picot) 7 times, sl st in top of beg ch-3. Fasten off.

Rnd 4: Join dark green with sl st in last sl st, ch 4 for first tr, tr in next dc, 5 dc in next dc, drop last lp from hook, insert hook in first st of grp, pick up dropped lp and pull through, ch 1 (popcorn made), keeping last lp of ea st on hook, tr in ea of next 2 sts, yo and pull through all lps on hook (2-tr cl made), * ch 5, 2-tr cl over next 2 dc, popcorn in next dc, 2-tr cl over next 2 dc, rep from * around, end with sl st in top of beg ch-4. Fasten off.

Rnd 5: Join gold with sl st in any ch-5 lp, ch 1, (4 sc, ch-3 picot, 4 sc) in same lp, * ch 6, sl st in 3rd ch from hook to make a picot, ch 3, (4 sc, ch-3 picot, 4 sc) in next lp, rep from * around, sl st in first sc. Fasten off.

Rnd 6: Join green with sl st in ch-3 picot bet 4-sc grps, ch 4 for first tr, 2-tr cl in same picot, ch 3, 3-dc cl in same picot for corner, * ch 3, sc in next picot, ch 3, sc in next sc, ch 3, sc in next picot, ch 3, sk 3 sc, sc in next sc, ch 3, sc in next picot, ch 3, (3-dc cl, ch 3, 3-tr cl, ch 3, 3-dc cl) in next picot for corner, rep from * around, end with 3-dc cl in beg picot, ch 3, sl st in top of beg ch-4. Fasten off.

Rnd 7: Join dark green with sl st in last sl st, ch 3 for first dc, 2 dc in same st, [* 3 dc in ea of next 2 ch-3 sps, (popcorn, ch 3, popcorn, ch 3, popcorn) in next ch-3 sp, rep from * once more, 3 dc in ea of next 2 ch-3 sps, (3 dc, popcorn, 3 dc) in corner 2-tr cl] around, sl st in top of beg ch-3. Fasten off.

Rnd 8: Join green with sc in corner popcorn, * (ch 5, sk next 3-dc grp, sc bet next 2 sts) twice, [ch 5, sk 3-dc grp and popcorn, pull up a lp in ea of next 2 ch-3 sps, yo and pull through all lps on hook (sc dec made), ch 5, sk popcorn and 3-dc grp, sc bet next 2 sts] twice, ch 5, sk 3-dc grp, sc bet next 2 sts, ch 5, (sc, ch 5, sc) in next corner popcorn, rep from * around, sl st in first sc. Fasten off.

2nd square: Rep rnds 1-7 as for first square.

Rnd 8 (joining rnd): Rep rnd 7 of first square to 3rd corner, sc in corner popcorn, ch 2, sl st in corner ch-5 lp on first square, ch 2, sc in same corner popcorn on 2nd square, * (ch 2, sl st in next ch-5 lp on first square, ch 2, sk 3-dc grp, sc bet next 2 sts on 2nd square) twice, [ch 2, sl st in next ch-5 lp on first square, ch 2, sk 3-dc grp and popcorn, sc dec over next 2 ch-3 sps on 2nd square, ch 2, sl st in next ch-5 lp on first square, ch 2, sk popcorn and 3-dc grp, sc bet next 2 sts on 2nd square] twice, ch 2, sl st in next lp on first square, ch 2, sk 3-dc grp on 2nd square, sc bet next 2 sts on 2nd square, ch 2, sc in next ch-5 lp on first square, ch 2, sc in corner popcorn on 2nd square, ch 2, sl st in corner lp on first square, ch 2, sc in same corner popcorn on 2nd square. Fasten off.

Cont to make and join squares as est for a throw 4 squares wide and 6 squares long.

Edging: **Rnd 1:** Join green with sc in any corner lp, ch 5, sc in same lp, * ch 5, sc in ea lp to next corner, (sc, ch 5, sc) in corner lp, rep from * around, sl st in first sc. Fasten off.

Rnds 2-4: Rep rnd 1, working 1 rnd ea gold, green, brown.

Rnd 5: With afghan turned to work across long edge, join green with sl st in corner lp, ch 4 for first tr, (2-tr cl, ch 3, 3-dc cl) in same lp, * (3-dc cl, ch 3, 3-dc cl) in next lp, ch 3, sc in next lp, ch 5, sc in next lp, ch 3 **, rep from * 4 times more, [(3-dc cl, ch 3, 3-dc cl) in next lp, rep from * to ** 3 times] 3 times, (3-dc cl, ch 3, 3-dc cl) in next lp, rep from * to ** 5 times, (3-dc cl, ch 3, 3-dc cl) in next lp, (3-dc cl, ch 3, 3-tr cl, ch 3, 3-dc cl) in corner lp, rep from * to ** 5 times, (3-dc cl, ch 3, 3-dc cl) in next lp, rep from * to ** 3 times, (3-dc cl, ch 3, 3-dc cl) in next lp, rep from * to ** 5 times, (3-dc cl, ch 3, 3-dc cl) in next lp, work corner as before, cont around afghan as est, end with 3-dc cl in beg corner lp, sl st in top of beg ch-4. Fasten off.

QUIET DAYDREAMS

Spend a quiet afternoon lost in a dreamworld inspired by this lavender, blue, and sparkling metallic throw.

FINISHED SIZE

Approximately 44″ x 64″.

MATERIALS

Worsted-weight cotton (93-yd. skein): 6 blue.
Bulky-weight viscose-wool blend metallic bouclé (72-yd. ball): 10 variegated blue/purple/pink/metallic.
Worsted-weight cotton (70-yd. skein): 12 lavender.
Size H crochet hook, or size to obtain gauge.

GAUGE

Panel B: 4 sts = 1″.

DIRECTIONS

Panel A: With first color, ch 168.

Row 1: Sc in 12th ch from hook, (ch 5, sk 5 ch, sc in next ch) across, turn = 27 lps.

Row 2: Ch 2 for first hdc, 5 hdc in first lp, (sc in next sc, 5 hdc in next lp) across, sc in last st, turn. Fasten off.

Row 3: Join next color with sc in last sc of row 2, (ch 5, sk 5 hdc, sc in next sc) across, turn.

Row 4: Ch 2 for first hdc, 5 hdc in first lp, (sc in next sc, 5 hdc in next lp) across, sc in last st, turn. Fasten off.

Rep rows 3 and 4 alternately, using colors as specified below. Fasten off after last row.

Row	A1 (make 2)	A2 (make 1)	A3 (make 1)
1-2	Blue	Blue	Blue
3-4	Lavender	Variegated	Variegated
5-6	Variegated	Lavender	Lavender
7-8	Blue	Blue	Blue
9-10	Variegated	Blue	Blue
11-12	Lavender	Lavender	Lavender
13-14	Blue	Blue	Blue
15-16	Blue	Variegated	Variegated
17-18	Lavender	Blue	
19-20	Blue	Lavender	
21-22	Variegated	Variegated	
23-24	Blue	Blue	
25-26	Lavender	Variegated	
27-28	Variegated	Lavender	
29-30	Blue	Blue	
31-32		Blue	
33-34		Lavender	

Panel B (make 4): With lavender, ch 162.

Note: Carry color not in use across the row by working over it with the next few sts. To change colors, work last yo of ea dc with new color.

Row 1: Join variegated, dc in 2nd ch from hook, dc in next ch, * drop variegated, pick up lavender, sc in next ch, drop lavender, pick up variegated, dc in ea of next 2 ch, rep from * across, drop variegated, turn.

Row 2: Pick up lavender, ch 3 for first dc, dc in next dc, * drop lavender, pick up variegated, dc in next sc, drop variegated, pick up lavender, dc in ea of next 2 dc, rep from * across, drop lavender, pick up variegated, dc in last st, drop variegated, turn.

Row 3: Pick up lavender, ch 2, * drop lavender, pick up variegated, dc in ea of next 2 dc, drop variegated, pick up lavender, sc in next dc, rep from * across, drop lavender, pick up variegated, dc in ea of last 2 sts, drop variegated, turn.

Rows 4-6: Rep rows 2 and 3 alternately, ending after row 2. Fasten off.

Assembly: With blue, whipstitch panels together in the following order from bottom to top: A1, B, A2, B, A3, B, A1, B.

Edging: **Rnd 1:** With right side facing and afghan turned to work across long edge of panel B, join variegated yarn in corner, ch 1, * sc in ea st to corner, (sc, ch 1, sc) in corner, rep from * around, sl st in beg ch-1. Ch 6, sk 5 sts, (sc in next st, ch 5) across to corner ch-1 sp, sc in corner sp = 27 lps. Fasten off.

HAVEN OF BLUE

*Velvety mohair yarns in calming shades
of blue become an afghan to harbor
you on cool evenings.*

FINISHED SIZE
Approximately 45″ x 50″.

MATERIALS
Worsted-weight wool (175-yd. skein): 9 blue tweed (A).
Sportweight wool (136-yd. ball): 6 dark blue (B).
Worsted-weight mohair-wool blend (99-yd. ball): 4 dark blue (C).
Worsted-weight wool (110-yd. ball): 2 medium blue (D).
Size H crochet hook, or size to obtain gauge.

GAUGE
7 sc = 2″.

DIRECTIONS
Panel (make 5): **Row 1:** With A, ch 16, sc in 2nd ch from hook and ea ch across = 16 sts, turn.

Row 2: Ch 1, sc in ea st across, turn.

Rows 3-7: Ch 2, sc in 2nd ch from hook (inc made), sc in ea st across, turn = 21 sts after row 7.

Row 8: Ch 2, sc in 2nd ch from hook and ea of next 9 sts, (yo and pull up a lp) 5 times in next st, yo and pull through all lps on hook (puff made), sc in ea of next 11 sts = 22 sts, turn.

Row 9: Ch 1, sc in ea of next 21 sts, sk last st = 21 sts, turn.

Rows 10-14: Ch 1, sc in ea st to last st, sk last st, turn = 16 sts after row 14.

Row 15: Ch 1, sc in ea st across, turn.

Rows 16-21: Ch 2, sc in 2nd ch from hook and ea of next 16 sts, turn = 22 sts after row 21.

Row 22: Ch 1, sc in ea of next 10 sts, puff in next st, sc in ea of next 10 sts, sk last st = 21 sts, turn.

Row 23: Ch 1, sc in ea of next 20 sts, sk last st, turn.

Row 24: Ch 1, sc in ea of next 7 sts, puff in next st, sc in ea of next 3 sts, puff in next st, sc in ea of next 7 sts, sk last st = 19 sts, turn.

Row 25: Ch 1, sc in ea of next 18 sts, sk last st = 18 sts, turn.

Row 26: Ch 1, (sc in ea of next 5 sts, puff in next st) twice, sc in ea of next 5 sts, sk last st = 17 sts, turn.

Row 27: Ch 1, sc in ea of next 16 sts, sk last st = 16 sts, turn.

Row 28: Ch 1, sc in ea of next 4 sts, puff in next st, sc in ea of next 5 sts, puff in next st, sc in ea of next 5 sts = 16 sts, turn.

Row 29: Ch 2, sc in 2nd ch from hook and ea of next 16 sts = 17 sts, turn.

Row 30: Ch 2, sc in 2nd ch from hook and ea of next 4 sts, puff in next st, sc in ea of next 5 sts, puff in next st, sc in ea of next 6 sts = 18 sts, turn.

Row 31: Ch 2, sc in 2nd ch from hook and ea of next 18 sts = 19 sts, turn.

Row 32: Ch 2, sc in 2nd ch from hook and ea of next 6 sts, puff in next st, sc in ea of next 3 sts, puff in next st, sc in ea of next 8 sts = 20 sts, turn.

Row 33: Ch 2, sc in 2nd ch from hook and ea of next 20 sts = 21 sts, turn.

Row 34: Ch 2, sc in 2nd ch from hook and ea of next 9 sts, puff in next st, sc in ea of next 11 sts = 22 sts, turn.

Rows 35-40: Ch 1, sc in ea st to last st, sk last st, turn = 16 sts after row 40.

Row 41: Ch 1, sc in ea st across, turn.

Rows 42-45: Ch 2, sc in 2nd ch from hook and ea st across, turn = 20 sts after row 45.

Row 46: Ch 2, sc in 2nd ch from hook and ea of next 9 sts, puff in next st, sc in ea of next 10 sts = 21 sts, turn.

Row 47: Ch 2, sc in 2nd ch from hook and ea of next 21 sts = 22 sts, turn.

Rows 48-53: Ch 1, sc in ea st to last st, sk last st, turn = 16 sts after row 53.

Row 54: Ch 1, sc in ea st across, turn.

Rows 55-59: Ch 2, sc in 2nd ch from hook and ea st across, turn = 21 sts after row 59.

Row 60: Ch 2, sc in 2nd ch from hook and ea of next 9 sts, puff in next st, sc in ea of next 11 sts = 22 sts, turn.

Row 61: Ch 1, sc in ea of next 21 sts, sk last st = 21 sts, turn.

Row 62: Ch 1, sc in ea of next 7 sts, puff in next st, sc in ea of next 3 sts, puff in next st, sc in ea of next 8 sts, sk last st = 20 sts, turn.

Row 63: Ch 1, sc in ea of next 19 sts, sk last st = 19 sts, turn.

Row 64: Ch 1, (sc in ea of next 5 sts, puff in next st) twice, sc in ea of next 6 sts, sk last st = 18 sts, turn.

Row 65: Ch 1, sc in ea of next 17 sts, sk last st = 17 sts, turn.

Row 66: Ch 1, sc in ea of next 4 sts, puff in next st, sc in ea of next 5 sts, puff in next st, sc in ea of next 5 sts, sk last st = 16 sts, turn.

Row 67: Ch 1, sc in ea st across, turn.

Row 68: Ch 2, sc in 2nd ch from hook and ea of next 4 sts, puff in next st, sc in ea of next 5 sts, puff in next st, sc in ea of next 5 sts = 17 sts, turn.

Row 69: Ch 2, sc in 2nd ch from hook and ea of next 17 sts = 18 sts, turn.

Row 70: Ch 2, sc in 2nd ch from hook and ea of next 6 sts, puff in next st, sc in ea of next 3 sts, puff in next st, sc in ea of next 7 sts = 19 sts, turn.

Row 71: Ch 2, sc in 2nd ch from hook and ea of next 19 sts = 20 sts, turn.

Row 72: Ch 2, sc in 2nd ch from hook and ea of next 9 sts, puff in next st, sc in ea of next 10 sts = 21 sts, turn.

Row 73: Ch 2, sc in 2nd ch from hook and ea of next 21 sts = 22 sts, turn.

Rows 74-79: Ch 1, sc in ea st to last st, sk last st, turn = 16 sts after row 79.

Row 80: Ch 1, sc in ea st across, turn.

Rows 81-158: Rep rows 3-80.

Rows 159-172: Rep rows 3-16. Fasten off.

Edging: **Row 1:** With right side facing and panel turned to work across long edge, join B in side of first row, ch 4 for first tr, tr in side of ea of next 2 rows, (dc in ea of next 2 sts, hdc in ea of next 2 sts, sc in ea of next 2 sts, hdc in ea of next 2 sts, dc in ea of next 2 sts, tr in ea of next 3 sts) 13 times. Fasten off.

Row 2: Join C in top of beg ch-4 of row 1, ch 1, sc in ea of next 2 tr, (hdc in ea of next 2 dc, dc in ea of next 2 hdc, tr in ea of next 2 sc, dc in ea of next 2 hdc, hdc in ea of next 2 dc, sc in ea of next 3 tr) 13 times. Fasten off.

Row 3: Join A in top of beg ch-1 of row 2, rep row 1. Fasten off.

Rep rows 1-3 across ea long edge of ea panel.

Assembly: Whipstitch panels together through both loops.

Border: With right side facing and afghan turned to work across short edge, join A with sl st in corner, ch 2 for first hdc, * hdc across to next corner working 3 hdc in side of ea tr and 1 hdc in ea sc, (hdc, ch 1, hdc) in corner, hdc in ea st to next corner, (hdc, ch 1, hdc) in corner, rep from * around, end with hdc in beg corner, ch 1, sl st in top of beg ch-2.

Fringe: Cut 24″-long strands of yarns A, C, and D, and 36″-long strands of yarn B. Knot 1 tassel in ea st across ea short edge of afghan in the foll order: 5 tassels with 1 strand ea of A and D, 2 tassels with 2 strands of C, 3 tassels with 2 strands of B, * 15 tassels with 1 strand ea of A and D, 3 tassels with 2 strands of B, 2 tassels with 2 strands of C, 5 tassels with 1 strand ea of A and D, 2 tassels with 2 strands of C, 3 tassels with 2 strands of B, rep from * across ea short edge. Knot B tassels tog across joinings of panels.

WOVEN ELEGANCE

The lattice-type edging on this afghan is easily achieved by working rows of chain-loops covered with half double crochet stitches.

FINISHED SIZE

Approximately 46″ x 64″.

MATERIALS

Worsted-weight cotton (70-yd. skein): 15 beige (A), 6 off-white (D).

Worsted-weight viscose-lamé-cotton blend (80-yd. skein): 9 variegated pink/blue/silver metallic (B), 8 variegated beige/silver metallic (C).

Metallic embroidery thread (1000m spool): 1 pearl (E).

Size K crochet hook, or size to obtain gauge.

GAUGE

4 sc and 4 rows = 1″.

DIRECTIONS

Note: When working with beige (A) and off-white (D) yarns, use 1 strand of yarn and 1 strand of pearl embroidery thread (E) held together as 1.

Afghan: With 1 strand ea of A and E, ch 202.

Row 1: Sc in 2nd ch from hook and ea ch across, turn.

Rows 2-4: Ch 1, working in bk lps only, sc in ea st across, turn. Fasten off.

Row 5: Join B with sl st in top of last st of prev row, ch 1, sc in same st, pull up a lp in same st and ea of next 2 sts, yo and pull through all 4 lps on hook (cl made), ch 1, * pull up lp in same st as last lp of prev cl and ea of next 2 sts, yo and pull through all 4 lps on hook (cl made), rep from * across to last st, sc in last st, turn. Fasten off = 101 cl.

Row 6: Join C with sl st in top of last st of prev row, ch 1, sc in same st, pull up 1 lp ea for next cl as foll: in same st as sc, in top of next cl, and in ch-1 sp, yo and pull through all 4 lps on hook (cl made), * pull up 1 lp ea for next cl as foll: in same st as last st of prev cl, in top of next cl, and in ch-1 sp, yo and pull through all 4 lps on hook (cl made), rep from * across to last st, sc in last st, turn. Fasten off.

Rows 7-18: Rep row 6, working 1 row ea using foll color sequence: A and E, B, C, A and E, B, C, A and E, B, C, A and E, B, C.

Rows 19-27: Join 1 strand ea of A and E, ch 1, sc in ea st and ch across, turn. Fasten off after row 27.

Row 28: Join B and rep row 5.

Rows 29-40: Rep row 6, working 1 row ea using foll color sequence: C, A and E, B, C, A and E, B, C, A and E, B, C, A and E, B.

Rows 41-46: Join 1 strand ea of D and E in last st of prev row, ch 1, sc in ea st across, turn. Fasten off after row 46.

Row 47: Join B and rep row 5.

Rows 48-55: Rep row 6, working 1 row ea using foll color sequence: C, D and E, B, C, D and E, B, C, D and E.

Rows 56 and 57: Join 1 strand ea of A and E, ch 1, sc in ea st across, turn. Fasten off after row 57.

Rows 58-63: Join 1 strand ea of D and E, ch 1, sc in ea st across, turn. Fasten off after row 63.

Row 64: Join B and rep row 5.

Rows 65-71: Rep row 6, working 1 row ea using foll color sequence: C, D and E, B, C, D and E, B, C.

Rows 72 and 73: Join 1 strand ea of D and E, ch 1, sc in ea st across, turn. Fasten off after row 73.

Rows 74-76: Join 1 strand ea of A and E, ch 1, sc in ea st across, turn. Fasten off after row 76.

Rows 77-81: Join 1 strand ea of D and E, ch 1, sc in ea st across, turn. Fasten off after row 81.

Rows 82 and 83: Join 1 strand ea of A and E, ch 1, sc in ea st across, turn. Fasten off after row 83.

Row 84: Join B and rep row 5.

Rows 85-96: Rep row 6, working 1 row ea using foll color sequence: A and E, C, B, A and E, C, B, A and E, C, B, A and E, C, B.

Rows 97-105: Join 1 strand ea of A and E, ch 1, sc in ea st across, turn. Fasten off after row 105.

Row 106: Join C and rep row 5.

Rows 107-119: Rep row 6, working 1 row ea using foll color sequence: B, A and E, C, B, A and E, C, B, A and E, C, B, A and E, C, B.

Rows 120-123: Join 1 strand ea of A and E, ch 1, sc in ea st across, turn. Do not fasten off A or turn after row 123. Fasten off E.

With A, sc in side of ea row across short edge of afghan. Fasten off. Rep to work 1 row of sc across rem short edge of afghan.

Lattice edging: **Row 1:** With wrong side facing, join 1 strand of A in 66th st before corner on long edge of afghan, (ch 9, sk 7 sts, sc in next st) 7 times to corner, ch 9, sc in corner st, (ch 9, sk 5 sts, sc in next st) 8 times across short edge of afghan, turn.

Row 2: Ch 2 for first hdc, (11 hdc in next lp, hdc in sc bet lps) 16 times, end with sc in same st as joining, turn. Fasten off.

Row 3: Working in front of prev lp, join 1 strand of A with sc in center sk st on afghan under first lp of prev row (4th st from prev joining), [* ch 9, working behind prev lp, sc in center sk st on afghan under next lp **, ch 9, working in front of prev lp, sc in center sk st on afghan under next lp], rep from * to corner, ch 13, working in front of prev lp, sc in center sk st under next lp after corner, rep bet [ ] to center sk st under last lp, end last rep at **, turn.

Row 4: Ch 2 for first hdc, (11 hdc in next lp, hdc in sc bet lps) 7 times, 15 hdc in corner lp, hdc in sc, rep bet ( ) 7 times, end with sc in same st as joining, turn. Fasten off.

Row 5: Join C with sc in center hdc of 2nd lp of first lp row, (ch 9, sc in center st of next lp of same row of lps) 6 times, ch 13, sc in center st of next lp of same row, rep bet ( ) 6 times, turn.

Row 6: Ch 2 for first hdc, (11 hdc in next lp, hdc in sc bet lps) 6 times, 15 hdc in corner lp, hdc in next sc, rep bet ( ) 6 times, turn. Fasten off.

Row 7: Join 1 strand of A with sl st in center hdc of 2nd lp of 2nd lp row, [* ch 9, working in front of prev lps, sc in center st of next lp of same row **, ch 9, working behind prev lps, sc in center st of next lp of same row], rep from * twice more, end last rep at **, ch 13, working behind prev lps, sc in center st of corner lp, ch 13, working in front of prev lps, sc in center st of next lp, ch 9, working behind prev lps, sc in center st of next lp, rep bet [ ] twice, turn.

Row 8: Ch 2 for first hdc, (11 hdc in next lp, hdc in next sc) 5 times, (15 hdc in next lp, hdc in next sc) twice, (11 hdc in next lp, hdc in next sc) 5 times, turn. Fasten off.

Row 9: Join B with sc in center hdc of 2nd lp of 3rd lp row, (ch 9, sc in center st of next lp of same row) 4 times, ch 13, sc in center st of corner lp, ch 13, sc in center st of next lp of same row, (ch 9, sc in center st of next lp of same row) 4 times, turn.

Row 10: Ch 2 for first hdc, (11 hdc in next lp, hdc in

next sc) 4 times, (15 hdc in next lp, hdc in next sc) twice, (11 hdc in next lp, hdc in next sc) 4 times, turn. Fasten off.

Row 11: Join B with sl st in center hdc of 2nd lp of 4th lp row, ch 9, working behind prev lps, sc in center st of next lp of same row, cont around corner as est in row 9, working in front of and behind prev lps as before, turn.

Row 12: Hdc in ea lp around as est in row 10. Fasten off.

Row 13: Join C with sl st in center st of 2nd lp of 5th lp row and work lps around corner as est.

Row 14: Rep row 12. Fasten off.

Row 15: Join 1 strand of A with sl st in center st of 2nd lp of 6th lp row and work lps around corner as est.

Row 16: Rep row 12. Fasten off.

Row 17: Join B with sl st in center st of 2nd lp of 7th lp row and work lps around corner as est.

Row 18: Rep row 12. Fasten off.

Sk 9 sts on short edge of afghan and work 2nd corner section, reversing shaping.

Work lattice edging at ea corner on opposite short edge of afghan in same manner.

Edging: Join 1 strand of A in joining of first lp of first corner, ch 1, sc in same st and ea of next 8 hdc of first lp, (5 sc across center sts of next lp) across corner section to 2 lps before corner, sk first 2 sts of next lp, sc in ea of next 9 sts of same lp, sc in ea hdc of next 2 lps of corner, sc in ea of next 9 hdc of next lp, (5 sc across center sts of ea of next 7 lps, sk first 3 sts of last lp, sc in ea rem st of same lp, sc in ea st across afghan to next corner section, work around next corner section as est. Fasten off. Work across opposite short edge of afghan in same manner.

Tassel (make 4): *Note:* See page 141 for tassel diagrams. For each tassel, wind yarns A, D, and B around an 11″ piece of cardboard, 33 times. Wrap tassel with yarn A. Stitch a tassel to lattice edging at each corner of afghan.

PAINTER'S PALETTE

*Draw on the techniques of the Impressionist artists
and use your crochet hook to paint with
the unusual yarns in this afghan.*

FINISHED SIZE

Approximately 68″ x 88″.

MATERIALS

Worsted-weight cotton (125-yd. ball): 4 celery (A).

Worsted-weight cotton (98-yd. ball): 3 pale green (N).

Sportweight cotton (192-yd. ball): 1 silver (O).

Bulky-weight wool-acrylic blend (55-yd. skein): 2 light green (B).

Bulky-weight cotton (55-yd. ball): 3 green (C), 2 purple (L).

Worsted-weight wool (175-yd. skein): 1 blue (D).

Bulky-weight wool (120-yd. skein): 2 variegated green and lavender (M).

Fingering-weight mercerized cotton (184-yd. ball): 1 purple (E).

Sportweight rayon ribbon (150-yd. spool): 2 green/gray/blue ombre (F).

Sportweight mohair-acrylic-wool blend (137-yd. ball): 2 purple (G).

Worsted-weight viscose-acrylic blend (77-yd. ball): 5 variegated purple and black (H).

Worsted-weight cotton-wool blend (85-yd. skein): 4 lavender (I).

Worsted-weight mohair-wool blend (90-yd. skein): 1 gray (K).

Worsted-weight cotton (176-yd. ball): 1 medium green (P).

Worsted-weight wool-mohair blend (150-yd. ball): 7 dark green (J).

Bulky-weight mohair-blend (70-yd. skein): 1 variegated blue (Q).

Size H crochet hook, or size to obtain gauge.

GAUGE

Square = 19″.

DIRECTIONS

Lp st: Insert hook in next st, place a 1½″ lp of yarn over left index finger, pick up back thread of lp with hook, pull through st, push lp to right side of work, yo and pull through 2 lps on hook.

Sc dec: Pull up a lp in ea of next 2 sts, yo and pull through all 3 lps on hook.

Hdc or dc dec: Keeping last lp of ea st on hook, hdc or dc in ea of next 2 sts, yo and pull through all lps on hook.

Popcorn: Work specified sts in next st, drop last lp from hook, insert hook in first st of grp, pick up dropped lp and pull through.

Reverse popcorn (rev popcorn): Worked on wrong side rows. Work popcorn as described above, except insert hook from back to front in first st of grp and push popcorn to right side.

4-dc bobble: Keeping last lp of ea st on hook, work 4 dc in next st, yo and pull through all lps on hook.

Puff: (Yo and pull up a lp) 5 times in next st, yo and pull through all 11 lps on hook.

Note: Because the number of stitches per row varies slightly, stitch counts for some rows are included as checkpoints. To change colors, work last stitch of previous color with both yarns held together as 1. To carry yarn not in use across the row, work over it with the next group of stitches. Use 2 strands of E held together as 1.

Square: Make 6 using colors as specified in table on page 128. **Square A: Row 1:** With A, ch 62, dc in 4th ch from hook and ea ch across, ch 2, turn = 60 sts.

Row 2: Hdc in ea of next 4 sts, dc in ea of next 2 sts, sk next st, 2 dc in ea of next 2 sts, 2 tr in next st, 2 dc in ea of next 2 sts, sk next st, hdc in ea of next 6 sts, sc in ea of next 4 sts, (sc dec over next 2 sts) 3 times, sc in ea of next 3 sts, hdc in ea of next 4 sts, dc in ea of next 18 sts, tr in ea of next 5 sts. Drop A. Do not turn or fasten off.

Row 3 (partial row): With wrong side facing, join B in first st of row 2, ch 2, hdc in ea of next 5 sts, dc in next st, sk next st, 2 dc in next st, dc in ea of next 2 sts, 2 tr in ea of next 2 sts, dc in ea of next 2 sts, 2 dc in next st, sk next st, dc in next st, hdc in ea of next 3 sts, sc in ea of next 5 sts, (sc dec over next 2 sts) twice, sc in ea of next 4 sts, ch 1, turn, leave rem row-2 sts unworked.

Row 4 (partial row): Working in row-3 sts, sc in first st, hdc in ea of next 33 sts, ch 1, turn.

Row 5: Sc in first st, hdc in ea of next 33 sts, sc in next st of row 2, dc in ea of next 2 sts, hdc in ea of next 9 sts, sc in ea of next 13 sts, turn. Fasten off B.

Row 6 (right side): Pick up A, sl st in top of last st of row 5, sc in same st, hdc in ea of next 4 sts, dc in ea of next

7 sts, tr in ea of next 4 sts, 2 tr in next st, tr in ea of next 5 sts, dc in ea of next 12 sts, hdc in ea of next 3 sts, sc in ea of next 17 sts, hdc in ea of next 3 sts, dc in ea of next 3 sts, ch 2, turn.

Row 7: Dc in ea of next 2 sts, hdc in ea of next 2 sts, sc in ea of next 13 sts, hdc in ea of next 5 sts, dc in ea of next 4 sts, tr in ea of next 5 sts, dc in ea of next 4 sts, hdc in next st, sc in ea of next 10 sts, sc dec over next 2 sts, hdc in ea of next 5 sts, dc dec over next 2 sts, dc in ea of next 4 sts, hdc in next st, ch 3, turn.

Row 8: Dc in ea of next 8 sts, join C, with A and C tog, dc in next st, drop A, using C, sc in next st, lp st in ea of next 18 sts, sc in ea of next 2 sts, join D, with C and D tog, sc in next st, drop C, using D, sc in ea of next 4 sts, dc in ea of next 5 sts, hdc in ea of next 4 sts, sc in ea of next 5 sts, hdc in ea of next 10 sts, ch 2, turn.

Row 9: Hdc in ea of next 28 sts, pick up C, with C and D tog, hdc in next st, drop D, using C, sc in next st, dc in ea of next 20 sts, pick up A, with A and C tog, dc in next st, drop C, using A, dc in ea of next 7 sts, ch 3, turn = 59 sts.

Row 10: Dc in ea of next 7 sts, pick up C, with A and C tog, dc in next st, drop A, using C, lp st in ea of next 15 sts, sc in next st, hdc in ea of next 3 sts, pick up D, with C and D tog, hdc in next st, drop C, using D, hdc in ea of next 2 sts, dc in ea of next 4 sts, tr in next st, dc in ea of next 4 sts, hdc in ea of next 20 sts, ch 2, turn = 59 sts.

Row 11: Hdc in ea of next 7 sts, dc in ea of next 4 sts, tr in next st, dc in ea of next 4 sts, hdc in ea of next 15 sts, pick up C, with C and D tog, hdc in next st, drop D, using C, hdc in ea of next 2 sts, dc in ea of next 15 sts, pick up A, with A and C tog, hdc in next st, drop C, using A, hdc in ea of next 9 sts, ch 2, turn.

Row 12 (right side): Hdc in ea of next 9 sts, pick up C, with A and C tog, hdc in next st, drop A, using C, lp st in ea of next 10 sts, hdc in ea of next 3 sts, pick up D, with C and D tog, hdc in next st, drop C, using D, hdc in ea of next 6 sts, join 2 strands of E, with D and E tog, dc in next st, work with E and carry D across, (5-dc popcorn in next st, ch 1, sk next st, dc in ea of next 2 sts) 3 times, pick up D, with D and E tog, dc in next st, drop E, using D, hdc in ea of next 15 sts, ch 3, turn.

Row 13: Dc in ea of next 14 sts, pick up E, with D and E tog, dc in next st, drop D, using E, (5-dc rev popcorn in next st, ch 1, sk next st, dc in ea of next 2 sts) 4 times, pick up C, with C and E tog, dc in next st, drop E, using C, dc in ea of next 15 sts, pick up A, with A and C tog, dc in next st, fasten off C, using A, dc in ea of next 11 sts, ch 3, turn.

Row 14: Dc in ea of next 3 sts, 2 dc in ea of next 2 sts, 2 tr in next st, 2 dc in ea of next 2 sts, sk next st, dc in next st, join B, with A and B tog, dc in next st, fasten off A, using B, dc in ea of next 2 sts, (dc dec over next 2 sts, dc in next st) 3 times, dc in ea of next 6 sts, pick up E, with B and E

tog, dc in next st, drop B, using E, dc in ea of next 2 sts, (5-dc popcorn in next st, ch 1, sk next st, dc in ea of next 2 sts) 3 times, pick up D, with D and E tog, dc in next st, fasten off E, using D, dc in ea of next 4 sts, sk next st, tr in ea of next 2 sts, 2 tr in ea of next 2 sts, tr in ea of next 2 sts, sk next st, dc in ea of next 3 sts, ch 2, turn.

Row 15: Hdc in ea of next 2 sts, sk next st, dc in ea of next 2 sts, 2 dc in ea of next 2 sts, dc in ea of next 2 sts, sk next st, hdc in ea of next 18 sts, pick up B, with B and D tog, hdc in next st, drop D, using B, hdc in ea of next 6 sts, hdc dec over next 2 sts, hdc in next st, hdc dec over next 2 sts, hdc in ea of next 9 sts, 2 dc in ea of next 2 sts, hdc in ea of next 8 sts, ch 2, turn = 60 sts.

Row 16: Hdc in ea of next 5 sts, sk next st, dc in ea of next 2 sts, 2 dc in ea of next 2 sts, dc in ea of next 2 sts, sk next st, hdc in ea of next 15 sts, pick up D, with B and D tog, hdc in next st, drop B, using D, hdc in ea of next 18 sts, sk next st, dc in ea of next 3 sts, 2 tr in ea of next 2 sts, dc in ea of next 3 sts, sk next st, hdc in ea of next 2 sts, turn = 60 sts.

Row 17: Join F in last st of row 16, with D and F tog, ch 2, work with F and carry D across, hdc in next st, sk next st, dc in ea of next 3 sts, 2 dc in ea of next 2 sts, dc in ea of next 3 sts, sk next st, hdc in next st, sc in next st, pick up D, with D and F tog, sc in next st, work with D and carry F across, hdc in ea of next 5 sts, drop F, using D, hdc in ea of next 9 sts, pick up B, with B and D tog, hdc in next st, drop D, using B, hdc in ea of next 15 sts, sk next st, dc in ea of next 3 sts, 2 dc in ea of next 2 sts, dc in ea of next 3 sts, sk next st, hdc in ea of next 5 sts, ch 2, turn = 60 sts.

Row 18 (partial row): With right side facing, drop B, join G with sc in 16th st from right-hand edge, sc in ea of next 2 sts, hdc in ea of next 2 sts, dc in ea of next 3 sts, tr in ea of next 3 sts, dc in ea of next 2 sts, hdc in next st, sc in next st, pick up and carry D across, using G, sc in ea of next 2 sts, fasten off G, drop D. Do not turn.

Row 19: With right side facing, pick up B, hdc in ea of next 3 sts, sk next st, dc in ea of next 2 sts, tr in next st, 2 tr in ea of next 2 sts, tr in ea of next 2 sts, dc in ea of next 2 sts, sk next st, sc in first row-18 sc, sc in ea of next 2 sts, hdc in ea of next 2 sts, dc in ea of next 2 sts, tr in ea of next 3 sts, dc in next st, hdc in ea of next 2 sts, sc in ea of last 3 row-18 sts, pick up D, with B and D tog, sc in next st, drop B, using D, hdc in ea of next 7 sts, pick up F, with D and F tog, hdc in next st, drop D, using F, hdc in ea of next 6 sts, sk next st, dc in ea of next 3 sts, tr in next st, 2 tr in ea of next 2 sts, tr in next st, dc in ea of next 3 sts, sk next st, hdc in next st, ch 2, turn.

Row 20 (wrong side): Hdc in ea of next 18 sts, pick up D, with D and F tog, hdc in next st, work with D and carry F across, hdc in ea of next 7 sts, drop F, pick up B, with B and D tog, hdc in next st, fasten off D, using B, hdc in ea of next 4 sts, dc in ea of next 2 sts, tr in ea of next 4 sts, dc in ea of next 2 sts, hdc in ea of next 2 sts, sc in next st, hdc in ea of next 16 sts, turn. Fasten off B.

Row 21 (right side): Join H in last st of row 20, ch 3, dc in ea of next 5 sts, hdc in next st, sc in ea of next 4 sts, hdc in next st, dc in ea of next 3 sts, tr in ea of next 3 sts, dc in ea of next 2 sts, hdc in ea of next 2 sts, sc in ea of next 2 sts, hdc in ea of next 2 sts, dc in ea of next 3 sts, tr in ea of next 2 sts, dc in next st, pick up F, with F and H tog, hdc in next st, drop H, using F, dc in ea of next 5 sts, tr in ea of next 5 sts, dc in ea of next 6 sts, hdc in ea of next 2 sts, sc in ea of next 4 sts, hdc in ea of next 2 sts, dc in ea of next 2 sts, ch 3, turn = 59 sts.

Row 22: Dc in ea of next 3 sts, hdc in ea of next 6 sts, dc in ea of next 7 sts, hdc in ea of next 5 sts, dc in ea of next 3 sts, hdc in ea of next 2 sts, pick up H, with F and H tog, hdc in next st, drop F, using H, hdc in ea of next 31 sts, turn. Fasten off H.

Row 23: Join I in last st of row 22, ch 1, hdc in ea of next 26 sts, dc in ea of next 5 sts, pick up F, work with I and carry F across, dc in ea of next 15 sts, hdc in ea of next 2 sts, sc in ea of next 3 sts, pick up F, with I and F tog, sc in next st, drop I, using F, dc in next st, tr in ea of next 5 sts, ch 1, turn = 59 sts.

Row 24: Sc in ea of next 4 sts, 2 sc in next st, pick up I, with F and I tog, sc in next st, fasten off F, using I, dc in ea

of next 4 sts, hdc in ea of next 2 sts, sc in ea of next 20 sts, dc in ea of next 26 sts, ch 3, turn.

Row 25 (partial row): With right side facing, join G in 21st row-24 st, sc in same st, (sk next 3 sts, 11 tr in next st, sk next 3 sts, sc in next st) 3 times. Fasten off G. Do not turn.

Row 26: With right side facing, pick up I, dc in ea of next 6 sts, sc in ea of next 6 sts, sk next st, hdc in next st, 2 dc in next st, tr in ea of next 4 sts, dc in first row-25 st, * ch 2, (sk next tr, sc in next tr, ch 2) 5 times, dc in next sc, rep from * twice more, dc in ea of next 7 sts, hdc in ea of next 4 sts, sc in ea of next 4 sts, ch 2, turn.

Row 27 (wrong side): Hdc in ea of next 3 sts, dc in ea of next 11 sts, sc in next st, (ch 3, sc in ch-2 sp) 18 times, ch 3, sc in ea of next 4 sts, fasten off I, join J, sc in ea of next 3 sts, hdc in ea of next 2 sts, sk next st, 2 dc in ea of next 2 sts, sk next st, hdc in ea of next 8 sts, ch 3, turn.

Row 28: Dc in ea of next 7 sts, tr in ea of next 4 sts, dc in ea of next 8 sts, (sc in next st, 2 sc in ch-3 lp) 5 times, * sc in next st, sk next ch-3 lp, 7 dc in next ch-3 lp, sk next ch-3 lp **, (sc in next st, 2 sc in next ch-3 lp) 3 times, rep from * to ** once, (sc in next st, 2 sc in next ch-3 lp) 5 times, (sc dec over next 2 sts) 4 times, drop J, join K, hdc in ea of next 8 sts, ch 3, turn.

Row 29: Dc in ea of next 8 sts, pick up J, with J and K tog, dc in next st, drop K, using J, (dc dec over next 2 sts)

twice, (dc in next st, sk next st) twice, dc in next st, * (sk next st, dc in next st) twice, 4-dc bobble in next st, sk next 3 sts, (sc in next st, sk next st) twice, sc in next st, sk next 2 sts, 4-dc bobble in next st, dc in next st, rep from * once more, (sk next st, dc in next st) twice, dc in next st, (sk next st, dc in next st) twice, (dc dec over next 2 sts) twice, dc in next st, join D, with J and D tog, hdc in next st, drop J, using D, hdc in ea of next 7 sts, sk next st, 2 dc in ea of next 2 sts, sk next st, hdc in ea of next 9 sts, ch 2, turn.

Row 30: Hdc in ea of next 6 sts, sk next st, dc in next st, 2 tr in ea of next 2 sts, dc in next st, sk next st, hdc in ea of next 6 sts, pick up J, work with D and carry J across, hdc in ea of next 5 sts, pick up J, with J and D tog, hdc in next st, drop D, using J, dc in ea of next 10 sts, tr in ea of next 10 sts, dc in ea of next 5 sts, pick up K, with K and J tog, dc in next st, drop J, using K, dc in ea of next 9 sts, ch 3, turn.

Row 31: Dc in ea of next 9 sts, pick up J, work with K and carry J across, dc in ea of next 5 sts, tr in ea of next 4 sts, hdc in ea of next 5 sts, pick up J, with K and J tog, hdc in next st, drop K, using J, sc in ea of next 11 sts, pick up D, with D and J tog, sc in next st, fasten off J, using D, sc in ea of next 9 sts, sk next st, dc in ea of next 2 sts, 2 tr in ea of next 2 sts, dc in ea of next 2 sts, sk next st, sc in ea of next 6 sts, ch 3, turn.

Row 32: Dc in ea of next 14 sts, tr in next st, ch 2, [sk next 2 sts, tr in next st, ch 1, working behind prev st, tr in first sk st (cross st made)] 5 times, tr in next st, dc in next st, hdc in ea of next 2 sts, pick up K, with D and K tog, hdc in next st, drop D, using K, hdc in ea of next 24 sts, ch 3, turn.

Row 33 (wrong side): Dc in ea of next 7 sts, ch 3, turn, dc in ea of next 7 sts, ch 3, turn, dc in ea of next 7 sts (ledge made), working in side of ledge rows, 2 dc in side of ea of next 3 rows, hdc in ea of next 2 sts, fasten off K, join L, hdc in ea of next 7 sts, dc in ea of next 8 sts, pick up D, with L and D tog, dc in next st, drop L, using D, hdc in ea of next 3 sts, (hdc in next st, hdc in ch-1 sp, hdc in next st) 5 times, hdc in next ch-2 sp, sc in ea of next 16 sts, ch 2, turn.

Row 34 (right side): Hdc in ea of next 14 sts, dc in ea of next 20 sts, pick up L, with D and L tog, sc in next st, drop D, using L, dc in next st, (5-tr popcorn in next st, ch 2, sk next 2 sts) 5 times, sc in st about halfway up side of ledge, sc in ea of next 3 ledge sts, sc in corner of ledge, sc in ea of next 7 sts, ch 1, turn.

Row 35: Sc in ea of next 7 sts, (ch 2, work 5-tr rev popcorn in next popcorn) 5 times, ch 4, sc in next st, ch 2, dc in next st, pick up D, work with L and carry D across, (dc dec over next 2 sts, dc in ea of next 2 sts) 3 times, sc in ea of next 10 sts, pick up D, with L and D tog, sc in next st, drop L, using D, dc in ea of next 12 sts, ch 3, turn.

Row 36: Dc in ea of next 6 sts, hdc in ea of next 4 sts, sc in ea of next 2 sts, fasten off D, join M, pick up L, work with M and carry L across, lp st in ea of next 17 sts, pick up

L, with L and M tog, sc in next st, drop M, using L, dc in ea of next 2 sts, sc in next st, 3 sc in ch-4 lp, (sc in popcorn, 2 sc in next ch-2 sp) 5 times, sc in ea of next 8 sts, ch 1, turn.

Row 37 (wrong side): Sc in ea of next 22 sts, dc in ea of next 6 sts, pick up M, with L and M tog, sc in next st, fasten off L, using M, lp st in ea of next 16 sts, hdc in ea of next 14 sts, ch 2, turn.

Row 38: Hdc in ea of next 15 sts, dc in ea of next 18 sts, hdc in ea of next 16 sts, sc in ea of next 10 sts, ch 1, turn.

Row 39: Sc in ea of next 30 sts, hdc in ea of next 7 sts, (sk next st, 2 hdc in next st) 5 times, sc in ea of next 12 sts, ch 1, turn.

Row 40: Sc in ea of next 11 sts, hdc in ea of next 7 sts, dc in ea of next 16 sts, hdc in ea of next 10 sts, sc in ea of next 15 sts = 60 sts. Fasten off.

Row	Square B	Square C	Square D	Square E	Square F
1	D	P	J	J	A
3	I	G	O	O	B
8	L	F	B	M	C
8	J	N	A	A	D
12	A	I	Q	Q	D
14	I	H	D	D	M
17	B	D	I	I	F
18	H	C	G	G	K
21	F	K	O	K	H
23	N	A	F	F	I
25	D	E	E	H	J
27	O	Q	N	N	E
28	G	M	D	D	A
29	P	J	P	P	D
33	B	C	H	G	Q
36	L	F	C	C	M

Border: **Square A: Rnd 1:** With right side facing and square turned to work across top edge, join J in corner, * (sc, ch 1, sc) in corner, sc in ea of next 58 sts to corner, rep from * around, sl st in first sc, sl st into corner sp.

Rnd 2: Ch 3 for first hdc and ch 1, hdc in same sp, * hdc in ea st to next corner, (hdc, ch 1, hdc) in corner, rep from * around, sl st in 2nd ch of beg ch-3, sl st into corner sp.

Rnd 3: Rep rnd 2.

Rnd 4: Ch 3, keeping last lp of ea st on hook, 2 dc in next st, yo and pull through all lps on hook (2-dc cl made), ch 3, 3-dc cl in next st, ch 2, sk 2 sts, sc in next st, [* ch 2, sk next st, (3-dc cl, ch 3, 3-dc cl) in next st, ch 2, sk next st, sc in next st, rep from * to 2 sts before corner sp, ch 2, sk 2 sts, (3-dc cl, ch 3, 3-dc cl, ch 3, 3-dc cl) in corner sp, ch 2, sk 2 sts, sc in next st] around, sl st in top of beg ch-3 = 14 cl bet corner-cl grps. Fasten off.

Rnd 5 (accent sts): Join F with sc in corner sp of rnd 2, * ch 3, dc around post of 2nd corner sc of rnd 1, sk 2 hdc of

rnd 3, (sc around post of next hdc of rnd 3, sk next sc of rnd 1, dc around post of next sc of rnd 1, sk next hdc of rnd 3) to corner, ch 3, sc in corner sp of rnd 2, rep from * around, sl st in first sc. Fasten off.

Square B: With P, rep rnds 1-3 as for first square. Fasten off after rnd 3.

Rnd 4: Join C with sc in any corner sp of rnd 2, * (working beside rnd-3 sts, lp st in top of ea of next 5 sts of rnd 2, working beside rnd-2 sts, lp st in ea of next 5 sts of rnd 1) 6 times, 3 lp sts in corner sp of rnd 2, rep from * around, sl st in first sc. Fasten off.

Square C: With I, rep rnds 1 and 2 as for first square. Fasten off after rnd 2.

Rnd 3: *Note:* Pull ea dc up 1½" and work loosly. Join M with sl st in corner sp, ch 3 for first dc, 2 dc in same sp, * [sk 2 sts, dc in next st, ch 1, working behind prev st, dc in first sk st (cross st made)] to corner, 5 dc in corner sp, rep from * around, sl st in top of beg ch-3. Fasten off.

Square D: With G, rep rnds 1 and 2 as for first square.

Rnd 3: Ch 3, 5-dc popcorn in same sp, * dc in next st, (5-dc popcorn bet next 2 sts, dc in ea of next 2 sts) to corner, (5-dc popcorn, ch 3, 5-dc popcorn) in corner sp, rep from * around, sl st in top of beg ch-3. Fasten off.

Square E: With H, rep rnds 1 and 2 as for first square.

Rnd 3: Turn to wrong side, sc in same corner sp, * lp st in ea st to corner sp, 3 lp sts in corner sp, rep from * around, sl st in first sc, turn.

Rnd 4: With right side facing, ch 2, sc in corner, * sc in ea st to next corner, (sc, ch 1, sc) in corner, rep from * around, sl st in 2nd ch of beg ch-2. Fasten off.

Square F: With J, rep rnds 1 and 2 as for first square.

Rnd 3: [* Ch 3, puff in same st, ch 2, sk 2 sts, sc in next st, rep from * to corner, ch 3, puff in same st, ch 2, sc in corner sp, ch 3, puff in same sp, ch 2, sk 2 sts] around, sl st in first ch of beg ch-3. Fasten off.

Assembly: Whipstitch squares together in the following order: squares A and B in top row, C and D in middle row, E and F in bottom row.

Edging: **Rnd 1:** With right side facing and afghan turned to work across top edge, join J with sl st in corner of square B, ch 3 for first dc, 2 dc in same corner sp, dc in ea of next 62 sts of square B, dc in first ch-3 sp of corner of square A, (2 dc in next ch-3 sp, dc in ea of next 2 sps) 15 times across square A, dc in next ch-3 sp of corner, 3 dc in corner cl, dc in next sp of corner, (dc in ea of next 2 sps, 2 dc in next sp) 15 times, dc in joining bet squares A and C, dc in ea of next 62 sts of square C, dc in ea of next 62 sts of square E, 3 dc in corner, dc in ea of next 62 sts of square E, dc in joining bet squares E and F, (2 dc in next sp, dc in next sp) 21 times, 3 dc in next corner, (dc in next sp, 2 dc in next sp) 20 times, dc in joining bet squares F and D, dc in next puff, dc in next dc, (dc in next puff, dc in ea of next 2 dc) 19 times, dc in next puff, sk next dc, dc in next puff, dc in corner of square D, dc in ea of next 62 sts of square B, sl st in top of beg ch-3.

Rnd 2: Sl st into center dc of corner, ch 3 for first dc, [(puff, ch 3, puff) in same st, * ch 2, sk 2 sts, (sc, ch 3, puff) in next st **, rep from * across to corner, ch 2, sk 3 sts, sc in center dc of corner, (puff, ch 3, puff) in same st, rep from * to ** across to corner, work corner as est] around, sl st in top of beg ch-3. Fasten off.

Rnd 3: Join A with sl st in corner sp, ch 3 for first dc, 4 dc in same sp, * [ch 1, sk next ch-2 sp, dc in next ch-3 sp, ch 1, working behind prev st, dc in sk sp (cross st made)] across to corner, ch 1, 5 dc in corner sp, rep from * around, sl st in top of beg ch-3, sl st into center dc of corner.

Rnd 4: Ch 3 for first dc, (2 dc, ch 2, 3 dc) in corner, tr in sp of next cross st, ch 2, working behind prev st, tr in last dc of corner (cross st made), [* tr in sp of next cross st, ch 2, working behind prev st, tr in same sp as first leg of prev cross st, rep from * to corner, tr in first dc of corner, ch 2, working behind prev st, tr in same sp as first leg of prev cross st, (3 dc, ch 2, 3 dc) for shell in center dc of corner] around, sl st in top of beg ch-3. Fasten off.

Rnd 5: Join H with sl st in corner sp, ch 3 for first dc, (2 dc, ch 3, 3 dc) in same corner, * ch 3, sk 3 dc, sc in sp before next cross st, (ch 3, sc in sp of cross st, ch 3, sc in sp bet cross sts) to corner, ch 3, shell in corner sp, rep from * around, sl st in top of beg ch-3, sl st into corner sp.

Rnd 6: Ch 3 for first dc, 4-dc popcorn in same sp, ch 3, 5-dc popcorn in same sp, * (dc in next ch-3 sp, ch 1, dc in next ch-3 sp, 5-dc popcorn in next ch-3 sp) to 1 sp before corner, (dc, ch 1, dc) in next sp, (5-dc popcorn, ch 3, 5-dc popcorn) in corner sp, rep from * around, sl st in top of beg popcorn. Fasten off.

Rnd 7: Join I with sl st in corner sp, ch 3 for first dc, (2 dc, ch 3, 3 dc) in same sp, ch 5, * (sc in next ch-1 sp, ch 5, sc in next popcorn, ch 5) to corner, sc in next ch-1 sp, ch 5, shell in corner sp, ch 5, rep from * around, sl st in top of beg ch-3. Fasten off.

Rnd 8: Join M with sc in corner sp, ch 6, sc in same sp, * (ch 5, sc in next ch-5 lp) to corner, ch 5, (sc, ch 6, sc) in corner sp, rep from * around, sl st in first sc. Fasten off.

Rnd 9: Join I with sl st in corner lp, * 9 sc in same corner lp, (ch 6, sc dec over next 2 ch-5 lps) to corner, ch 6, rep from * around, sl st in first sc. Fasten off.

Rnd 10: Join N with sc in first sc of corner, sc in ea of next 8 sc, * ch 5, (5-dc popcorn in sc dec, ch 2) to corner, ch 3, sc in ea of next 9 corner sc, rep from * around, sl st in first sc. Fasten off.

Rnd 11: Join D with sc in 4th sc of corner, (ch 5, sk next st, sc in next st) twice, * (ch 5, sc in next sp) to corner, sc in next sc, ch 5, sk first sc of corner, sc in next sc, (ch 5, sk next sc, sc in next sc) 3 times, rep from *

around, sl st in first sc. Fasten off.

Rnd 12: Join H with sl st in center corner lp, ch 3 for first dc, (dc, ch 1, 2 dc) in same corner lp, * ch 2, sk next lp, dc in next lp, ch 1, working behind prev st, dc in sk lp (cross st made), (ch 2, dc in next lp, ch 1, working behind prev st, dc in same lp as first leg of prev cross st) to corner lp, ch 2, (2 dc, ch 1, 2 dc) in corner lp, rep from * around, sl st in top of beg ch-3, sl st into corner sp.

Rnd 13: Ch 3 for first dc, (2 dc, ch 2, 3 dc) in same corner, * ch 1, tr in sp of next cross st, ch 2, working behind prev st, tr in last dc of corner, (ch 1, tr in sp of next cross st, ch 2, working behind prev st, tr in same sp as last leg of prev cross st) to corner, ch 1, tr in first dc of corner, ch 2, work 2nd leg of cross st in same sp as prev cross st as est, ch 1, (3 dc, ch 2, 3 dc) in corner sp, rep from * around, sl st in top of beg ch-3. Fasten off.

Rnd 14: Join D with sl st in corner sp, ch 3 for first dc, (2 dc, ch 3, 3 dc) in same sp, * (ch 3, sc in next ch-1 sp, ch 3, sc in next ch-2 sp) to corner, ch 3, sc in next ch-1 sp, ch 3, (3 dc, ch 3, 3 dc) in corner sp, rep from * around, sl st in top of beg ch-3. Fasten off.

Rnd 15: Join M with sl st in corner sp, ch 4 for first dc and ch 1, (dc, ch 1, dc, ch 1, dc) in same sp, * ch 1, sk 2 dc, dc in next dc, (ch 1, dc in next lp) to corner, ch 1, dc in first dc of corner, ch 1, (dc, ch 1, dc, ch 1, dc, ch 1, dc) in center corner sp, rep from * around, sl st in 3rd ch of beg ch-4. Fasten off.

Rnd 16: Join I with sl st in center sp of corner, ch 2, (puff, ch 4, puff) in same sp, * ch 3, sk 2 dc, puff in next sp, (ch 3, sk next sp, puff in next sp) to corner, ch 3, sk 2 dc of corner, (puff, ch 4, puff) in center sp of corner, rep from * around, sl st in top of beg ch-2. Fasten off.

Rnd 17: Join A with sc in corner sp, * 6 sc in same sp, (sc dec over same sp and next sp, 2 sc in same sp) to corner, sc dec over last sp before corner and corner sp, rep from * around, sl st in first sc. Fasten off.

Rnd 18: Join J with sc in dec before corner, sc in ea of next 8 sts, * [ch 2, sk 2 sts, (sc, puff) in next st] to corner, ch 2, sk 2 sts, sc in ea of next 9 sts, rep from * around, sl st in first sc.

Rnd 19: Ch 1, sc in same st, * (ch 3, sc in first ch for picot, sk next st, sc in next st) 4 times, [(2 hdc, picot, 2 hdc) in next sp] to corner, sc in first sc of corner, rep from * around, sl st in first sc. Fasten off.

Accent rnd: *Note:* Work foll sts in rnd-10 sts. Join J with sc in first sc of corner, * (ch 3, sc in first ch for picot, sk next st, sc in next st) 4 times, 3 hdc in next lp, picot, 3 hdc in same lp on other side of rnd-11 sc, (sk popcorn, 2 hdc in next sp, picot, 2 hdc in same sp on other side of rnd-11 sc) to sp after popcorn before corner, 3 hdc in next lp, picot, 3 hdc in same lp on other side of rnd-11 sc, sc in first sc of corner, rep from * around, sl st in first sc. Fasten off.

SWIRLING LEAVES

Leaves and vines, crocheted in cotton thread, enhance a soft throw of burgundy and navy wool yarns.

FINISHED SIZE

Approximately 41″ x 49″.

MATERIALS

Bulky-weight wool (105-yd. skein): 15 burgundy (A), 9 variegated navy/red (B).

Size H crochet hook, or size to obtain gauge.

Size 5 pearl cotton (53-yd. ball): 10 garnet.

Size 5 pearl cotton (27-yd. skein): 2 navy.

Sizes 0 and 1 steel crochet hooks.

GAUGE

3 dc and 2 rows = 1″ with size H hook.

DIRECTIONS

Throw: With size H hook and A, ch 141.

Row 1: Join B, carry A across by working over it with the next few sts, dc in 4th ch from hook, pull up a lp in next ch, (yo and pull through 1 lp on hook) 3 times, yo and pull through both lps on hook (lg ch-st made), dc in next ch, lg ch-st in next ch, dc in next ch, drop B, * pick up A and pull up a lp in next ch, (yo and pull through 1 lp on hook) twice, yo and pull through both lps on hook (sm ch-st made), dc in next st, rep from * across, dc in last ch = 139 sts, turn.

Row 2: Ch 3 for first dc, dc in ea st across to last 7 sts, drop A, pick up B, dc in ea of last 7 sts, turn.

Row 3: Ch 3 for first dc, (lg ch-st in next st, dc in next st) 3 times, lg ch-st in next st, drop B, pick up A, (dc in next st, sm ch-st in next st) across, dc in last st, turn.

Row 4: Ch 3 for first dc, dc in ea st across to last 10 sts, drop A, pick up B, dc in ea of last 10 sts, turn.

Row 5: Ch 3 for first dc, (dc in next st, lg ch-st in next st) 4 times, dc in next st, drop B, pick up A, (sm ch-st in next st, dc in next st) across, turn.

Row 6: Ch 3 for first dc, dc in ea st across to last 11 sts, drop A, pick up B, dc in ea of last 11 sts, turn.

Cont in pat as est, working lg ch-sts with B and sm ch-sts with A and using colors as specified below.

Row 7: 11 B, 127 A.

Row 8: 125 A, 13 B.

Row 9: 14 B, 124 A.

Row 10: 123 A, 15 B.

Row 11: 16 B, 122 A.

Row 12: 120 A, 18 B.

Row 13: 19 B, 119 A.

Row 14: 117 A, 21 B.

Rows 15-24: Cont as est working 1 more st with B and 1 fewer st with A ea row = 107 A, 31 B after row 24.

Row 25: 33 B, 105 A.

Rows 26-30: 104 A, 34 B.

Rows 31 and 32: 33 B, 105 A.

Row 33: 32 B, 106 A.

Row 34: 107 A, 31 B.

Row 35: 29 B, 109 A.

Row 36: 110 A, 28 B.

Row 37: 26 B, 112 A.

Rows 38 and 39: 111 A, 27 B.

Rows 40 and 41: 110 A, 28 B.

Rows 42 and 43: 109 A, 29 B.

Rows 44 and 45: 108 A, 30 B.

Row 46: 107 A, 31 B.

Rows 47-56: Cont as est working 1 more st with B and 1 fewer st with A ea row = 97 A, 41 B after row 56.

Rows 57 and 58: 41 B, 97 A.

Row 59: 42 B, 96 A.

Row 60: 95 A, 43 B.

Row 61: 44 B, 35 A, 5 B, 54 A.

Row 62: 51 A, 12 B, 29 A, 46 B.

Row 63: 46 B, 26 A, 17 B, 49 A.

Row 64: 48 A, 21 B, 23 A, 46 B.

Row 65: 46 B, 20 A, 25 B, 47 A.

Row 66: 46 A, 28 B, 18 A, 46 B.

Row 67: 46 B, 15 A, 32 B, 45 A.

Row 68: 44 A, 35 B, 13 A, 46 B.

Row 69: 47 B, 11 A, 37 B, 43 A.

Row 70: 42 A, 96 B.

Rows 71-74: Cont as est working 1 more st with B and 1 fewer st with A ea row = 38 A, 100 B after row 74.

Rows 75-80: 101 B, 37 A.

Row 81: 35 A, 103 B.

Row 82: 105 B, 33 A.

Rows 83 and 84: 7 A, 131 B.

Rows 85-89: Cont as est working 1 more st with B and 1 fewer st with A ea row = 2 A, 136 B after row 89. Fasten off A after row 89.

Rows 90-99: Cont working with B in pat as est. Fasten off after row 99.

Small leaf spray (make 13 garnet, 4 navy): **Outer leaf** (make 2): With size 1 hook, ch 13.

Row 1: Sl st in 2nd ch from hook, sl st in next ch, sc in ea of next 9 ch, 2 sc in last ch, working down opposite side of foundation ch, sc in ea of next 9 ch, turn.

Row 2: Sl st in first sc, sc in ea of next 8 sc, 2 sc in ea of next 2 sc, sc in ea of next 7 sc, ch 2, turn.

Row 3: Sl st in first sc, sc in ea of next 7 sc, 2 sc in ea of next 2 sc, sc in ea of next 7 sc, ch 2, sl st in 2nd ch from hook for picot, turn.

Row 4: Sl st in first sc, sc in ea of next 7 sc, 2 sc in ea of next 2 sc, sc in ea of next 6 sc, picot, turn.

Row 5: Sl st in first sc, sc in ea of next 6 sc, 2 sc in ea of next 2 sc, sc in ea of next 3 sc, turn.

Row 6: Sk first sc, sc in ea of next 7 sc, turn.

Row 7: Sk first sc, sc in ea of next 6 sc, turn.

Row 8: Sk first sc, sc in ea of next 5 sc. Fasten off.

Center leaf (make 1): **Rows 1-5:** Work as for outer leaf.

Row 6: Sl st in ea of next 3 sts, sc in ea of next 3 sts, turn.

Rows 7 and 8: Sk first st, sc in ea of next 3 sts, turn.

Row 9: Sl st in ea of next 2 sts, ch 25 for stem, sl st in 2nd ch from hook and ea of next 22 ch, sl st in next st at base of leaf. Fasten off.

Stitch 2 outer leaves to center leaf at base (see photo).

Large leaf spray (make 8 garnet): **Outer leaf** (make 2): With size 0 hook, ch 16.

Row 1: Sl st in 2nd ch from hook, sl st in ea of next 2 ch, sc in ea of next 11 ch, 2 sc in last ch, working down opposite side of foundation ch, sc in ea of next 10 ch, sl st in next ch, ch 4, turn.

Row 2: Sl st in first sc, sc in ea of next 10 sc, 2 sc in ea of next 2 sc, sc in ea of next 9 sc, ch 4, turn.

Row 3: Sl st in first sc, sc in ea of next 9 sc, 2 sc in ea of next 2 sc, sc in ea of next 8 sc, ch 4, turn.

Row 4: Sl st in first sc, sc in ea of next 7 sc, 2 sc in ea of next 2 sc, sc in ea of next 7 sc, ch 4, turn.

Row 5: Sl st in first sc, sc in ea of next 15 s

Row 6: Sl st in first sc, sc in ea of next 10

Row 7: Sl st in first sc, sc in ea of next 6 s

Rows 8 and 9: Sc in ea of next 6 sc, turn. Fasten off after row 9.

Center leaf (make 1): **Rows 1-6:** Work as for outer leaf.

Row 7: Sc in ea of next 4 sc, turn.

Row 8: Sk first sc, sc in ea of next 3 sc, turn.

Row 9: Sc in ea of next 3 sc, turn.

Row 10: Sl st in ea of next 2 sc, ch 30 for stem, sl st in 2nd ch from hook and ea of next 27 ch, sl st in next st at base of leaf. Fasten off.

Stitch 2 outer leaves to center leaf at base (see photo).

Vine: With size H hook and A, make a chain 4 yards long, sl st in ea ch across. Fasten off. Make another vine using size H hook and B. Make another vine using size 0 hook and garnet.

Finishing: Stitch leaf sprays and vines to afghan as desired (see photo).

133

RIBBONS & BOWS

*Give a special little girl a throw
of pretty pink squares adorned with baskets
of ribbon flowers, lace fans, and bows.*

FINISHED SIZE
Approximately 41" x 51".

MATERIALS
Sportweight cotton (109-yd. ball): 16 dark pink.
Sportweight brushed acrylic (170-yd. skein): 1 pink/gray ombre.
Size H crochet hook, or size to obtain gauge.

GAUGE
Block = 13½" x 12½".

DIRECTIONS
Block (make 12): With dark pink, ch 51.

Row 1: Hdc in 3rd ch from hook and ea ch across = 50 hdc, turn.

Rows 2 and 3: Ch 2 for first hdc, hdc in ea st across, turn.

Row 4: Ch 2 for first hdc, * yo and insert hook from front to back around post of next hdc 1 row below, complete st as a dc (fpdc made), hdc in next hdc, rep from * 23 times more, dc in last st, turn.

Rows 5-9: Ch 2 for first hdc, hdc in ea st across, turn. Fasten off after row 9.

Row 10: Join ombre with sl st in last hdc of row 9, rep row 4. Fasten off.

Row 11: Join dark pink with sl st in last st of row 10, ch 2 for first hdc, hdc in ea st across, turn.

Row 12: Ch 4 for first tr, * yo twice and pull up a lp in next st, yo and pull through 2 lps on hook, sk next st, yo and pull up a lp in next st, (yo and pull through 2 lps on hook) 4 times, ch 1, yo and insert hook in joint halfway down long st just made, yo and pull up a lp, (yo and pull through 2 lps on hook) twice (X-st made), rep from * 15 times more, tr in last st, turn.

Row 13: Ch 4 for first tr, keeping last lp of ea st on hook, 3 dc in ch-1 sp of next X-st, yo and pull through all lps on hook (bobble made), ch 2, rep from * 15 times more, end with ch 1, dc in last st, turn.

Row 14: Ch 2 for first hdc, hdc in ch-1, * hdc in bobble, 2 hdc in ch-2 sp, rep from * across, turn. Fasten off.

Row 15: Join ombre with sl st in last hdc of row 14, ch 2 for first hdc, hdc in ea st across, turn.

Row 16: Rep row 4. Fasten off.

Rows 17-22: Join dark pink with sl st in last st of row 16, rep row 2.

Row 23: Ch 2 for first hdc, hdc in ea of next 2 sts, (yo and pull up a lp) 5 times in next st, yo and pull through all lps on hook (puff made), * hdc in ea of next 3 sts, puff in next st, rep from * across, hdc in ea of last 2 sts, turn.

Rows 24 and 25: Rep rows 2 and 3. Fasten off after row 25.

Row 26: Join ombre with sl st in last st of row 25, rep row 4. Fasten off.

Row 27: Join dark pink with sl st in last st of row 26, rep row 2.

Rows 28-31: Rep rows 2-5.

Border: Ch 2 for first hdc, * hdc evenly to next corner, 3 hdc in corner, rep from * around, end with 2 hdc in beg corner, sl st in top of beg ch-2. Fasten off.

Assembly: Afghan is 3 blocks wide and 4 blocks long. Whipstitch blocks together through back loops only.

Edging: With right side facing, join dark pink with sl st in corner, ch 1, * sc in ea st to corner, (sc, ch 1, sc) in corner, rep from * around, sl st in beg ch-1. Fasten off.

Finishing: If desired, decorate afghan with ribbons, lace, and other trims, referring to photo for inspiration.

NIGHT SKY

*For this playful but stylish throw, scatter
a quarter moon and a few stars in
a deep blue sky.*

FINISHED SIZE

Approximately 43″ x 57″.

MATERIALS

Sportweight acrylic (175-yd. ball): 13 deep blue.
Size 5 crochet cotton (218-yd. ball): 2 yellow.
Sizes E and F crochet hooks, or size to obtain gauge.

GAUGE

4 dc = 1″ with size F hook.

DIRECTIONS

Block (make 35): **Row 1** (right side): With size F hook and blue, ch 31, dc in 4th ch from hook and ea ch across, turn = 29 dc.

Row 2: Ch 1, (dc in next st, sl st in next st) across, turn.

Row 3: Ch 3 for first dc, dc in ea dc and sl st across, dc in ch-1, turn = 29 dc.

Rows 4-19: Rep rows 2 and 3 alternately. Fasten off after row 19.

Assembly: Afghan is 5 blocks wide and 7 blocks long. Arrange blocks in a checkerboard pattern, rotating every other block a quarter turn, so that stitch patterns are at right angles. With right sides facing, whipstitch blocks together.

Edging: **Rnd 1:** With right side facing and size E hook, join blue with sc in any corner, ch 1, work * 29 sc across ea block to next corner, (sc, ch 1, sc) in corner, rep from * around, end with sl st in beg ch-1.

Rnd 2: Sl st backward into corner ch-1 sp, ch 3 for first dc, dc in same sp, * dc in ea st to next corner ch-1 sp, (2 dc, ch 1, 2 dc) in corner sp, rep from * around, end with sl st in top of beg ch-3.

Rnd 3: Sl st backward into corner ch-1 sp, ch 1, * dc in next st, sl st in next st, rep from * around, end with sl st in beg ch-1.

Rnd 4: Ch 4, * sc in next sl st, ch 3, rep from * around, end with sl st in first ch of beg ch-4.

Rnd 5: Ch 3 for first dc, dc in same st, * 2 dc in ea ch-3 lp to corner, (2 dc, ch 1, 2 dc) in corner st, rep from * around, end with sl st in top of beg ch-3.

Rnd 6: Ch 4, * sc in sp bet 2-dc grps, ch 3, rep from * around, end with sl st in first ch of beg ch-4.

Rnds 7-9: Rep rnds 5 and 6 alternately, ending after rnd 5.

Rnd 10: Rep rnd 3. Fasten off.

Moon (make 1): **Row 1:** With 2 strands of yellow held tog as 1 and size E hook, ch 100, sc in 2nd ch from hook and ea ch across, turn.

Row 2: Ch 1, pull up a lp in ea of next 2 sts, yo and pull through all lps on hook (sc dec made), * sc in ea of next 3 sts, sc dec over next 2 sts, rep from * across, turn.

Row 3: Ch 1, sk next st, sl st in ea of next 15 sts, sc in ea of next 10 sts, hdc in ea of next 5 sts, dc in ea of next 5 sts, tr in ea of next 5 sts, dc in ea of next 5 sts, hdc in ea of next 5 sts, sc in ea of next 10 sts, sl st in ea of next 3 sts, turn.

Row 4: Ch 1, sk next st, sl st in ea of next 2 sts, sc in ea of next 5 sts, hdc in ea of next 5 sts, dc in ea of next 5 sts, tr in ea of next 15 sts, dc in ea of next 5 sts, hdc in ea of next 5 sts, sc in ea of next 5 sts, sl st in ea of next 12 sts, turn.

Row 5: Ch 1, sk next st, sc in ea of next 5 sts, hdc in ea of next 5 sts, dc in ea of next 45 sts, hdc in ea of next 5 sts, sc in ea of next 5 sts, turn.

Row 6: Ch 1, sk next st, sc in next st, hdc in ea of next 5 sts, dc in ea of next 15 sts, keeping last lp of ea st on hook, dc in ea of next 2 sts, yo and pull through all lps on hook (dc dec made), dc in ea of next 5 sts, dc dec over next 2 sts, dc in ea of next 5 sts, dc dec over next 2 sts, dc in ea of next 15 sts, hdc in ea of next 5 sts, sc in ea of next 3 sts, sl st in next st, turn.

Row 7: Ch 1, sk next st, sc in ea of next 5 sts, hdc in ea of next 5 sts, (dc in ea of next 2 sts, dc dec over next 2 sts) 11 times, dc in ea of next 2 sts, hdc in ea of next 5 sts, sc in ea of next 5 sts, sl st in next st, turn.

Row 8: Ch 1, sk next st, sc in ea of next 12 sts, hdc in ea of next 5 sts, dc dec over next 2 sts, dc in next st, dc dec over next 2 sts, dc in ea of next 12 sts, dc dec over next 2 sts, dc in next st, dc dec over next 2 sts, hdc in ea of next 5 sts, sc in ea of next 12 sts, sl st in ea of next 5 sts, turn.

Row 9: Ch 1, sc in ea of next 25 sts, hdc in next st, dc in next st, (dc, ch 2, sc) in next st, sc in next st, hdc in next st, dc in ea of next 3 sts, (3 tr, ch 3, sc) in next st, sc in next st, hdc in next st, dc in next st, (dc, sc, hdc) in next st, ch 2, sc in ea st to last st, sl st in last st. Fasten off.

Star (make 3): With 2 strands of yellow held tog as 1 and size E hook, ch 4, join with a sl st to form a ring.

Rnd 1: Ch 3 for first dc, 14 dc in ring, sl st in top of beg ch-3.

Rnd 2: Ch 4 for first tr, 2 dc in same st, * hdc in ea of next 2 sts, (2 dc, tr, 2 dc) in next st, rep from * around, end with sl st in top of beg ch-4.

Rnd 3: * Ch 12, sl st in 3rd ch from hook, sc in next st, hdc in next st, dc in ea of next 2 sts, tr in ea of next 2 sts, dtr in ea of next 2 sts, tr tr in next st, sl st in next rnd-2 tr (point of star made), rep from * 4 times more, end with sl st in base of beg ch-12. Fasten off.

Finishing: Stitch moon and stars to throw as desired (see photo).

GENERAL DIRECTIONS

CROCHET ABBREVIATIONS

beg	begin(ning)
bet	between
bk lp(s)	back loop(s)
ch	chain(s)
ch-	refers to chain previously made
cl	cluster(s)
cont	continu(e) (ing)
dc	double crochet
dec	decrease(s) (d) (ing)
dtr	double triple crochet
ea	each
est	established
foll	follow(s) (ing)
ft lp(s)	front loop(s)
grp(s)	group(s)
hdc	half double crochet
inc	increase(s) (d) (ing)
lp(s)	loop(s)
pat(s)	pattern(s)
prev	previous
qdtr	quadruple triple crochet
rem	remain(s) (ing)
rep	repeat(s)
rnd(s)	round(s)
sc	single crochet
sk	skip(ped)
sl st	slip stitch
sp(s)	space(s)
st(s)	stitch(es)
tch	turning chain
tog	together
tr	triple crochet
tr tr	triple triple crochet
yo	yarn over

GAUGE

Before beginning a project, work a 4″-square gauge swatch using the recommended-size hook. Measure 1″ or 2″ (as given in the gauge note); count and compare the number of stitches in the swatch with the designer's gauge. If you have fewer stitches in your swatch, try a smaller hook; if you have more stitches, try a larger hook.

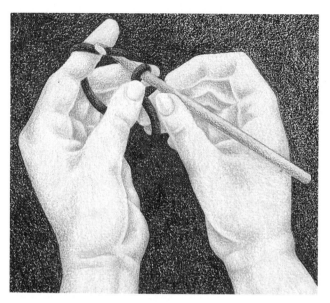

WORKING TOGETHER

Hold the hook as you would a pencil (shown here) or a piece of chalk. If your hook has a finger rest, position your thumb and opposing finger there for extra control. Weave the yarn through the fingers of your left hand to control the amount of yarn fed into the work and to provide tension. Once work has begun, the thumb and middle finger of the left hand come into play, pressing together to hold the stitches just made.

SLIP STITCH DIAGRAM

Here a slip stitch (sl st) is used to join a ring. Taking care not to twist chain, insert hook into first chain, yarn over and pull through chain and loop on hook (sl st made).

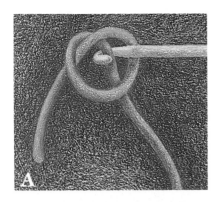

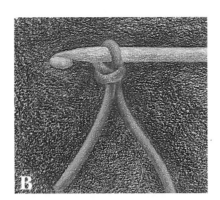

SLIP KNOT DIAGRAM
Loop the yarn around and let the loose
end of the yarn fall behind the loop to
form a pretzel shape as shown. Insert the
hook (**A**) and pull both ends to close the
knot (**B**).

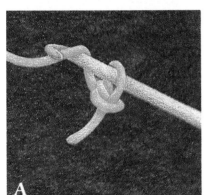

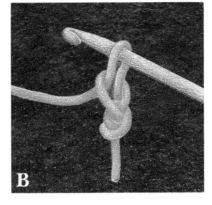

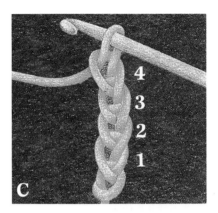

CHAIN STITCH DIAGRAM
A. Place a slip knot on your hook. With
hands in the position shown above, and
with the thumb and middle finger of the
left hand holding the yarn end, wrap the
yarn up and over the hook (from back
to front). This movement is called a
"yarn over (yo)" and is basic to every
crochet stitch.

B. Use the hook to pull the yarn through
the loop (lp) already on the hook. The
combination of yo and pulling the yarn
through the lp makes 1 chain stitch (ch).

C. Repeat until the ch is the desired
length, trying to keep the movements
even and relaxed, and all the ch stitches
(sts) the same size. Hold the ch near the
working area to keep it from twisting.
Count sts as shown in diagram. (Do not
count lp on hook or slip knot.)

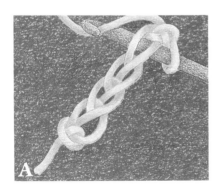

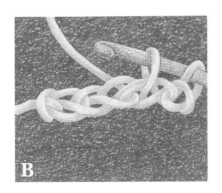

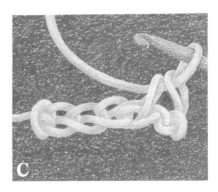

SINGLE CROCHET DIAGRAM
A. Insert hook under top 2 lps of 2nd ch
from hook and yo. (Always work sts
through the top 2 lps of a stitch unless
directions specify otherwise.)

B. Yo and pull yarn through ch (2 lps on
hook).

C. Yo and pull yarn through 2 lps on
hook (1 sc made).

DOUBLE CROCHET DIAGRAM
A. Yo, insert hook into 4th ch from hook, and yo.

B. Pull yarn through ch (3 lps on hook).

C. Yo and pull through 2 lps on hook (2 lps remaining). (*Note:* When instructions say "keeping last lp of ea st on hook," this means to work the specified st to the

final yo. This is done to make a cluster or to work a decrease.)

D. Yo and pull through 2 remaining (rem) lps (1 dc made).

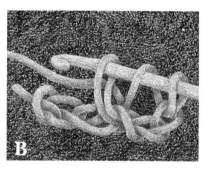

HALF DOUBLE CROCHET DIAGRAM
A. Yo and insert hook into 3rd ch from hook.

B. Yo and pull through ch (3 lps on hook).

C. Yo and pull yarn through all 3 lps on hook (1 hdc made).

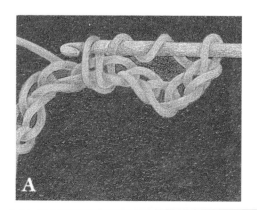

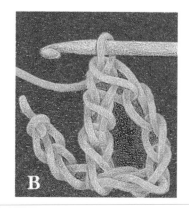

TRIPLE CROCHET DIAGRAM
A. Yo twice, insert hook into 5th ch from hook. Yo and pull through ch (4 lps on hook).

B. Yo and pull through 2 lps on hook (3 lps rem). Yo and pull through 2 lps on hook (2 lps rem). Yo and pull through 2 lps on hook (1 tr made).

TASSEL DIAGRAM

A. Wrap the yarn around a piece of cardboard as specified in the pattern. At 1 end, slip a 5″ piece of yarn under the loops and knot. Cut the loops at the other end.

B. Loop a 38″ piece of yarn around the tassel as shown.

C. Wrap the yarn tightly around the tassel several times. Secure the yarn ends as shown and tuck them into tassel. Trim all yarn ends even.

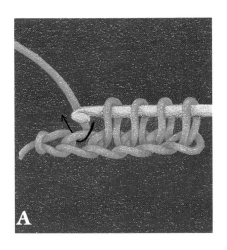

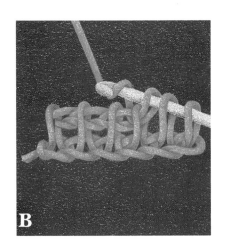

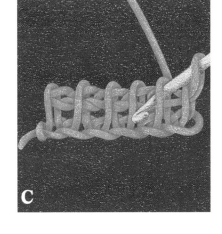

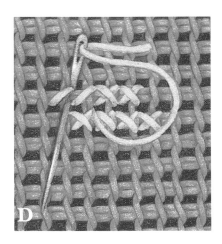

AFGHAN STITCH DIAGRAM

A. *Row 1: Step 1:* Keeping all lps on hook, pull up a lp through top lp only, in 2nd ch from hook and each rem ch across (at end of base ch, number of lps on hook should equal number of ch in base ch). Do not turn.

B. *Step 2:* Yo and pull through first lp on hook, * yo and pull through 2 lps on hook, rep from * across (1 lp rem on hook for first lp of next row). Do not turn.

C. *Row 2: Step 1:* Keeping all lps on hook, pull up a lp from under 2nd vertical bar, * pull up a lp from under next vertical bar, rep from * across. Do not turn.

    Step 2: Rep step 2 of row 1.

    Rep both steps of row 2 for the required number of rows. Fasten off after last row by working a sl st in each bar across.

D. When the fabric is finished, it is a perfect grid for cross-stitch.

YARN INFORMATION

The following is a complete list of the yarns used for each project pictured in the book. Visit your local yarn shop to obtain the yarn shown or for help in substituting another yarn. If you are unable to locate the yarn in your area or for further information, write the yarn company at the address listed below.

Pink Dogwoods, page 8, Brunswick Yarns, Pearl (50-gr., 110-yd. ball): 33 Eggshell #59100.

Sweet Dreams, page 10, Brunswick Yarns, Windrush (100-gr., 230-yd. skein): 3 each Cherry Blossom #90172, Peach Blossom #9071, Yellow #9003, Juniper #9057, Light Blue #9002.

Rickrack Revival, page 12, Bucilla, Softex Spectrum (85-gr., 165-yd. skein): 4 Rose Ombre #131; Softex (100-gr., 280-yd. skein): 2 each Brown #97, Rose #86; 4 Light Rose #123.

Flower Garden, page 14, Brunswick Yarns, Pearl (50-gr., 110-yd. ball): 11 Willow #5920, 6 Blue #5921.

Picots & Pearls, page 17, Brunswick Yarns, Windmist (50-gr., 135-yd. skein): 17 Candy Mint #2807. Avocet, Soireé (103-yd. ball): 2 Turquoise #520.

Simply Country, page 20, Aarlan, Fleurette (50-gr., 120-yd. ball): 6 each Olive #4489, Beige #4490.

Lavender Fields, page 22, Schewe, Filigrana (50-gr., 137-yd. ball): 9 Lavender #4189, 8 Pink #4180. Avocet, Soireé (103-yd. ball): 7 White #504.

Evening Ombre, page 24, Brunswick Yarns, Windmist (50-gr., 135-yd. skein): 18 Evening Ombre #2893.

Victorian Finery, page 26, Classic Elite Yarns, La Gran Mohair (43-gr., 90-yd. skein): 8 Dark Pink #6562, 9 Pink #6519; Sharon Mohair (43-gr., 90-yd. skein): 10 Pink #2519.

Flowery Fantasy, page 30, Pingouin, Corrida 3 (50-gr., 230-yd. ball): 7 White #301. Lily, Baby and Fashion Sugar 'n Cream (36-gr., 150-yd. ball): 8 Fairytales #99.

Cotton Candy, page 32, Brunswick Yarns, Monterey (50-gr.,

105-yd. ball): 10 Pink with White Accents #2603. Unger Yarns, Fluffy (50-gr., 156-yd. ball): 1 White #460.

Twining Ivy, page 34, Brunswick Yarns, Pearl (50-gr., 110-yd. ball): 25 Dark Green #5925.

Homespun Classic, page 36, Aarlan, Cotonella (50-gr., 115-yd. ball): 7 Blue #6108, 10 Brown #6113, 6 Green #6103.

Rich Rose Lace, page 39, Schewe, Fil D'Ecosse No. 16 (50-gr., 440-yd. ball): 4 Rose #118.

Lacy Daffodils, page 42, Schewe, Fil D'Ecosse No. 16 (50-gr., 440-yd. ball): 4 Yellow #157. DMC Corporation, Size 20 Cebelia (405-yd. ball): 1 Ecru.

Block Party, page 44, Emu Yarns, Superwash DK (50-gr., 124-yd. ball): 1 each Dark Rust #3050, Light Rust #3015, Medium Rust #3014, Medium Red #3051, Dark Red #3002, Coral #3005. Brunswick Yarns, Pearl (50-gr., 110-yd. ball): 1 each Dark Blue #5917, Dark Green #5925, Lavender #5904, Orchid #5916. Schewe, Damasco (50-gr., 154-yd. ball): 1 each Light Brown #8503, Purple #8507. Aarlan, Cotonella (50-gr., 115-yd. ball): 1 each Blue #6108, Orange #6200, Medium Orange #6204, Red #6205. Schewe, Coton A Tricoter (190-yd. ball): 1 Gold #13889. Filatura Di Crosa, 501 (50-gr., 137-yd. skein): 3 Black #115.

Blue Heather, page 48, Filatura Di Crosa, Sympathie (50-gr., 150-yd. ball): 18 each Dark Green #938, Green #934; 6 Blue #914.

Ruffled Comfort, page 50, Unger Yarns, Roly Sport (50-gr., 190-yd. ball): 4 Pink #4576. Brunswick Yarns, Windmist (50-gr., 135-yd. skein): 28 Pastel Ombre #2895.

Sunshine Kisses, page 52, Robin, Bambino DK with Cotton (100-gr., 344-yd. ball): 5 Yellow #1641, 6 Green #1650.

Rose Medallions, page 54, DMC Corporation, Size 5 Perle Cotton (27-yd. skein): 10 each Yellow #745, Mauve #3688; 59 Pistachio Green #367; Size 5 Perle Cotton (53-yd. ball): 5 each Peach #353, Rose #3326.

Vivid Waves, page 56, Filatura Di Crosa, Sympathie (50-gr.,

150-yd. ball): 5 Aqua #929. Bernat, Ultrawash Worsted (50-gr., 110-yd. ball): 4 Plum #12552. Filatura Di Crosa, 501 (50-gr., 137-yd. skein): 10 Teal #111, 4 Black #115.

Gypsy Paths Afghan, page 58, Schewe, Fil D'Ecosse No. 16 (50-gr., 440-yd. ball): 7 each Tan #164, Taupe #160; 4 each Blue #151, Brown #166; 1 each Ecru #115, Rose #118, Khaki #140, Blue-green #163, Yellow #157, Apricot #142, Periwinkle #161.

Bunnies 'n Carrots, page 61, Filatura Di Crosa, Sympathie (50-gr., 150-yd. ball): 4 Green #934, 10 Light Blue #940. Unger Yarns, Fluffy (50-gr., 156-yd. ball): 1 White #460. Brunswick Yarns, Sportmist (50-gr., 170-yd. skein): 1 each Powder Pink #8812, Silver Gray #8836.

Memory Lane, page 64, Schewe, Contessa (50-gr., 137-yd. ball) 8 each Purple #7812, Brown #7810.

Luxurious Lace, page 66, Classic Elite Yarns, Newport Light (50-gr., 93-yd. skein): 13 Light Green #3387, 7 Peach #3363; Applause (50-gr., 70-yd. skein): 13 Variegated Green/Gray/Peach #1801.

Champagne Toast, page 68, Pingouin, Douceur (50-gr., 75-yd. skein): 20 Beige #715. Trendsetter Yarns, Calypso (50-gr., 80-yd. skein): 2 Caramel #4.

Falling Stars, page 70, Aarlan, Swa Laine (50-gr., 105-yd. skein): 7 Navy #BL1. Reynolds Yarns, Saucy (100-gr., 185-yd. ball): 3 White #800. Kreinik Mfg. Co. Inc., Balger Japan Threads Ombres, an 8-ply soft-twist metallic thread (300m spool): 1 Solid Gold #2000.

Touches of Gold, page 72, Reynolds Yarns, Sunrise (50-gr., 110-yd. ball): 37 White #02 for afghan; 4 White #02 for pillow. Phildar, Sunset (20-gr., 163-yd. ball): 4 Gold Metallic for afghan; 1 Gold Metallic for pillow.

Diamonds, page 76, Aarlan, Charmeuse (50-gr., 185-yd. skein): 9 Black #4967; 4 each Purple #4973, Dark Green #4959.

Holiday Plaid, page 78, Brunswick Yarns, Pearl (50-gr., 110-yd. ball): 23 Dark Green #5925.

Spring Dawn, page 80, Brunswick Yarns, Pearl (50-gr., 110-yd. ball): 2 Willow #5920, 8 Dusty Pink #5922, 6 Orchid #5916, 12 Lavender #5904, 7 Jewel Ombre #5996.

Snowmen, page 83, Brunswick Yarns, Pearl (50-gr., 110-yd. ball): 18 Navy #5908. Unger Yarns, Fluffy (50-gr., 156-yd. ball): 3 White #460.

Buttercup Blanket, page 86, Aarlan, Fleurette (50-gr., 120-yd. ball): 20 Yellow #4471.

Fall Wreath, page 89, Brunswick Yarns, Fore-'n-Aft (50-gr., 175-yd. ball): 17 Ecru #6444.

Vintage Aran, page 92, Brunswick Yarns, Pearl (50-gr., 110-yd. ball): 32 Burgundy #5924.

Fancy Filigree, page 94, Tahki Imports, Designer Homespun Tweed (110-gr., 175-yd. skein): 4 Light Blue Tweed #203. Berger du Nord, Kid Mohair #5 (50-gr., 70-yd. skein): 5 Variegated Blue #8323.

Shades of Coral, page 96, Emu Yarns, Superwash DK (50-gr., 124-yd. ball): 9 Dark Rust #3050, 7 Light Coral #3055, 3 Medium Rust #3014, 9 Dark Red #3002, 1 Light Rust #3051, 3 Light Red #3003, 9 Coral #3005.

Crochet Touché, page 98, DMC Corporation, Size 5 Cebelia, (141-yd. ball): 21 White; Size 5 Perle Cotton (53-yd. ball): 1 each Peach #353, Pink #776, Blue #519, Violet #554, Green #954; 2 Yellow #744; Size 5 Perle Cotton (27-yd. skein): 2 each Light Blue #828, Lavender #211, Light Pink #819; 4 Light Green #955.

Pastel Patchwork, page 101, Plymouth Yarn Company, Cleo (50-gr., 109-yd. ball): 21 Aqua #401, 8 Pink #391, 6 Yellow #372.

Wisteria Arbor, page 104, Brunswick Yarns, Fore-'n-Aft (50-gr., 175-yd. ball): 20 White #6000.

Hints of Autumn, page 114, Classic Elite Yarns, Newport (50-gr., 70-yd. skein): 4 Brown #2344, 6 Gold #2341, 10 Green #2364. Schewe, Contessa (50-gr., 137-yd. ball): 10 Dark Green #7807.

Quiet Daydreams, page 116, Classic Elite Yarns, Newport Light (50-gr., 93-yd. skein): 6 Blue #3392. Schewe, Anne Claire (50-gr., 72-yd. ball): 10 Variegated Blue/Purple/Pink /Metallic #3256. Classic Elite Yarns, Newport (50-gr., 70-yd. skein): 12 Lavender #2367.

Haven of Blue, page 118, Tahki Imports, Designer Homespun Tweed (100-gr., 175-yd. skein): 9 Blue Tweed #204. Filatura Di Crosa, Stella (50-gr., 136-yd. ball): 6 Dark Blue #422. Schewe, Mohair Superio (50-gr., 99-yd. ball): 4 Dark Blue #6227. Bernat, Ultrawash Worsted (50-gr., 110-yd. ball): 2 Medium Blue #12574.

Woven Elegance, page 120, Classic Elite Yarns, Newport (50-gr., 70-yd. skein): 15 Beige #2345, 6 Off-white #2316. Trendsetter Yarns, Calypso (50-gr., 80-yd. skein): 9 Pink #2, 8 Beige #13. Madeira USA Inc., Supertwist #30 (1000m spool): 1 Pearl #300.

Painter's Palette, page 124, Lily, Sugar 'n Cream (86-gr., 125-yd. ball): 4 Celery #53; Softball (57-gr., 98-yd. ball): 2

Tint Green; Sugar 'n Cream Cotton Mousse (50-gr., 192-yd ball): 1 Silver #5. Neveda Yarn Company, Cottage (50-gr., 55-yd. skein): 2 Light Green #9069. Pingouin, Biais de Coton (50-gr., 55-yd. ball): 3 Green #400, 2 Purple #600. Tahki Imports, Designer Homespun Tweed (100-gr., 175-yd. skein): 1 Blue #203; Ambrosia II (114-gr., 120-yd. skein): 2 Variegated Green and Lavender #622. Rowan Designer Collection, Cabled Mercerized Cotton (50-gr., 184-yd. ball): 1 Purple #310. Berroco, Glace (150-yd. spool): 2 Green/Gray/Blue Ombre #2128. Schewe, Contessa (50-gr. 137-yd. ball): 2 Purple #7812. Trendsetter Yarns, Bacio (50-gr., 77-yd. ball): 5 Variegated Purple and Black #5. Classic Elite Yarns, Cambridge (50-gr., 85-yd. skein): 4 Lavender #3905; La Gran Mohair (43-gr., 90-yd. skein): 1 Gray #6503; Batik Cotton (100-gr., 176-yd. ball): 1 Moss Green #1373. Filatura Di Crosa, Sympathie (50-gr., 150-yd. ball): 7 Dark Green #938. Berger Du Nord, Kid Mohair #5 (50-gr., 70-yd. skein): 1 Variegated Blue #8323.

Swirling Leaves, page 131, Aarlan, Swa Laine (50-gr., 105-yd. skein): 15 Burgundy #R1, 9 Variegated Navy/Red M1. DMC Corporation, Size 5 Perle Cotton (53-yd. ball): 10 Garnet #902; Size 5 Perle Cotton (27-yd. skein): 2 Navy #939.

Ribbons & Bows, page 134, Plymouth Yarns, Cleo (50-gr., 109-yd. ball): 16 Dark Pink #419. Brunswick Yarns, Sportmist (50-gr., 170-yd. skein): 1 Salmon Gray Ombre #8892.

Night Sky, page 136, Brunswick Yarns, Fore-'n-Aft (50-gr., 175-yd. ball): 13 Deep Blue Velvet #6081. DMC Corporation, Brilliant Knitting/Crochet Cotton (218-yd. ball): 2 Medium Yellow #743.

YARN COMPANIES

Berroco
Elmdale Road
P.O. Box 367
Uxbridge, MA 01569

Bernat Yarn and Craft
c/o Spinrite Yarns
320 Livingston Avenue South
Listowel, Ontario, Canada
N4W3H3

Brunswick Yarns
P.O. Box 276
Pickens, SC 29671

Bucilla
1 Oakridge Road
Hazelton, PA 18201

Classic Elite Yarns
12 Perkins Street
Lowell, MA 01854

DMC Corporation
107 Trumbull Street
Elizabeth, NJ 07206

Emu/Robin Yarns
c/o Plymouth Yarn Company
500 Lafayette Street
Bristol, PA 19007

Filatura Di Crosa
c/o Stacy Charles Collection
119 Green Street
Brooklyn, NY 11222

Kreinik Mfg. Co. Inc.
P.O. Box 1966
Parkersburg, WV 26102

Madeira USA Inc.
30 Bayside Court
Laconia, NH 03246

Neveda Yarn Company
c/o Mayflower Yarns
P.O. Box 1046
Clarksville, MD 21029

Phildar
16 Mahopac Village Center
Mahopac, NY 10541

Pingouin
c/o Laninter USA, Inc.
P.O. Box 1542
Mount Pleasant, SC 29465

Plymouth Yarn Company, Inc.
500 Lafayette Street
Bristol, PA 19007

Reynolds Yarns
A division of JCA, Inc.
35 Scales Lane
Townsend, MA 01469

Rowan Designer Collection
c/o Westminster Trading Company
5 Northern Boulevard
Amherst, NH 03031

Schewe
c/o Muench Yarns
118 Ricardo Road
Mill Valley, CA 94941

Tahki Imports
11 Graphic Place
Moonachie, NJ 07074

Trendsetter Yarns
16742 Stagg Street, #104
Van Nuys, CA 91406

Unger Yarns
William Unger and Company
A division of JCA, Inc.
35 Scales Lane
Townsend, MA 01469